中國特色話語：

——陳安論國際經濟法學　第四卷　上冊

陳安　著

簡目

▌第四卷▌

目錄

第四卷

第五編——國際經濟法熱點學術問題長、短評

第一章
改進我國國際法教育的「他山之石」*
——歐美之行考察見聞

❧ 內容提要

　　一九八四年三至四月，筆者應聯合國教科文組織邀請，作為中國派出的「國際法教育考察組」成員之一，出訪西歐和北美五國二十個城市，對西方發達國家的法學教育進行調研、考察，並與一百多位法學界相關人士進行交流。本文是依據此次考察見聞，結合中國國情，就國際法專業人才培養等方面的問題提出的具體改進建議。如今這些建議有的已被有關部門採納，並行之有效；有的則尚待借鑑他山之石，付諸實踐，俾使中國的國際法人才培養事業與時俱進，更上層樓。

❧ 目次

（四）提倡由優秀研究生主辦學刊——法學拔尖人才的搖籃

（五）注重開發利用外籍華人和港臺留學生中的法學人才資源

二、關於國際法資料中心的建立

三、關於國際法專業力量的合作

應聯合國教科文組織的邀請，中國國際法教育考察組一行三人，由北大國際法研究所所長王鐵崖教授率領[1]於一九八四年三月三日至四月二十一日對西歐和北美的五國進行了法學教育的考察。考察的目的是，了解和學習西方發達國家國際法教學與科研的主要經驗；爭取外來資助，為選送更多的青年教師與研究生出國深造而溝通管道；同時，也向國際同行介紹中國國際法教學與科研的現狀、我國在若干國際法問題上的原則立場以及我國涉外的政策法令。

考察期間，我們歷經比利時的布魯塞爾、魯汶，瑞士的日內瓦，聯邦德國的波恩、法蘭克福、海德堡，加拿大的渥太華、哈利法克斯、多倫多、蒙特利爾、埃德蒙頓，美國的紐約、紐黑文、羅萊、查洛斯維爾、華盛頓特區、舊金山等二十個城市，走訪了享有國際聲譽的大學法學院、國際法研究所、聯合國總部、聯合國歐洲總部、歐洲共同體總部等重要國際組織以及議會、法院、國會圖書館、國際性大型律師事務所、國際法專業書刊出版社等，約三十個單位，先後與一百多名國際法學界的知名人士和專家、學者進行了學術交流，並就開展國際學術協作、培養人才、交流資料等進行了初步的磋商。現將訪問考察過程的若干見聞和感想，結合中國國情，從國際法專業人才的培養、國際法資

料中心的建立以及國際法專業力量的合作這三個方面，綜合簡述如下：

一、關於國際法專業人才的培養

我國法學人才短缺，國際法人才尤其缺。現有國際法專業人才的數量和品質，與發達國家相比，差距很大。為了提高我國的國際地位，大力開展國際交往活動，我們必須加速國際法專業人才的培養。借鑑有關經驗，我國現有的培養方法宜在以下幾方面加以改進：

（一）派人員出國深造應考慮門類、品種和國別的多樣化

目前我國選派出國深造的國際法專業人員，絕大多數集中在美國，絕大多數攻讀法學碩士（L. L. M.）學位，選讀的課程和選定的學位論文題目，其計劃性、目的性、針對性也不夠強，未必完全切合我國開展國際鬥爭和擴大國際交往的急需。例如，歐洲共同體是我國對外交往中的主要對象之一，有些主攻歐洲共同體法律的出國人員不是派往西歐，卻送到美國去，這就不如派往比利時或聯邦德國、法國這些歐洲共同體成員國學習，從而耳濡目染，獲得更多感性認識和理性認識。

據了解，聯邦德國基於自身利益的考慮，亟欲擴大對中國的經濟、文化交流。阿登納基金會等組織對於提供資助吸收中國留學生前往聯邦德國學習法律很有積極性，所提供的資助也是比較優厚的。但國內選派的預備入選只有德語訓練，缺乏基本的法學

專業知識，不符合對方要求，故兩年來該基金會為中國學生留下的資助名額，至今還空著。它們的要求是寧可德語差些，也要先具備基本法學知識，在聯邦德國可以進行德語速成訓練，進而專攻歐洲共同體法律或聯邦德國法律。因此，國內有條件的法律系中，不妨自一年級起就要求部分學生修習德、法、日、俄、西班牙等語種，作為第一外語必修課，便於從中選派前往相應國家深造的人員，這是很有必要的。

在聯邦德國、加拿大和美國的若干大學裡，學習中國法律已成為「熱門」，但我國現有的法律系，卻極少開設德國法、加拿大法或美國法的專門課程。這些國家的政府或投資者在與中國交往中，多半聘有熟知中國法律的本國專家或律師參加談判或立約，而我國現有法學人員中，既掌握國際法又熟知對方國內法者幾乎完全闕如。例如，近年來我國對美國經濟關係中就發生過「蘑菇貿易官司」、紡織品配額糾紛、湖廣鐵路債券案件等，在有關訟爭中，我方往往不得不花費重金聘請美國律師提供法律幫助，其不得力、不相稱是可想而知的。所以，我們從現在起，應以較大的注意力，有計劃地選送適量的留學生專攻中國對外交往重點對象國家的國內法。以美國為例，就是攻讀J. D.學位而不是攻讀L. L. M.或S. J. D.學位。而在攻讀L. L. M.或S. J. D.學位的留學生中，也應根據我國的現實需要，在國際公法、國際私法、國際經濟法（國際貿易法、國際投資法、國際貨幣金融法、國際稅法、國際組織法等等）以及有關的重要分支專業（諸如海洋法、外層空間法、國際環境保護法、國際海事法等等）各門各類中，分別有所側重，有所專攻。通過上述措施，使我國的國際法專業

人才「品種齊全，配套成龍」，有能力在各種國際場合打各種「國際官司」，以維護我國權益。

此外，鑒於我國國內目前的培養力量（國際法專家、師資）嚴重不足，圖書資料奇缺，而國際法專業訓練又具有特別強的國際性，因此，即使是國內在學的國際法研究生，如能獲得外國學術資助，又不增加國家負擔，也宜儘量多地送往國外培養，以求迅速成才。我國目前有關「在學研究生不得出國」的現行規定，自有一定道理，但考慮到國際法專業人才的特殊情況，似乎不宜「一刀切」，而宜靈活掌握或對原規定加以調整。

（二）應積極參加國際性的學術討論會或學術團體

享有國際聲譽的聯邦德國馬普國際法研究所對於加強中、德國際法學術交流具有濃厚興趣，他們主動倡議一九八五年春在聯邦德國海德堡或中國北京舉辦一次國際法學術討論會，主題是有關國際投資保護條約的理論和實踐，建議中、德雙方各提供五六篇學術論文，並歡迎中國青年學者屆時出席會議。他們還建議把這類學術討論會制度化，今後每兩年定期舉行一次。我們建議首次討論會最好在北京舉行，對方初步表示同意，並即將派專人前來北京進一步找中國國際法學會會長宦鄉同志具體磋商確定。如果此種形式果真制度化，我們應有與之相應的準備。

美國國際法學會是一個國際性的學術組織，擁有許多其他國家的會員。其年會討論的問題豐富多彩，多半是國際法學科中新出現的疑難問題或有爭論的問題，事後又將有關的專題論文和講稿彙編出版。會議期間，不但國內外國際法學者雲集，而且全美

經營國際法專業書刊的各家大出版商也擺出二十餘個書攤，推銷最新出版和即將出版的各種國際法讀物專著，可謂琳琅滿目。據了解，來自發展中國家的學會會員，每年只需繳納三十美元的會員費，即獲免費贈閱《美國國際法雜誌》（美國權威性學術雜誌，一年六期，原定價為78美元）一份，還可以用四十美元的訂閱價獲得一份《國際法學資料》（一年四冊，原定價為85美元）。以上兩種雜誌，是當前我國各大學法律系國際法課程的重要參考讀物，各校多按原訂閱價付款訂購，而沒有人利用入會會員資格獲得上述半價優待。看來這是一種可以避免的浪費，而其「思想障礙」則可能是認為「中國人不宜參加美國學會」。其實，我國國際法專業人員以個人名義參加這種實際上是國際性的學術組織作為會員，有利於維護我國的權益。適當地有組織地選派我國部分國際法學者加入這種學會，實質上有如派人出國留學、進修一樣，符合魯迅先生所提倡的「拿來主義」精神。利用會員資格和派人參加這種會議，我們可以從中了解國際法學科的最新動態。

（三）國際法課程的教學應注重培養學生解決實際問題的能力——大量的課前預習和活躍的課堂對話

我國法律系各科目前的教學內容，大多側重於理論體系的分析講解，在一定程度上存在著「純理論」的偏向，對引導學生研究與分析典型的實際案例，是不夠注意的。在教學方法上，則相當普遍地採取「滿堂灌」的辦法。課堂上自始至終，全是主講教員的「一言堂」，學生則全神貫注，忙於記錄，無暇思考，形成「課上記筆記、課後對筆記、考試背筆記、考後全忘記」的消

極、被動、低效率的學習局面。可以說，這是文科教學中常見的積弊，亟待改革。

西方發達國家的教學內容和教學方法，頗可以借鑑。一般說來，他們的課堂教學主要採取兩種方式：二十人以上的大班，採取以教師為主的講授式；二十人以下的小班，採取教師指導下的討論式。當然，根據課程的性質和教師個人的喜好，也有採用講授式的小班。但不論採取何種方式，全都要求學生事先進行大量的預習，由教師指定閱讀範圍，每兩節課要求事先預習六十至八十頁（16開）的圖書和資料，其內容主要是典型案例及有關的原始文檔。討論式教學中，學生圍繞典型案例各抒己見，教師加以引導。講授式教學中，也有大量時間用於師生對話，即教師就預習內容和案例提問，要求學生當堂闡述自己的看法；或者由學生隨時舉手，經教師許可，就教師講授內容中的疑點提出質詢、問難或發表自己不同的意見。因此，教師事先也必須充分備課，以便隨時對付這種「半路殺出來的程咬金」。這種以大量預習為基礎，課堂上穿插大量師生對話的講授，對師生雙方都提出了更高的要求，在課堂上能充分激發學生的積極思維，利於師生思想和知識的及時交流。這樣，不但課堂氣氛生動活潑，而且學生學得積極主動，大大加深了對所學內容的理解，同時培養了獨立思考的習慣和能力。

他們認為，教師應當了解學生心理，講究教學藝術，鼓勵學生「自我表現」：在刻苦鑽研的基礎上，敢於探索新知識，提出新見解。青年學生精力旺盛，在課前經過刻苦鑽研，往往有許多新鮮的看法、獨特的觀點和豐富的聯想。他們在課堂上當眾表

述、答疑或質疑，不但可以鍛煉他們的口頭表達能力（這也是一種重要的基本功），而且可以使他們帶著一種高漲、激動的情緒進行學習和思考，既在學習和辯難中意識到自己的智慧和力量，體驗到開拓與創造的歡樂，也在同一過程中發現自己的缺陷和不足，「知不足而後學」，從而獲得新的提高。在課堂上讓他們闡發歧議、開展爭論，還可以進一步激發學生群體的思考，擴大和加深對有關問題的理解；與此同時，教師也從課堂上的辯難中，大大增強備課和講授的廣度、深度和針對性，十分有利於教學水準的提高。這種教學相長、師生互促共進的效果，是那種「臺上播音員，臺下打字員」的老辦法所無法達到的。

西方法學院重視培養學生的實踐能力，還體現在普遍開設模擬法庭課（Moot Court）、法律門診課（Clinical Program in Legal Aid）或學生法律援助服務專案（Student Legal Aid Service）上。

模擬法庭課在許多學校法學院是一年級學生（研究生）的必修課。自第二年開始，則有「模擬法庭競賽」選修課。它由選修學生自行結合為許多二人小組，就教師所指定的案例案情，輪流充當原告或被告的代理人（或辯護人）出庭辯論，採取淘汰賽的辦法，最後勝訴者獲得「競賽冠軍」稱號。初賽中的法官（審判員）由畢業班學習成績突出者擔任，複賽中的法官由授課老師或聘請律師事務所有名望的律師志願擔任（義務工作，無報酬，受聘者引為一種榮譽），決賽時則請法院現職老法官裁判。最後的勝訴競賽冠軍小組取得獎品銀盃或銀盾後，把姓名鐫刻其上，交還學校保管，以供下屆競賽之用，一如國際性球賽獎盃的頒發與收藏。學校當局往往把這種優勝銀杯或銀盾作為一種學習榮譽展

品，放在大會客廳或公共圖書館最顯眼處，陳列展覽，供歷屆入學新生和外賓參觀。

模擬法庭競賽也常在校際進行。美國國際法學會年會則每年舉辦模擬國際法庭競賽最後階段的複賽和決賽，這是全國性的校際競賽，獎盃命名為「傑塞普杯」，爭奪十分激烈。對學生來說，模擬法庭中複賽或決賽的優勝者，不唯是一項榮譽，而且是日後獲得良好職業崗位的初步保證。因為各大律師事務所前來法學院徵聘新人員時，畢業生在模擬法庭課中的成績和表現，往往是主管人（雇主）決定取捨的一項重要標準。

至於法律門診課或學生法律援助服務專案，實際上就是類比的律師事務所。前者由有關師生聯合組成，另由學校出資聘請數位開業律師兼任部分指導工作，對前來尋求法律援助的托辦人（當事人）收取低廉費用或完全免費，主要目的在於訓練在學學生初步學會開業律師的「基本功」；後者則純是學生自行組織的免費服務項目，為社會上無力支付律師費用的人解答法律上的疑難，提供法律援助，學生們從免費服務中獲得運用課堂知識的實踐鍛煉，提高了獨立分析和解決實際問題的能力。

目前，我國法律系一般只要求高年級學生參加司法實習，而低年級學生則很少有實習鍛煉的機會。實習成績在四年學習總成績中所占的比重很低，畢業生中往往出現「高分低能」的現象。離校從事司法工作或經辦法律事務，在相當一段時期內，往往不能適應實際工作需要，審案辦案能力不強或案情分析能力欠佳，抓不住要害，或庭辯談鋒不健，說不清論點論據。這與在校期間的訓練方法欠妥有密切關係。

（四）提倡由優秀研究生主辦學刊——法學拔尖人才的搖籃

　　一般說來，西方每所法學院都有一種以上的法學學術雜誌，而校辦法學學術雜誌一般都是由該校學習成績最優的研究生擔任主編和編委，這尤其是美國校辦法學刊物的一大特點。他們的一般做法是：法學院二年級研究生可以自願報名，要求參加該校法學刊物編輯工作，然後由刊物的主編、編委（都是高年級研究生）共同進行考核和審批。考核的主要根據是一年級的學生成績以及當場出題測試的成績，擇其最優者參加編輯工作。頭年的工作主要是查對來稿的腳註，稱為「腳註編輯」，要求把作者投寄的論文來稿中的所有腳註一一查對出處，弄清是否言之有據，是否符合原文原意，並對作者的引證和論證，從內容到方法，作出自己的評論，提交「論文編輯」審議。一篇法學論文，腳註一般在一百至二百個之間，腳註編輯每審畢一稿，等於是「被迫」認真細緻地閱讀了大量的原始資料和有關書刊，大大開闊了學術視野，鍛煉了縝密思考的習慣，培養了一絲不苟的學風。

　　腳註編輯工作成績優良者，次年（即研究生三年級）始能被編委會提升為論文編輯，擔任論文編輯所經受的學術鍛煉和專業知識水準的提高，較之腳註編輯，自然更勝一籌。整個編委會，全由學習成績優異的高年級研究生組成，來稿的取捨，全由編委民主決定。若干學術精深的教授，則被編委會禮聘為刊物顧問，為專業疑難問題提供諮詢意見，但並不干預編務工作。編委中大約半數逐年畢業離校，因而逐年更新一半，使更多新人獲得鍛煉的機會。據了解，曾經擔任過校辦學術刊物編委的畢業生，本身就是高才生的標誌之一，一般是各家大律師事務所爭相羅致的物

件。因此，儘管擔任編委純是無償的義務性社會工作，但美國諸法學院的研究生卻競相爭取入選，樂此不疲。看來，法學院、法律系多辦法學刊物，並由成績優異的高年級研究生主辦的方式，既有利於法學學術繁榮，也是促使青年人早日成才和培養拔尖法學人才的有效途徑之一。

在世界民族之林中，中國人的智慧、勤勞和開拓精神，素來享有盛譽。「拿來主義」更是魯迅先生所一貫宣導的信條。「他山之石，可以攻玉。」在法學人才培養的措施和方法上，我們不妨借鑑他人的經驗，拓出自己的新路，使法苑新苗茁壯成長，人才輩出。

（五）注重開發利用外籍華人和港臺留學生中的法學人才資源

在國外，不時可以遇到開業的外籍華人律師、法學教授以及正在法學院攻讀J. D.或L. L. M.或S. J. D.學位的港臺研究生。他們的共同點是：（1）英文根底深厚，法學基本知識較好，對所在國的法律學有專長或較為熟悉；（2）對我黨十一屆三中全會以來所釐定和貫徹的基本政策表示贊同，民族凝聚力和向心力與日俱增；（3）有的已在國外立足，有的正在爭取並有很大可能在國外就業。由於國外物質待遇遠較內地優厚，而且他們對內地還存在不同程度的疑慮或誤解，所以不願長期回國工作，但不少人很想短期回國講學、工作或居留，既為祖國法學繁榮和法制建設出點力，也便於他們自己更深入具體地學習中國法律，提高在國外執業的能力和充當中外交往中的法律橋梁。鑒於我國現有法學人才短缺，能熟練掌握外文而且熟知外國國內法的法學人才尤

缺，因此，上述人才資源頗有開發利用的必要與可能。如何適應他們的業務特點和思想特點，擬訂相應的政策，採取相應的措施（包括建立短期招聘的制度），是值得考慮的。

二、關於國際法資料中心的建立

在國內從事國際法教學和研究的人員，常苦於專業資料奇缺，難為無米之炊。再加上國內現有的外文圖書資料分散收藏，互不通氣，單位「壟斷」「保密」不願外傳的現象亦非絕無僅有，這些都是我國國際法學並不繁榮昌盛的重要原因。而國外有些著名的國際法研究所之所以成果纍纍，原因之一就在於注意資料的長期積累和廣泛收集。訪德期間，馬普國際法研究所的圖書館人員在引導客人參觀時，檢索書目，發現了王鐵崖教授一九四五年所撰寫的英文小冊子《論外國人與外國企業的地位》。他們為表示友好情誼，經有關領導同意，當即複印一份收藏，而將原本當面奉贈原作者。原作者此書當年出版於中國戰亂時期，早已散失；此次竟在國外偶獲樣書，實屬喜出望外。該研究所收集資料之廣泛，由此可見一斑。

為儘快改變我國國際法資料奇缺的狀況，似可採取以下辦法：

（1）建立一兩個全國性的國際法資料中心。以我國現有的北京大學國際法研究所和武漢大學國際法研究所為基礎，給以採購專業圖書資料的外匯保證和自主使用權，並指定專人負責，陸續收集和統一整理目前我國各大學、研究所以及外交、外貿等實

務部門所收藏的國際法外文圖書資料目錄，陸續印發各有關單位。同時，在資料中心配備較好的影印機，便於各地專業單位或專業人員前來複製使用。這樣做，既可大量節省外匯，避免外文書刊採購上的重複和疏漏，又能大大提高外文書刊的使用效率。

（2）有些外國法學院、研究所或學術基金會表示願意免費贈送法學書刊，但也要求我方免費贈送公開出版的中文法學書刊資料。為此，應當給資料中心定期撥付專款，供採購中文書刊和對外郵寄交流之用。

（3）訪問聯合國歐洲總部（即聯合國駐日內瓦辦事處）時，該部總負責官員E. Suy表示願將私人收藏多年的全套《美國國際法雜誌》（自1946年迄今，計38年，二百餘冊）贈送給我國大學。訪美時，紐約大學的圖書館負責人表示願將館中收藏的多餘複本圖書資料，免費贈送我國大學，以便騰出藏書空間。此外，聯合國總部法律事務局的負責人也有免費贈書的同類表示。對於我國國際法教學和科研來說，這些圖書資料都是難得的、珍貴的，但問題是這些書刊的運費須由我方負擔。這一問題亟待有關部門研究解決。

三、關於國際法專業力量的合作

西方發達國家的國際法學術機關（大學、研究所）與國家政府的涉外實務部門，往往是互相通氣、聯繫密切的。許多學有專長的國際法教授和專家，往往同時是政府有關部門的常年顧問或談判代表；在政府涉外部門工作多年的專家或實務人員，也經常

受聘到大學講學或到研究所從事研究工作，總結工作經驗，著書立說。教授、研究員的研究成果和有關建議，常為政府涉外部門所採納，而政府涉外部門也經常提出一些實務問題交付教授、研究員研究討論，並撥出專款，以供徵聘研究工作助手和購置圖書資料等項開支。大學與獨立研究所之間的分工合作和人才交流，也是常見現象。專職研究人員往往到大學兼課，講授研究成果；而大學教授也往往是獨立研究所的兼職研究員。聯邦德國的馬普國際法研究所、加拿大的麥吉爾比較法研究所和外層空間法研究所，其人員結構，都是如此。因此，這些研究成果纍纍，人才輩出，飲譽世界，頗為國際同行所稱道。看來，上述這類體制，頗有利於理論與實際的結合，也有利於國際法學術的繁榮，值得師法。

結合我國的現狀，下述辦法似乎也是可行的：

（1）在外交部、外經貿部、司法部、最高人民法院等實務部門同各大學、研究所之間建立密切聯繫的體制：由前者定期向後者介紹涉外事務和涉外案件中的實況和存在的問題，布置研究的課題和任務，在不違反保密原則的前提下，盡可能提供必要的文檔資料，要求大學、研究所定期寫出研究報告。目前，我國國務院設有國家科委，專司自然科學方面研究任務的布置和下達，在社會科學（包括國際法學）方面，也不妨設立類似的機構，主持研究專案的布置下達和研究經費的調撥。

（2）大學和研究所可隨時聘請外交部、外經貿部等實務部門在職或離休、退休的老幹部和專業人員，擔任兼職教員或研究人員，舉辦專題講座、講學授課或參加研究工作。

（3）現有的北大國際法研究所與武大國際法研究所，除編制以內的專職研究人員外，可以聘請外校、外單位的國際法教授、講師作為兼職的研究人員，以加強校際、所際的互相通氣和分工合作。在研究課題上，力求成龍配套，以適應國家對外交往中的各種需要，避免重複和疏漏；在圖書資料上，互通資訊，互通有無，避免耳目不靈不周，學術情報閉塞無知；在治學經驗和研究方法上，向老前輩、老專家學習，並提倡校際交流，互相取長補短，避免「近親繁衍」，見聞受囿，不利創新。

注釋

* 本文原題為《對我國國際法教育的芻議》，發表於原國家教委主辦的《國際學術動態》（內部刊物）1985年第4期「考察綜述」專欄。其中部分內容曾以《歐美之行看西方法學院對學生實踐能力的培養》為題，先期發表於《福建高教研究》1985年第1期。此次輯入本書，綜合上述兩文，對標題和若干提法稍加調整改訂。
〔1〕　除王鐵崖先生和筆者外。還有一人是西南政法學院的劉鴻惠教授。

第二章
從難從嚴訓練成果人才並出

↘ 內容提要

　　培養研究生的目的是為國家輸送高層次的專業人才，為了快出人才，出好人才，很有必要把出成果作為培養人才的手段。從研究生入學伊始，就從難從嚴出發，狠抓基本功訓練，力爭實現成果與人才同時並出，其基本訓練方式包括：實行「大運動量」訓練，敢於堅持嚴格要求，力排怕苦「眾議」和畏難「惰性」，過法學專業英語關；多學科交叉滲透，提倡兼修相關相鄰課程，建立合理的知識結構；理論聯繫實際，參加各類實踐，提高實務工作能力；充分信賴，畀以「重擔」，嚴密組織，嚴格把關；賦予新設專業較大「成才自留權」，加速形成「人才生產基地」，提高人才生產力。

↘ 目次

　　培養研究生的目的是為國家輸送高層次的專業人才，因而人們通常認為：衡量研究生培養工作的優劣，端視所出人才的品質和數量。至於**出科研成果**，則是培養**成才之後的事**，必須待以時日。我們在培養研究生過程中認識到，出人才與出成果，其先後次序並非如此截然分明。在從嚴訓練基本功的基礎上，應適時地給年輕人**壓擔子**，讓他們承擔一定的科研任務，早出成果，多出成果，**把出成果作為培養人才的手段**，或者說，力求創成果與出人才二者互相促進，**同時並舉**。從研究生入學伊始，我們就確定了這麼一條原則：從難從嚴出發，狠抓基本功訓練，以便為創成果與出人才奠定堅實、必要的基礎。

一、實行「大運動量」訓練，過法學專業英語關

　　本專業研究生的培養目標是造就從事國際經濟法律教學、科研和涉外經濟法律實務的高層次專門人才。這一培養目標決定了外語基本功的重要性，甚至可以說是一切基本功的首要前提。尤其是在目前，我國實行對外開放的時間還不長，造成了對國際經濟往來所適用的國際慣例不夠了解，對各國的涉外經濟法律知之甚少。要在較短時間內迎頭趕上，了解最新學術動態和實務，及時引進最新專業知識，就必須能夠熟練地閱讀、準確地理解外文資料和**原始文檔**。

　　在有限時間內練好外語基本功，不宜在聽、說、讀、寫四方面平均花力氣，而應側重於**閱讀—理解—翻譯**這一主要環節。我們招收的研究生，外文底子比較好，但即使是外語專業畢業的本

科生，也同樣面臨無法熟練閱讀和準確翻譯的問題。因為所接觸的已不是一般的文藝讀物、政論文章，而是專業性很強的國際經濟法文獻。法律語言的特點是準確、精練，但表達的思想又深邃複雜，對句式、語法都有很高的要求，往往一字之差，含義全變。要準確透澈地理解，就得發狠下一番苦功夫。我們在抓外語基本功訓練時，主要注意兩點：一是認真扎實，一絲不苟，逐詞逐句地弄通弄懂；二是要廣泛接觸，大量閱讀，準確地譯成中文。具體的訓練過程要環環緊扣。我們從近年出版的最新文檔資料中選取國際經濟法律的重要參考文獻，或者讓學生們根據自己的研究課題選取有關參考資料，由學生在認真閱讀、深刻理解之後譯成中文，並隨時記下翻譯過程中碰到的疑難問題，包括語言難點和學術上有爭議的問題。譯稿謄寫三份，一份交給導師，一份留底，一份給同班研究生搞「循環校對」。一方面要在校對中發現他人譯文中的錯誤、不妥之處，予以修改更正；另一方面要解答他人翻譯過程中懸而未決的難題。這就體現和發揮了同窗的作用，相互切磋，共同提高。隨後，在導師指導下進行小組講評，發揮集體的智慧協力攻關，解決疑難。這樣做，既擴大了研究生的知識面，又促使他們認真地去思考問題，發揮學習的積極主動性。

翻譯、互校、講評、答疑、討論，每一個步驟都要求學生認真對待，實行「綜合評分」。實踐表明，經過這幾個環節的反覆訓練，學生的專業外語閱讀理解能力以及專業知識水準都能在較短時間內得到明顯提高。因為在閱讀外文專業文獻中，從似懂非懂到透澈理解，是一個飛躍；從只能意會、無法言傳到克服障

礙、正確地表達，又是一個飛躍；就翻譯而言，從逐詞逐句對譯、佶屈聱牙，到修改成通順規範的現代漢語，又是一個飛躍。我們的專業外語訓練並不停留於此。由於學生接觸、閱讀的都是近期的外文資料，這些資料反映了國際上本專業的最新學術動態和研究成果，因而有必要予以引進、消化、吸收並介紹給國內學術界。再者，研究生的訓練中還有教學實踐這一環，還要進一步要求他們把從專業外文新資料中獲得的知識條理化，經過融會貫通，寫成講稿，傳授給同窗和本專業的本科生。因此，備課、試講這些環節，又是一次新的飛躍。簡言之，研究生的專業外語基本功的訓練是與日後的教學、科研緊密聯繫在一起的。總的要求就是**熟練地閱讀、深刻地理解、準確地翻譯、流暢地表達**。要達到這一境界，需要付出艱苦的勞動。導師的職責，不僅在於從方法上給予指導，還在於嚴格要求，使研究生在訓練過程中養成一絲不苟的、嚴謹的學風。

　　抓專業外語基本功訓練，要堅持「大運動量」原則。起初，研究生對「大運動量」訓練的意義認識不足，壓力大些，鑽研辛苦些，就頗有牢騷，用他們自己的話來說，「有時甚至會『怨聲載道』」！但導師秉持「教不嚴，師之惰」的古訓，從不「姑息」遷就，敢於力排怕苦「眾議」和畏難「惰性」，堅持嚴格訓練的原則。同時，又常常援引當年周恩來總理特聘日本「狼」教練大松博文嚴格培訓中國女排，苦練基本功，打下堅實基礎，從而使她們在後來的國際大賽中連連奪取冠軍的故事，對「叫苦不迭」的青年同學加以啟發誘導，促使他們提高勇於吃苦的自覺性。反覆引導他們思考：中國女排成功的秘訣何在？為什麼能在短期內

不但達到國際水平，而且奪得「五連冠」？顯然，其主要經驗之一就在於日常堅持大量的、嚴格的、單調的摸、爬、滾、打。只有在基本功訓練中不怕大量流汗、不怕皮破血流，才能練出過硬的水準，贏得勝利和榮譽。總之，基本功的訓練絕對不能「講價錢，打折扣」。就這樣，促使每個研究生在短短一年中，精讀細譯十萬字以上的原始資料，循環校對他人十萬字以上的譯稿，之後，閱讀理解能力普遍得到提高。正如俗話所說：「磨刀不誤砍柴工。」他們也嘗到了基本功訓練的甜頭。不少研究生事後反映：為寫作論文或專著而收集資料時，能從浩瀚的外文專業書刊中較快地檢索所需材料，略加流覽，便可決定取捨。撰寫論文時，也取得了時間上的效益，因為得心應手地使用專業外語這個工具，為他們的科研提供了很大的便利。自此以後，歷屆研究生都心悅誠服地接受了這一整套的嚴格訓練方案。

二、多學科交叉滲透，建立合理的知識結構

　　建立合理的知識結構，是每一學科都可能面臨的問題。國際經濟法是新興的邊緣學科，與世界經濟、國際經濟關係、法學都有密切的關係；同時，它雖然是一個獨立的法律部門，但與國際公法、國際私法又都具有許多互相交叉滲透之處。因此，就知識結構而言，從上到下，應該包含三個層次：

　　第一個層次，是國際經濟法這一學科的核心知識。從課程設置來說，國際經濟法總論、國際貿易法、國際投資法、國際貨幣金融法、國際稅法、國際海事法等應作為國際經濟法專業的主幹

課程，是本專業碩士研究生必須系統學習、牢固掌握的。

第二個層次，包括一般法律基礎課和國際經濟法的專業基礎課。一般法律基礎課指法學基礎理論、憲法、民法、民事訴訟法等課程，專業基礎課則包括國際公法、國際私法、比較民商法、涉外經濟合同法等課程。這些基礎課都在不同程度上與國際經濟法具有內在的聯繫，對本專業的學習和研究也是必不可少的。

第三個層次是政治經濟學、世界經濟、國際貿易、國際金融等學科的基礎理論和知識。國際經濟法作為一門邊緣學科，植根於國際經濟關係，它的產生和發展，必然受到世界經濟形勢的影響。要把握國際經濟法的本質和規律，只有上述兩個層次還不夠，必須對國際經濟學作一番深入的探討。涉外經濟實務方面的知識，對於本專業的學習也有很大的幫助。為了使本專業的研究生具有堅實的基礎知識，我們總是鼓勵他們跨系、跨學院選修並學好相鄰學科的課程，打好基礎，擴大知識面。我們認為，就法學法，就法論法，不利於本專業研究生建立合理的知識結構。因此，對相鄰學科知識的學習和掌握，也應包括在基本功訓練的範圍裡，而且是本專業研究生訓練基本功的重要內容之一。

擴大知識面與有所專攻，如能妥善處理，二者並不矛盾，也可以同時並舉。前幾批招收的十餘名研究生相繼進入高年級後，我們就在確定學位論文選題時有意識地把他們分布在國際經濟法的五個主要分支，讓他們把各自的科研、學習與本專業本科生課程設置的需要結合起來，分別選定國際貿易法、國際投資法、國際貨幣金融法、國際稅法、國際海事法等為重點學習和研究的範圍。這樣，在打好基礎的同時又各有所長，畢業後，很快就能承

擔本專業本科生各門主幹課程的教學工作。通過自力更生，「成龍配套」地培養了廈大國際經濟法專業本科的第一代師資力量，不但在短期內就開齊了本專業的應有課程，使教學逐步系統化，而且準備了促使本專業科研成果逐步系統化的有利條件。

三、理論聯繫實際，提高實務工作能力

國際經濟法這門學科的實踐性很強。我們利用學校地處經濟特區的有利條件，結合本省市的具體情況，學術界當前爭論的現實、理論問題，國家決策方面的疑難問題，進行學習和研究。廈門特區的涉外經濟活動比較多，從客觀條件來看，可謂「得天獨厚」，有利於在國際經濟法的教學與科研中培養理論與實際相結合的優良學風。

廈大設有律師事務所，法律系多數教師都參加了兼職律師工作，律師事務所成了他們很好的實踐基地。我們也安排研究生從在學期間起就在律師事務所實習，在兼職律師指導下，參加涉外經濟法律的實務工作，如涉外經濟合同的草擬、談判，提供涉外經貿問題的法律諮詢，參加涉外經貿糾紛的訴訟活動等，充分運用所學的知識，在分析和解決實際問題的過程中，深化理論知識，並不斷得到提高。另外，組織高年級研究生參加經濟特區的立法活動，為特區法制建設做貢獻。如廈門市人大草擬廈門經濟特區條例時，就請廈大法律系教師提供諮詢意見，我們也安排研究生參加討論，探討和權衡各項有關條文規定的利弊得失，鍛煉和提高他們分析實際問題的能力。我們還曾接受福建省有關領導

部門的委託，組織研究生翻譯校訂本省為貫徹執行《國務院關於鼓勵外商投資的規定》所制定的地方性法規。在為地方政府提供服務的過程中，鍛煉了運用專業英語對外商宣傳我國有關政策法令的實務本領。這些工作實踐都為研究生日後從事涉外經濟、法律工作積累了有益的經驗。

近年來，隨著我國進一步實行對外開放政策，許多新的法律問題也不斷出現。我們獲悉：我國正在考慮是否參加一九六五年制定的《華盛頓公約》，即《解決國家與他國國民之間投資爭端公約》。對此，國內學術界意見不一，眾說紛紜。我們認為，爭論雙方都有一定理由，但均從一般原則出發立論，缺乏足夠的事實根據。除了應該進一步深入研究仲裁機構（ICSID）的體制以外，還應了解它設立以來是怎麼運轉的，處理過哪些具體的案件，處理過程中對發達國家有哪些偏袒，對發展中國家是否有過歧視等等，據以判斷我國作為發展中國家是否應該參加。根據這種認識，我們組織研究生結合他們的外語基本功訓練和學位論文寫作，翻譯了大量有關ICSID的基本文獻，分工撰寫專題研究報告，並擬將研究成果彙集成冊出版，供我國有關決策部門和立法部門參考。這項研究課題，由於緊密聯繫實際，切合國家急需，已得到有關部門重視。同時，對於本屆研究生也是一次有益的嘗試，使他們從解決現實問題出發，開展科研、集體攻關。

四、充分信賴，畀以「重擔」，嚴密組織，嚴格把關

經過兩三年嚴格的基本功訓練之後，研究生的視野擴大了，

思維、表達、寫作各方面的能力也都有了一定程度的提高，再加上年輕人特定的優勢，諸如精力充沛、思維敏捷、善於接受新知識等等，因此具有較大的潛力。如果把他們組織起來，適時地給他們壓擔子，並加以引導，就可以成為一支具有**攻堅實力**和**開拓精神**的科研隊伍。我們認為，應充分估計到這支隊伍蘊藏的能量，信賴他們，熱情地鼓勵他們承擔科研任務，**勇於「自討苦吃」，敢於超過常規負荷**，從在學期間，就把學習的心得體會、知識積累、專題研究與日後的實際工作、教學任務、科研專案結合起來，經過不斷努力，力爭多出成果，快出人才。

在出成果中培養人才是一個行之有效的辦法，但這同樣需要在導師的精心組織、悉心指導之下，才能達到預期的目標。若放任自流，就形不成一股強勁的攻堅實力，也不利於對研究生個人的培養。一九八五年，我們接受了國家教委博士點基金的重點科研專案，編寫一套國際經濟法系列專著，包括國際貿易法、國際投資法、國際貨幣金融法、國際稅法、國際海事法等。這在當時是一個大膽的設想，因為要對國際經濟法這一學科的五個分支部門同時進行深入的研究，在短短兩年內寫出共約一百五十五萬字的系列專著，成套推出，這在國內尚屬初次嘗試，任務是相當艱巨的，更何況我們的第一批專業師資隊伍當時才剛剛建立，人員和力量顯然都不足。但我們對這些年輕人的潛能作了實事求是的估量。接受任務之後，就以這批初出茅廬的碩士畢業生為骨幹，同時也挑選了幾名較優秀的在學研究生，組成攻關小組，既「**異想天開**」，又**腳踏實地**，立足於刻苦的學習和研究，充分發揮潛力，要求他們盡可能廣泛地收集國內外最新的研究成果，潛心鑽

研。另外，在充分估量年輕碩士生潛力的同時，也清醒地看到他們的弱點，如學術上不夠成熟，不同程度地存在治學經驗不足，學風不夠嚴謹，知識面不夠寬等，這些都有待於及時得到同行、前輩的指導。針對這些弱點，本專業點導師又分別邀請國內各有關分支學科的**知名學者**、教授（如安徽大學朱學山教授、復旦大學董世忠教授、南開大學潘同龍教授和高爾森教授、中國政法大學吳煥甯教授等）給予具體指導和**嚴格把關**。在審訂年輕作者的書稿時，不符合要求者退回重寫，有疏漏處退回補充，錯誤的予以改正，累贅者予以刪除。在青年碩士生勤奮筆耕、同行前輩學者嚴格把關之下，終於完成了國家教委下達的科研任務。一九八七年十一月，全套五本系列專著正式出版，不但成書品質得到保證，而且使年輕人在寫作過程中經受了較全面的嚴格鍛煉。

學界人士認為，這套系列專著問世，對於國際經濟法這門邊緣性學科在中國的興起，在一定程度上發揮了開拓創新的作用。它們具有兩個鮮明的特點：（1）材料新：引進了國際經濟法的新知識和新資訊，因為它們直接取材於近期外文書刊有關國際經濟法的最新學術動態和科研成果；（2）見解新：站在第三世界國家的共同立場上，從中國的實際出發，評析國際經濟往來中的法律問題，提出自己的見解，為建立具有中國特色的國際經濟法學體系作了添磚加瓦的努力，也得到有關部門的重視。一九八六年，司法部教育司教材編輯部組織編寫國際經濟法學科系列教材，除了本專業導師擔任《國際經濟法總論》《國際經濟法參考資料》兩本書的主編以外，還有五位青年教師應邀參加其他五本教材的編寫工作。這說明他們的刻苦勞動已經得到了一定的社會

承認；也說明了在嚴密組織、嚴格把關的前提下，這些**新生力量**是可以信賴的，他們將在實踐中不斷地得到鍛煉，取得進步和提高。

五、賦予較大「成才自留權」，加速形成「人才生產力」

幾年來，我們的培養工作取得了一些成績，這與國家教委和學校領導的關心和重視是分不開的。我們希望再經過若干年的努力，利用現有的基礎和有利的客觀條件，把廈大國際經濟法專業建設成為我國培養國際經濟法高層次專門人才的主要「生產」基地之一，進入全國同類專業的前列，為國家輸送更多的人才。

就目前的情況來看，我們認為首先有必要允許新興學科的新設專業在畢業研究生的使用和分配方面適用靈活政策，擁有更多的自主權和「自留權」，對畢業研究生的使用應該相對地集中，組織他們集體攻關，相互配合，分工協作，以便在較短的期間內，迅速形成培養人才的生產力，從而源源不斷地為國家輸送這方面的人才。新學科與老學科、白手起家的學校與積累有餘的學校應該區別對待。對新學科中的新設專業，應當像對剛開始贏利的外資、合資企業一樣，允許它們享有「二年免稅、三年減半納稅」的優惠待遇。在成才研究生的分配上，允許培養單位多留些人，這才有利於他們在沒有外來援助的情況下，通過自力更生，加速形成生產力。對老學科、老專業來說，「防止近親繁衍」是對的，但不能絕對化，不分青紅皂白地推行於新設的專業。成才研究生的分配使用如果過於分散，就有如一架拆散的工作母機，

東一個馬達，西一條皮帶，南一個齒輪，北一個螺絲釘，不利於更多地製造新機器，不可能建設起人才培養的生產基地。

其次，學校的物質待遇比起涉外經貿部門、政府機關、企事業單位來要相對差些，研究生的「從政熱」「從商熱」在各個專業不同程度地存在著，而在國際經濟法專業尤甚。要使研究生安心在教學、科研機構工作，還有待於各級領導部門採取合理的、切實有效的措施解決待遇差距問題，以便「穩定軍心」「提高士氣」。此外，高職稱的比例和名額限制，也直接影響到學術梯隊的形成以及教學、科研人員的工作積極性。對確有才華，又經過努力取得頗佳科研成果的年輕人，應該努力創造條件，讓他們上。這個問題，對於新興學科的發展影響較大，希望能夠引起有關部門和領導的重視。

注釋

* 本文於一九八八年由當時的廈門大學博士生劉智中根據筆者的講話錄音整理，原載於國務院學位委員會和國家教委聯合主辦的《學位與研究生教育》1988年第5期。因篇幅所限，原文稿在該刊發表時曾有所刪節，現恢復全文，輯入本書。

第三章
「博士」新解*

◥ 內容提要

「博士」應當是博學之士、博采之士與博鬥之士的「綜稱」或「合成體」。一個合格的「博士」，其學識範圍應擴及本專業的中、外、古、今；應能瞄準本學科的中外最新前沿新知，消化吸收後創出新高度；應刻苦拼搏，「自討苦吃」，方能有成。

◥ 目次

「傻博士」曾與「窮教授」並列，一度是用以嘲人或自嘲的一對「美稱」。嘲的大概是其耕耘之艱辛與其收穫之菲薄，反差甚大，因而感慨於分配之不公。然而，曾經「蕭條」一時的「博士業」，近來卻出現了「考博熱」，而且迅猛升溫。這標誌著人們在體制改革深化過程中價值觀念的重要改變，自屬可喜。不過，據報導，也有業內人士擔心在這種新氣象下不無某種隱憂，「使博士教育嚴格的管理體系面臨著從未有過的考驗」[2]。

　　五六年前的這種隱憂，如今竟在某種程度上「不幸而言中」。在商品經濟大潮的衝擊下，在某種腐敗風氣的侵蝕下，一向相對「清高」甚至擁有「名牌」的某些高校，某些管理者和被管理者也放鬆了應有的學術自律，其教授和博士的知識「含金量」明顯下滑，甚至出現了鍍金冒稱「足赤」剛剛入學就大量印發名片，赫然自封「J. D.」或「博士」，以攫取某種「效益」；存心混過三年，就文憑到手，也果真有如願以償的。諸如此類，說輕些，是「短斤缺兩」，說重些，恐怕近乎摻假偽劣產品及虛假廣告。對此類現象，社會正直人士已經公開質問：「教授貶值為哪般？」並且大聲吶喊：「該擠擠學術泡沫了！」[3]

　　單就博士而言，看來問題就出在其「嚴格的管理體系」在某些學校日漸鬆弛了。在強調「依法治國」的宏觀環境下，攻讀法學博士學位乃是「博士熱」中之一大熱。追求者眾，難免也面臨著嚴格管理體系是否日漸鬆弛的現實問題。

　　說到「嚴格的管理」，無非是把好品質關，做到「嚴進」和「嚴出」，使博士之名與博士之實嚴格相符。這顯然應是管理者與被管理者的共同追求。

　　從這個意義上說，似不妨對「博士」一詞略作新解：它是**博學**之士、**博采**之士與**搏鬥**之士的「綜稱」或「合成體」。

　　「博士」必須博學，自是題中應有之義。一個合格的博士，其學識範圍自應擴及本專業的中、外、古、今。業務上的高精尖，離不開比較寬廣的基礎知識面和過硬的中文、外文基本功。如果博士閱讀外文資料的速度只比蝸牛略快，或筆下中文錯別字不斷，而又自解為「雕蟲小技，微不足道」，則此種「大將」風

度實在不敢恭維。

博學是目的，博采是手段。博采提倡瞄準本學科的中外最前沿新知，奉行「拿來主義」與「消化主義」相結合，創出新高度。有如蜜蜂，廣泛採集最新鮮的「花蜜」，絞盡腦汁，和以心血，釀成科學之新蜜。而不是如蜘蛛之懸空結網，貌似「體系完整」，卻華而不實；也並非如螞蟻之只善搬運和堆砌，卻不致力於開拓和創新。博采的前提之一，是虛懷若谷，具備「海綿」精神，善於吸收他人科學新知的涓涓滴滴，忌的是「自我感覺良好」，淺嘗輒止，或眼高手低，志大才疏。

「博」，古通「搏」，兩字同音同義。故「博士」亦指其「拼搏」的必備之素志恒心和必具之治學精神。「梅花香自苦寒來」，「學海無涯苦作舟」，所喻的都是務必刻苦拼搏和「自討苦吃」，方能有成。如此，平日「喝咖啡的時間」比別人少，卻心安理得；必要時通宵達旦，廢寢忘餐，也不喊累，卻自得其樂，甚至自覺活得很「瀟灑」，這就漸臻於「博士」的化境了。

一言以蔽之，如能致力於兼具此三「博」要素，則博士之名實嚴格相符，並不難預期。

附錄一　官員與老闆：心儀博士帽[*]

王曉暉

當幾位經理漫步在中國社會科學院研究生院秋日的校園時，共青團中央書記處第一書記李克強已經在未名湖畔戴過博士帽了。

海關總署副局級官員黃勝強今年以驕人成績叩開博士之門的時候，中國名牌三鳴養生王的總裁又報考了中國科技大學研究生院。

不知數學與養生之間有多少的距離和聯繫，但可以確認的是，近兩年的中國「考博熱」中，官員考博和老闆考博已成為此間一大景觀。

「考博熱」來得迅猛。前十年招不滿博士生的中國社會科學院近來招考比例激增到1：5。中國科學院招收的博士再次突破了歷史最高水準，今年入學的博士人數預計又很可觀。國家教委去年的計畫在眾多方面的要求之下被打破，實際招收人數超出預定人數兩千多，達到九千人以上。

計畫變更的原因有多少是因為官員與老闆的介入，這個數字難以統計。不過事情正像中國社科院研究生院黨委副書記翁傑明所說的，戴上黑帽子的博士官居要職的事實和身居星級賓館的老闆日夜兼程備考博士的消息已成為中國「考博熱」與生源多元化的重要依據。

平心靜氣，參與過中國政治經濟生活具體運作，官員與老闆重返校園去讀書，這中間的動力何在呢？在政府部門供職的李先生說，我們必須先期致力於自身知識結構的完善。因為，經濟給政治帶來的影響無法回避，因為國家的現代化首先要求人的現代化。

按照翁傑明估計，二十年後，中國的領導群體將由一批具有碩士、博士頭銜的職業、半職業管理者組成，而一個健全的知識結構是他們所必需的。

至於老闆對博士帽的嚮往則隱約折射出他們對儒商的嚮往。另外，在商言利，有一頂博士帽戴在公司頭頂，公司的信譽即可瞬間陡增，屆時，知識的力量便可以在公司的生意上以數字的形式表現出來。

其實，以考博為愚鈍之舉還只是昨天的事情，「傻博士」的稱呼仍依稀響在耳畔，考博士的熱潮就迅猛地來到了眼前。無論是嚮往健全的知識結構，還是借助博士桂冠達到實利的目的，究其根本，還是知識的力量越來越被人們認識。翁傑明說，中國的市場經濟逐步有序化，靠機遇和冒險去獲取超額利潤不會再是一種普遍現象了。不過，也有業內人士指出「考博熱」引出招博方式的多樣化。據稱，操作過程中各種利益的驅動使博士教育嚴格的管理體系面臨著從未有過的考驗。

附錄二　「教授」貶值為哪般 *

苗體君

近年來，「教授滿街走」已成為高校的普遍現象。北京大學著名學者季羨林教授曾極而言之：「如今不管是誰，只要能在北大謀一個教書的位子，就能評上教授。」而在七八十年前，連魯迅、梁漱溟這樣的大學者也只能被聘為講師。今天，稍有名氣的大學多在拼命增加教授的數量，一些院系甚至提出「告別有講師」的奮鬥目標，廣東還有大學趁合併之機一次性突擊評出了四十多個博導。這不禁使人想起「大躍進」時期全民煉鋼鐵的那一幕。

筆者日前在南京大學檔案館查閱有關校中資料時發現，一九

二七年時的南京大學（時稱「第四中山大學」）竟沒有一位教授，即使是從國外回來的諸如芝加哥大學畢業的吳有訓博士、哈佛大學畢業的竺可楨博士、法國國家科學院畢業的嚴濟慈博士，也都只被聘為副教授。而到新千年來臨之際，南京大學的教授已達千餘名。難怪那裡的一位博導對學生說：「別稱我教授，現在的教授一分錢能買好幾個。」

當今社會對教授們的期望值總是很高，其實高校也並非什麼理想、乾淨的知識殿堂。十年前畢業的優秀本科生、研究生很少有人願意到高校當教師，因為這個職業太清貧，連不太優秀留下來做教師的，也被視作進了「鬼門關」。教師隊伍的整體素質亟待提高已是不爭的事實。筆者認為，現在的高校教師大致可分為兩類：一類真正有本事且熱心教育；另一類沒什麼本事，因能力不足從社會大舞臺退到學校，只圖混口飯吃而已。

在新中國的五十多年歷史中，「文化大革命」前對教授的評審，在數量和品質上都有所限制，教授是潛心做學問的象徵，含金量大，中央教育部直接參與對教授的評審與任命。「文化大革命」結束，在恢復高校職稱評審制度的開始幾年還比較正規，後來隨著職稱評審的最終權力下放，「濫評」現象就出現了。

一些學校對教授的評審不重視學術水準和教學能力，而要按教師的工作年限排隊。有些學校為了解決教師職稱，竟由校領導出面編寫教材及教學指導書目，再強賣給學生使用，其實有些教授們編的教材幾乎都是照抄別人的，實在沒有多少學術價值。

我國現行的官本位體制是導致教授貶值的一大原因。在高校僅做個專職教師還不夠，想盡快提升職稱不從政不行，多數人稱

之為「曲線提升」。有了行政職務就有了「學術」，就可以憑藉手中的權力占有科研經費，出版專著都可以找人代筆。

學貫中西的大學者錢仲聯，可謂江蘇省學術界的一塊金招牌。二十年前國家首次審批申報博導時，他所在的學校向北京申報了不包括他的一百餘人，甚至該校的膳食科長也名列其中。北京的評審者沒有找到他的名字，就通知江蘇省火速上報他的材料。結果當只有錢仲聯一人為博導的批文回到該校，大家都呆了。這個真實的故事很快傳遍了全國學術界，當時中央評審之正規可見一斑。

這類事情同時反映了我國「不患寡而患不均」的傳統觀念對評聘教授工作的滲透。天津某大學的一個好友告訴我，他取得博導的成功秘訣是在學術上「團結領導和廣大群眾」。原來他每次撰寫著作或論文，總是添上領導或一些教師的名字，如此把自己辛勤獲得的成果均分，以求得大家的支持和擁護。

不能破除教授終身制是造成教授貶值的又一個原因。教授頭銜多是高校教師最終的追求目標，一旦得到，他們中的不少人便要享受教授頭銜帶來的諸多好處，而對教學、科研不會再有多少興趣。

眼下拉關係、送禮在職稱評審時也成為時尚，最具學術說服力的博導評審都不例外。筆者今年在北京參加一個學術會時，才得知一個多年未見的好友成了博導。他的學術資本只是兩篇品質一般的論文，此次榮升的關鍵是他占據教務處處長的職位。他私下裡對我說，他們學校剛成為博士點的某專業，是花了二十萬元買來的。

附錄三　該擠擠「學術泡沫」了 *

周大平

據教育部去年底統計，在我國高校的四十六點三萬名教師中，教授和副教授占32.4%。高級教學職稱頭銜的人數指標符合國家標準，而其中是否如這篇來稿中所言「教授」貶值，恐怕只有透過「學術泡沫」去洞察它的深層。

近兩年有的高校擴招，實際上是把大量高考分數中等偏下的考生擴招進了學校，因為考分較高的考生不必擴招也能考入大學。面對新生品質的參差不齊，高校普遍出現了教師的結構性短缺，致使一些本科專業的教師達到滿負荷授課的極限，有的基礎課甚至由在校研究生講授。這種現狀使人想起兩年前北京大學高教研究所的一個預言：就供給的角度說，要大規模擴大招生，必定以降低教育品質為代價。

瑞士洛桑國際管理開發研究院發表的《2000年度國際競爭力報告》表明，中國的國際競爭力已由一九九八年的第二十四位降到第三十一位。清華大學的一個課題組在調查兩個工科系後認為，這與當前我國高等教育品質嚴重下滑有關，其中教師的教學品質下滑是一個關鍵因素。教育部一位官員也委婉地表示，這支隊伍的整體素質有待提高。

儘管誰也無從知道到底有多少高校教師所擁有的教學職稱與實際能力不符，然而教師教學品質下滑的現狀，使我們仍有理由作出這樣的推斷：是那些形形色色無法定論為學術腐敗的行為，導致了當今高校中一些名不副實的「教授」們在「濫竽充數」。

高校的根本任務是培養人。從經濟學的角度講，學生好比是產品，評定其品質是否合格，首先必須擁有一些基礎性的標準，這與教育部所稱的建立教育品質的多樣化模式並不矛盾。其次必須擁有施教者個人的良好素質，如果施教者的教學職稱是注了水的，他本人也就沒有了「可靠度」，所謂「人而無信不知其可」。原復旦大學校長楊福家院士曾舉過一個同類型的例子：前些年上海有個很有名的年輕教授，後來被人發現他的許多論文都是抄別人的，於是他失去了所有的光環。

　　目前高校教學職稱中所以存在「假冒」，一個重要原因是教學品質評價機制的自我封閉，其運作的客觀性和公正性完全取決於體系內主管者的道德自律。一旦這種自律失控，教學職稱評定的「學術泡沫」必然發生。廣東某大學去年一次性突擊評出四十多個博導的事情，就被業內人士判定是一個「內行包庇同行」的典型。

　　我國不是沒有教師職務聘任方面的規定，也不是沒有強調教師教學業績表現的政策導向，然而為什麼還是對混跡在教師隊伍中的「濫竽」無能為力？這的確是一個值得反思的問題。

　　多年來，我們的教育督導往往側重於評價學校的各項硬體達沒達標，各項投入符不符合法定的標準等，而對教師的教學效果如何，學校對師資的管理是否有利於培養人（包括對教授這樣的高級職稱有沒有按需設崗，有沒有面向社會、公開招聘，有沒有平等競爭、擇優錄用、合同管理）等有所忽視。如果教育督導沒有把「人」放在督導的核心，實際上就是在客觀上為那些違反道德準則的行為網開一面。

　　高校的自主辦學權正在逐年擴大，教學品質是教育永恆的話題。從進一步強化監管職能考慮，教育部已著手建立高校教學品質的監控體系。從未來走上社會就業考慮，苦讀幾年的學生最關心的莫過於高校的教學品質「能使自己學到多少東西」。而從自身的生存和競爭考慮，一些學校如果沒有危機感，置學校教學品質於不顧，頻頻在教學職稱評定上違規做手腳，終究要自食其果，被市場淘汰，只是到時候他們有何顏面面對為此付出了沉重代價的在校生們？

注釋

＊ 本文原輯於《專家論壇：中國法學教育的改革與未來》，載《中國大學教學》2001年第4期，高等教育出版2001年版。

〔2〕 參見《官員與老闆：心儀博士帽》，載《人民日報》（海外版）1995年11月24日。

〔3〕 參見以上述質問和吶喊為題的兩篇文章。已作為本文附錄二、三。

＊ 本文原載於《人民日報》（海外版）1995年11月24日。

＊ 本文原載於《瞭望新聞週刊》2001年5月21日第21期。經征得該刊總編室楊桃源主任同意，轉錄於此，以饗讀者。謹向該刊和本文原作者致謝。

＊ 本文原載於《瞭望新聞週刊》2001年5月21日第21期。經征得該刊總編室楊桃源主任同意，轉錄於此，以饗讀者。謹向該刊和本文原作者致謝。

是「棒打鴛鴦」嗎？
——就「李爽案件」評《紐約時報》報導兼答美國法學界同行問[*]

↳ 內容提要

　　一九八一年秋，時值中國實行對外開放基本國策之初，北京發生了一起涉及法國駐華外交官昂瑪努·貝耶華（E. Bellfroid）的「緋聞」和拘留中國女青年李爽的事件。經外國媒體炒作，在國際上鬧得沸沸揚揚，成為轟動一時的「外交事件」。當時，美國法學界有些人士也借題發揮，對中國的「人權」狀況和法制問題議論紛紛，或誤解，或指責，或抨擊，或質疑，不一而足。諸如，中國政府是否尊重和保護人身自由和婚戀自由？中國對駐華外交官的身份地位和外交特權是否給予應有的尊重和足夠的保護？中國政府及民眾是否具有強烈的盲目排外情緒？中國當局是否乘機製造藉口迫害前衛知識份子？此事在中國何以不公開審理並接受外國記者自由採訪和輿論監督？當時筆者正在美國哈佛大學從事國際經濟法學研究，並兼部分講學工作，遂應邀針對由此事件引發的一系列具體問題和質疑作了一次專題演講，依據中國當時有效的法律法規、有關的國際公約以及美國的相關法律和司

法實踐判例，對上述有關問題逐一作了評論和剖析。以下是此次專題演講的基本內容。

↘ 目次

《紐約時報》記者克利斯托弗・S. 雷恩（Christopher S. Wren）寫了一篇新聞特別報導，題為《中國拘禁了法國男人的情婦》[4]。一九八二年一月間，這篇特稿連同另一則短訊[5]，由任課的美國教授[6]加以複印，分發給哈佛大學法學院的博士研究生，供作「當代中國法律」這一熱門課程的參考資料。看來，這兩篇報導，特別是其中第一篇，現在已被當作研究中國現行法律制度的重要素材。

不久前，我從中華人民共和國應邀來到哈佛大學法學院。不少美國同行朋友和研究生得知我來自中國，先後向我提出了有關這一事件的許多問題。諸如李爽究竟是何許人？此案產生的背景

如何？她究竟觸犯了什麼法，犯下了什麼罪？中國政府何故干預她的婚姻自由，竟然「棒打多情鴛鴦」，不尊重基本人權？此案為什麼不公開審理？面對這形形色色的諸多問題，身為來自中國的法律學人，我感到有責任也很樂意同對這一事件感興趣的美國同行朋友們一起來展開討論。同時，鑒於《紐約時報》的上述兩篇報導有含糊不清、不正確或自相矛盾之處，我謹結合中國現行法律、法規的有關規定，提出個人看法，希望通過共同討論，把這一事件的真相和本質盡可能弄個一清二楚、水落石出。

一、李爽是何許人？「李爽案件」的背景如何？

雷恩先生撰寫的上述特別報導稱：

「李爽是一名年方二十四歲的前衛派美工人員，她與法國駐華大使館一名館員，即年已三十三歲的昂瑪努‧貝耶華墜入情網，並且已經訂婚。此間的朋友們都說，**中國人先前曾經許諾這一對情侶可以正式結婚**……但是，本星期二，中國當局公開宣布：這位李小姐已經被判處在一所懲罰機構中接受『勞動教養』兩年。」「貝耶華先生已經與他的妻子分居」。

這一段報導中含有不少誤解、失實和不確切之處。

根據中國的新聞報導，李爽本來是中國青年藝術劇院的一名美工人員，一九八一年一月辭職後，成為一名無業遊民和女「阿飛」。她在很長一段時間裡沒有正當職業，卻從事各種下流活動，違反公共道德，影響了社會秩序。特別應當指出：儘管有關當局曾反覆多次對她提出勸誡，但她卻置若罔聞，依然我行我

素，拒不改正；並且進一步發展到不顧一切後果，乾脆明目張膽地搬入法國外交官貝耶華的寓所，與他同居達兩個月之久，並利用貝耶華的外交官特權來庇護自己。因此，依據中國法律的有關規定，她被有關當局拘留，並由一家執法機關按照正當的執法程式處以兩年勞動教養。隨後，貝耶華就大喊大叫，歪曲事實真相，煽動輿論，猛烈抨擊中國有關當局針對李爽不軌行為依法採取的正當的措施。

針對這些抨擊，看來很有必要嚴格區分正當、合法的戀愛婚姻關係與不正當、不合法的男女兩性關係。眾所周知，中國是一個社會主義國家。國家要求具有勞動能力的每個公民都應當自食其力，並遵守公共秩序和社會道德。中華人民共和國的《憲法》明確規定，公民享有多種自由權利，諸如言論自由、出版自由、集會自由、結社自由、遊行示威自由等等。但是，《憲法》從來未曾規定個人可以享有從事不道德、不合法兩性腐化行為的「自由」。恰恰相反，在中國，一切不道德和不合法的兩性行為都會受到公眾的譴責；而情節嚴重者，則會受到法律的懲罰。毫無疑義，世界上一切正直的人士，包括一切理智的人權主義者和人權宣導者，都絕不會把通姦「自由」或賣淫「自由」認定為個人的正當「自由」，認定為公民「人權」的一個正當組成部分。因為諸如此類的不正當、不合法的兩性行為，早已被公認為違反公共道德、損害和危害民族健康。

自從粉碎「四人幫」之後，中國人民與世界各國人民的接觸日益頻繁。絕大多數外國人是中國人民的忠實朋友，他們致力於促進中國與其他各國的文化經濟交流。但是，也確實還有極少數

外國人仍然沿襲老殖民主義者居高臨下、傲慢無禮的態度，仍然視獨立自主的新中國如半殖民地的舊中國，仍然把新中國看作「外國冒險家的樂園」，他們往往在各種外衣的掩護之下，來到中國為非作歹，恣意欺凌中國老百姓。他們認為在這裡依然可以隨心所欲，尋花問柳。

　　遺憾的是，也確有少數中國女青年為某些外國來客的財富所誘惑，不顧民族的尊嚴和自己的人格，向外國人出賣自己的靈魂和肉體。換言之，她們竟然從事賣淫活動，或從事變相的賣淫活動。如所周知，自一九四九年新中國建立以後，娼妓賣淫活動在中國一直受到嚴禁，並曾一度銷聲匿跡。但是，自一九七九年中國實行對外開放政策以後，娼妓賣淫活動又開始在少數城市中死灰復燃。特別可惡的是，有一些賣淫或變相賣淫活動，竟是在某些外國人的強權地位和特權豁免掩護之下，明目張膽、肆無忌憚地進行的。這顯然是藐視和嘲弄了中國法律的莊嚴，嚴重地傷害了中國人民的民族自尊，並且激怒了中國民眾。因為，這種醜惡現象勾起了中國民眾對一九四九年以前遭受一百多年殖民地屈辱的痛苦回憶，他們強烈地希望在這種醜惡現象重新萌長的初期階段就予以嚴厲禁止。

　　可以說，這就是產生「李爽案件」的部分重要背景。人們如果能在這樣的背景下，結合其他各種因素來觀察這次事件，就不難理解中國有關當局何以採取如此嚴肅認真的態度來處理此事。這種態度正是準確地反映了中國民眾的共同願望，因而獲得了他們的全力支持。

　　誠然，也不難設想，在西方某些國家中，人們對此類現象的

第五編・國際經濟法熱點學術問題長、短評

看法和態度也許會與中國人有很大的差異。這是因為他們的歷史、文化、社會制度和道德觀念迥然不同於中國民眾。但是，我仍然確信，一切外國朋友定能充分理解：中國人曾經飽經憂患，飽受殖民主義者和帝國主義者強加的不勝枚舉的各種苦難、蹂躪、侵害、褻瀆和凌辱，因此，他們不能不時時回顧和總結過去的痛苦經歷，一切外國朋友也定能充分理解和自覺自願地充分尊重中國民眾正當的、無可非議的民族感情。

二、李爽觸犯了什麼法律？犯了什麼罪？

由於李爽是中國公民，她的違法行為發生於中國境內，因此，作為一個主權獨立的國家，中國當局依據中國法律處置李爽的違法行為，並且視之為純屬內國事務，與外交無涉，這是理所當然、無可非議的。看來，有關法律選擇或準據法的此項普通常識，目前已被某些人士置之腦後，因此，有必要重新強調此項常識，並把它作為評析本案的前提和基礎。

我個人的初步看法是李爽的行為觸犯了以下幾種中國法律法規：

首先，她可能觸犯了《中華人民共和國治安管理處罰條例》[7]該條例第五條規定：「有下列擾亂公共秩序行為之一的，處十日以下拘留、二十元以下罰款或者警告」其中所列的第八種違法行為，就是「違反政府取締娼妓的命令，賣淫或者奸宿暗娼」。作為一項十分重要的補充，該條例第三十條進一步規定：對於一貫遊手好閒、不務正業、屢次違反治安管理的人，在處罰執行完

畢後需要勞動教養的，可以送交勞動教養機關實行勞動教養。」

其次，她觸犯了中國國務院《關於勞動教養問題的決定》[8]。該決定第一條規定，對於不務正業，有流氓行為，違反治安管理，屢教不改的人，應當加以收容實行勞動教養。一九七九年，國務院又公布了《關於勞動教養的補充規定》[9]其中第三條載明：「勞動教養的期限為一年至三年。必要時得延長一年。節日、星期日休息。」

雷恩先生的報導中提到，中國駐法國大使館在一九八一年十一月十二日發表的一項聲明中「並未說明李爽小姐究竟犯了什麼罪」。這是不足為奇的。因為該大使館發表的聲明並不是一份裁決書或判決書，因此它無須逐一詳細列出被指控的違法行為和被援引的有關法律條文。但是，一九八一年十一月十四日新華社記者發表的評論中卻已經明確指出：根據中國國務院頒行的《關於勞動教養問題的決定》第一條，李爽被送去接受「勞動教養」兩年。[10]

有人質疑：李爽究竟是否觸犯了中國的刑法？

要回答這個問題，必須先指出以下兩點：

第一，根據我在美國所看到的有關新聞報導，中國政府並未認定李爽的行為是觸犯了中國刑法的犯罪行為，從而根據刑法的有關規定加以懲處；中國政府只是按照勞動教養的有關規定加以處罰。關於這一點，前面已經提到，本文的第三部分將進一步加以評析。

第二，李爽的行為是否觸犯了中國的刑法，取決於法國外交官貝耶華當時的婚姻狀態：在貝耶華與李爽公開同居的當時，這

位男人究竟是單身未婚、已經結婚、喪偶鰥居、已經離異，或是
正在分居之中？雷恩先生在報道中說「貝耶華已與他的妻子實行
分居」，但在同一篇報導的開頭，卻又說貝耶華和李爽「已經訂
婚」，而且「中國人先前曾經許諾這一對情侶可以正式結婚」。[11]
同一篇報導中出現的這兩種說法難道不是自相矛盾嗎？眾所周
知，「分居」是與「離婚」具有本質差異的一種婚姻狀態。即使
在美國的法律規定與官方檔中，前者與後者從來都是嚴格地加以
區分的。[12] 顯而易見，「離婚」意味著有關的法定婚姻關係已經
死亡，而「分居」則意味著有關的法定婚姻關係仍然存活著，只
不過是男女配偶雙方各自分別居住而已。既然如此，貝耶華作為
一個有著合法妻子的「有婦之夫」，在其並未正式依法離婚之
前，怎麼可以合法地與另外的一個女人——李爽「訂婚」？中國
人又怎能「許諾」他們兩人可以合法地「正式結婚」？由此可
見，如果雷恩先生關於貝耶華與其合法妻子「分居」的報導屬
實，那麼，貝耶華和李爽兩人就犯下了重婚罪。[13]

　　有人辯難說：李爽並未與貝耶華正式結婚，而只不過是與貝
耶華同居兩個月而已，因此，她的行為並未構成重婚罪。誠然，
根據一九八〇年公布的《中華人民共和國婚姻法》的規定，一項
合法的婚姻，必須由男女雙方前往婚姻登記機關進行結婚登記。
符合法定條件的，發給結婚證書，確立夫妻關係。[14] 但是，社會
實際生活中卻有不少這樣的事例：男方或女方已經有一個依法登
記在案的合法配偶，卻又與另一個異性住在一起，他和她不是秘
密地通姦，而是公開地儼然以夫妻相待，共同生活，而並不進行
另一次（第二次）結婚登記。在中國的司法實踐中，此類公開同

居往往被認定為「事實上的重婚」，並且按重婚罪處斷，以便更有效地控制這種犯罪行為。這種司法實踐已被總結成為一項公認的原則，並被輯入一九八〇年出版的《法學詞典》[15]中國官方主辦的一家週報《中國法制報》對這一原則也加以採納和宣傳。[16]

對照上述這類司法實踐中總結出來的斷案原則，可以看出，如果雷恩先生對於貝耶華當時婚姻狀態所作的描述準確無誤，那麼，李爽進入外交人員聚居的使館區，並在外交官住所內與貝耶華公開同居達兩個月，這一行為本來就已經構成了事實上的重婚罪。

當然，還應當補充說：如果貝耶華在與李爽公開同居之前，**確實**已經與他的法國妻子辦妥了離婚手續，那麼，李爽的行為可以不構成事實上的重婚。不過，她與貝耶華的所作所為，就其整體而言，仍然可以被認定為**流氓阿飛和娼妓行為**。[17]

三、是打擊「鴛鴦」的無情棒，還是拯救沉淪的救生圈？

雷恩先生報導說，中國「有關當局一向警告中國公民，不要和外國人廝混」。「十分明顯，處罰李爽的用意在於殺雞嚇猴，儆戒其他情侶。不過，現在還弄不清楚此事是否也表明當局有意對知識界的不馴分子採取更加嚴厲的鎮壓迫害措施。」雷恩這些模棱兩可、含糊其辭的評論，把中國人與外國人之間正常、合法的交往與兩者之間不正常、不合法的關係混為一談，也混淆了法律問題與政治問題的界限，並且把再就業培訓曲解為鎮壓迫害與

威脅恫嚇。

眾所周知，中國人民絕不會盲目排外，絕不會不分青紅皂白，反對一切來自外國的事物和人員，也從來不反對中國人與外國人之間進行正常、合法的接觸和交往，包括正常、合法的中外聯姻結親。這方面的事例可謂不勝枚舉，無須逐一列舉最近幾年來已經正式結成佳偶的許多中外情侶。最能說明問題的是：在同一個北京，屬於同一個法國駐華大使館的另一名外交官克里斯琴‧加依亞諾（Christian Galliano），就在一九八一年十月與一名中國女青年趙江愉快地結為夫妻。僅此一例，就足以說明：中國當局對於「中外合璧」型的美滿姻緣，向來是成人之美和樂觀其成的。關於這一項中外聯姻，雷恩先生在前述那篇新聞特稿中也如實地作了報導，這是令人高興的。遺憾的是，法國外交官貝耶華的所作所為卻迥異於這另一位法國外交官加依亞諾。貝耶華利用他所享有的外交官特權，包括司法管轄上的豁免權[18]藐視其派駐所在地東道國的法律法規，從事與其外交官身份極不相稱的不軌行為。具體說來，他作為有婦之夫，卻在正式離婚前就與李爽亂搞男女關係，從事兩性交易，任意觸犯中國法律，並且濫用他所享有的外交官住所不可侵犯的特權[19]以窩藏和包庇李爽。為什麼說是「濫用」外交特權呢？因為，《維也納外交關係公約》明文規定：「在不妨礙外交特權和豁免權的情況下，凡享有外交特權與豁免權的人員，均負有尊重接受國（東道國）法律規章的義務。這些人員並負有不干涉該國內政的義務。」[20]與此相關，一切使館館舍以及享有同等不可侵犯特權的一切外交官住所，也理所當然地「**不得充作**與本公約或一般國際法之其他規則或派遣

國與接受國間有效之特別協定所規定之**使館職務不相符合之用途**」[21] 貝耶華利用外交官住所窩藏和包庇李爽、非法同居的所作所為，顯然違反了《維也納外交關係公約》的禁止規定。

任何外交官員，如果濫用其享有的各種特權，從而嚴重觸犯了接受國（東道國）的法律，則按照《維也納外交關係公約》有關規定的精神，享有主權的東道國就有權根據國際公法的原則採取嚴肅的措施，對付該違法胡為的外交官員。諸如向社會公眾披露其不光彩行為（如貝耶華之不軌行為）的有關事實，宣布他為「不受歡迎的人員」（persona non grata），要求派遣國把他召回或撤換，實質上也就是東道國有權把他驅逐出境。[22] 但是，中國政府出於珍視中法兩國友誼的考慮，盡力避免如此行事。中國有關當局僅僅是局限於依據本國國內法的有關規定，對本國的違法公民（李爽）加以處罰，而並未對觸犯中國法律的貝耶華本人採取本來可以採取的嚴厲措施。

然而，貝耶華不但不領情，反而恩將仇報。他夥同他的一幫朋友，肆無忌憚地猛烈抨擊中國有關當局處置李爽是所謂「鎮壓迫害」知識份子，「壓制自由化」，並且標誌著「中國的改革發生變化」。諸如此類的信口雌黃、造謠中傷、捏造歪曲和大吵大鬧，顯然都是為了混淆視聽，藉以為貝耶華自己那些與外交官身份極不相稱的不軌行為遮羞蓋醜，藉以轉移中外社會公眾的視線和注意力。簡言之，貝耶華正是竭盡全力，妄圖把法律問題歪曲為所謂的「政治」問題，藉以為自己的醜行塗脂抹粉；把李爽下流放蕩的違法行為美化為所謂「政治自由化」，並把中國有關當局依法給予李爽的正當處罰詆毀為對知識份子施加所謂政治上的

「鎮壓迫害」。

顯而易見，所有這些誹謗無非是一場煙幕。明眼人一眼就看穿這場鬧劇的本質。即使有些人士暫時還不明白此事的真相，但只要不存在「先入為主」的偏見（或許雷恩先生也屬此類人士），則隨著時間的推移，也不難透過貝耶華所施放的煙幕，逐漸地看清此事的本來面目。

說到這裡，也有必要針對李爽受到處罰所依據的「勞動教養」法律制度，簡略地談談它的程式和性質。

許多外國朋友以為，在有關當局決定對李爽處以「勞動教養」之前，沒有經過什麼必要的程序，因為他們在雷恩先生的報導中沒有看到有關這方面的敘述。但是，據我所知，在中國駐法國大使館所發表的一項聲明中，卻已經明確指出，「中國的一家執法機關依據執法程式」決定對李爽處以兩年「勞動教養」[23]依據一九五七年與一九七九年由中國國務院先後公布施行的《關於勞動教養問題的決定》與《關於勞動教養的補充規定》，對於需要實行勞動教養的人，應由當地民政、公安部門及有關單位提出申請，報請勞動教養管理委員會認真審查批准後，送往勞動教養機關實行勞動教養。在各省、自治區、直轄市和大中城市分別設立勞動教養管理委員會，由當地民政、公安、勞動部門的負責人組成，領導和管理各該地區的勞動教養工作。勞動教養機關的各種活動，應由當地的人民檢察院實行監督。[24]

雷恩先生並沒有在報導中概述中國實施「勞動教養」的程式。人們當然不應為此而苛責於他。因為，在一篇短短的特別報導中，不可能說得面面俱到，巨細無遺。況且，他也未必熟悉有

關實行「勞動教養」的程式問題。即使他對此略有所知，也未必就有機會直接參加或採訪李爽案件的審訊過程。

在有關審訊問題上，依據《中華人民共和國刑事訴訟法》的有關規定，作為基本原則，人民法院審判案件，一律公開進行。但是，「有關國家機密或者個人陰私的案件，不公開審理」[25]。在案件涉及國家秘密或者個人隱私，如果公開審理可能對國家利益或者對公共道德和社會風氣產生不良影響的情況下，中國民眾和外國來客（包括外國新聞記者）都會被謝絕列席旁聽審理。因為，這些人既不是利害攸關的訴訟當事人，不是證人，也不是通常被允許進入法庭的訴訟當事人的近親、密友、法律顧問、陪審員、法官、法院職員以及與法院業務有關的其他人員。

誠然，前文已經提到，李爽案件並未作為一起刑事犯罪案件並且嚴格地依據刑事訴訟法的程式進行審理，但是，上述審理個人隱私案件有關規定的基本精神，顯然也是適用的，因為這些基本精神本來就應當適用於像李爽這樣的案件。

在這方面，有些美國朋友提出了一些重要的疑問：即使這些涉及個人隱私的案件不予公開審理只是一些例外，即使這些不公開審理的案件總數可能不多，但是，這種做法豈不是侵害了新聞出版自由？更為重要的是，此類不予公開審理的例外做法，使得法院在審理案件過程中不受社會公眾的監督，這豈不是把被告置於可能遭受到不公待遇的危境？

這些問題確實很有趣也很重要，值得進一步探討。如所周知，在這些問題上，人們向來見仁見智，意見分歧；而且就是在美國法學界，也一直聚訟紛紜。究竟應當如何看待不公開審理這

一例外做法，是一項有待深入研究和剖析的課題，就此足以寫出多篇學術論文。在這裡，我們只需要指出一點，即在對待公開審理的問題上，美國法本身也存在著**原則**和**例外**，並且採取類似於中國法的做法。

譬如，作為一項基本原則，美國《憲法》在其第一修正案中規定：「國會不得制定……剝奪言論自由或新聞出版自由……的法律。」第六修正案中進一步規定：在一切刑事訴訟中，被告有權要求實行快速和公開的審理。」第五修正案以及第十四修正案中反覆強調：非經「正當的法律程式」（due process of law），不得剝奪任何個人的生命、自由或財產。綜合這些規定，從整體上說，「新聞出版自由」和「被告公開審理權」兩者都受到憲法的保護，聯邦和各州當局都不得任意加以剝奪。

但是，美國的司法實踐表明，「新聞出版自由」和「被告公開審理權」這兩者都不是**絕對的**，兩者都必須結合其他方面的權益加以綜合權衡，而有些權益則可能證明：在法院審理某些案件時，不讓公眾和新聞界列席旁聽是合情合理的。在美國的司法實踐中，向來可以引據和論證各種各樣的權益，足以令人信服地承認：在某些情況下，完全地或部分地拒絕社會公眾和新聞記者列席旁聽庭審，是合理合法的，為此目的，甚至**可以不顧被告的反對意見**。這些曾經被引據和論證的各種權益中，就含有以下幾種情況：在許多強姦案件中，有必要切實保護少年受害人和出庭作證的少年目擊者[26] 在某類案件中，有必要防止暴露隱名代理人的身份[27] 有必要防止洩漏公司的商業秘密[28] 有必要對制止空中劫機的做法保密[29] 等等。同時，根據這些案例所述，完全地

或部分地不讓社會公眾和新聞記者列席旁聽審理並不是沒有憲法依據的。

除此之外，有些被告往往自願放棄獲得公開審理的權利，並且主動請求採取封閉式或半封閉式的審理，以便保護自己，免受新聞炒作、危言聳聽、獵奇嘩眾之苦，並且避免可能由此造成的審理不公的結果。

兩相比較，社會公眾和新聞記者列席旁聽法院審理的權利，其憲法依據和重要性，當然不會必然超過被告是否願意選擇公開審理的權利。因此，在上面列舉的類似情況下，前一種權利往往會被後一種權利所否定。

重溫這些法律規定和司法判例，人們就會獲得這樣的初步印象：在有關公開審理的問題上，立法機關或司法機關都應當仔細評估和全面權衡各種互相對抗的權益（competing interests），或者在每一起具體案件中，慎重考慮各種有利因素和不利因素，準確地劃分原則和例外，從而在審理和斷案進程中盡可能做到對社會、對國家、對涉案的個人都是公正和公平的。

最後，除了上述有關「封閉式」審理的問題之外，看來也很有必要進一步說明一下李爽所受到的處罰——「勞動教養」的性質和特點。

就其固有意義來說，「勞動教養」本來就不只是一種懲罰，而且是對被教養者實行強制性教育的一種措施。大家知道，中國是社會主義國家，中國《憲法》規定：「勞動是一切有勞動能力的公民的光榮職責」；國家實行「不勞動者不得食」的原則，公民必須「遵守勞動紀律，遵守公共秩序，尊重社會公德」。[30] 根

據憲法的上述基本精神，「勞動教養」制度的建立，目的在於改造那些雖有能力勞動，卻遊手好閒、違法亂紀、不務正業的人，通過勞動教養，把這些人員改造成為自食其力的新人，從而維護公共秩序，有利於社會主義建設。依據有關法規的明文規定，「勞動教養，是對於被勞動教養的人實行強制性教育改造的一種措施，也是對他們安置就業的一種辦法」。在實行勞動教養期間，對於被勞動教養的人，「應當按照其勞動成果發給適當的工資」；同時，為了避免他們在拿到工資後即時揮霍，吃光花光，管理機構可以酌量預先扣出其一部分工資，作為其家屬贍養費或者日後本人安家立業的儲備金。[31]

這些規定表明，「勞動教養」迥然不同於中國刑法所規定的「勞動改造」，這主要體現在兩個方面：（1）勞動改造是執行有期徒刑或無期徒刑的重要組成部分，本質上是一種刑罰；勞動教養在本質上卻不是簡單的處罰，它是一種強制性的教育和職業培訓措施。（2）勞動改造是不能領取工資的；而勞動教養則是有權領取適當工資的。

在中國，勞動教養制度行之已久，實踐證明：在改造和拯救失足青年，使他們轉變為對社會有益的勞動者過程中，勞動教養是特別有效的措施。許多國際知名的外國法官和法學家參觀、訪問了中國的勞動教養所，他們都肯定這種制度對社會進步能夠發揮積極、有益的作用，而且其中還體現了革命人道主義的精神。

因此，任何不存偏見的人自然會得出這樣的結論：中國當局對李爽個人採取的措施，既不是打擊「鴛鴦」情侶的無情棒，也不是恫嚇知識界不馴分子的殺威棒，而只是拯救沉淪青年的救生圈！

附錄一　中國拘禁了法國男人的情婦[*]

〔美〕克里斯多夫・S.雷恩

（北京1981年11月12日電）一個中國女人與一名法國外交官員在北京本地外國人圍牆住區中同居，隨後她被逮捕了。中國政府正在想方設法向西方世界證明：對這個女人進行的審判是合理合法的。

李爽是一名年方二十四歲的前衛派美工人員，她與法國駐華大使館的一名館員，即年已三十三歲的昂瑪努・貝耶華墜入情網，並且已經訂婚。此間的朋友們都說，中國人先前曾經許諾這一對情侶可以正式結婚。

但是，十一月九日，在李爽進入貝耶華先生的公寓同居兩個月之後，她在北京三里屯外交官圍牆住區的入口處被幾名便衣員警逮捕帶走了，當時貝耶華先生正在香港停留，隨後他已返回法國。

此後兩個月，李爽杳無音信。直到本星期二，中國當局公開宣布：這位李小姐已經被判處在一所懲罰機構中接受「勞動教養」兩年。

法國官員十分惱火

此事影響廣泛，涉及許多方面。因為，在宣布判處李爽勞動教養兩年之際，法國外貿部長蜜雪兒・約伯（Michel Jobet）正在北京和官員們會談。據報導，約伯曾為這對情侶出面干預，設法與中國的高級官員，包括鄧小平先生和趙紫陽總理進行交涉。但

他被告知此案純屬中國的內部事務。

據此間法國消息靈通人士說，約伯先生一怒之下，竟然取消了其日程上原定的一場新聞發布會和最後兩場技術性會談，並在當天傍晚拂袖而去，離開北京。另一位消息人士報導說，正值法國高官訪問北京之際，卻披露了李爽被判受罰的資訊，鄧小平認為這是一次「令人遺憾的偶然巧合」。

今天，中國官方的新華社發布了一份專為駐巴黎以及其他各地的中國大使館準備的聲明，針對此事提出了「北京版本」的說法。

這份聲明也由中國外交部提供給在北京當地的一些西方記者。據這份聲明說，「這個問題並不像某些人所說的，是什麼李爽與貝耶華之間的婚姻問題，而是李爽觸犯了中國法律」。

並未說明準確的罪名

這份聲明並未說明李爽小姐究竟犯了什麼罪。不過，有關當局一向警告中國公民，不要和外國人廝混。在北京，外國居民被指定聚居在用圍牆隔開的公寓裡，周圍有士兵保衛。在一些公共餐館，外國人往往被帶到另外的餐廳，與其他中國顧客分隔開來。

儘管此類接觸和結婚都受到阻攔，但都並非不可能實現。今天發表的聲明中就提到，法國駐華大使館中的另一名館員克里斯琴‧加依亞諾（Christian Galliano）就在上個月被許可與中國女青年趙江結為夫妻。今年早些時候，有一個加拿大人被許可與一名中國舞蹈演員結婚。

此間有些外國居民熟悉李小姐案件的有關情況，他們認為，中國的官員們一般持有清教徒般的思想觀念，反對與異己分子搞

男女關係，反對婚外私通行為。李爽明目張膽地搬進貝耶華的公寓和他同居，公開蔑視共產黨人的清規戒律，這就激怒了中國的官員們。貝耶華先生已經與他的妻子分居，她已返回法國。

此外，李爽在北京美術界一個前衛團夥中表現突出，這些美術界人員玩世不恭，政治上標新立異。十分明顯，處罰李爽的用意在於殺雞嚇猴，儆戒其他情侶，不過，現在還弄不清楚此事是否也表明當局有意對知識界的不馴分子採取更加嚴厲的鎮壓迫害措施。

貝耶華目前住在法國。當地正在圍繞李爽案件掀起陣陣喧囂，新華社發表的這份聲明表明這些喧囂使中國人感到困窘。

新華社這份聲明指出：「中國作為一個享有主權的國家，依據中國的法律處理李爽的犯法行為，這是完全正當的。」「此舉純屬中國內部事務，它同中法兩國關係毫不相干。我們相信法國的朋友們一定會也一定能夠理解。」

附錄二　法國外交官說中國拘留了他的未婚妻 *

（**美聯社北京1981年9月12日電**）　一位法國外交官說，員警今天把他的中國籍未婚妻拘留了。

昂瑪努・貝耶華，現年三十三歲，是法國駐華大使館的一名館員。他說，星期四這天他從國外回到北京，得知李爽星期三在外國人聚居的圍牆住區（使館區）外面被抓走了。他們倆就住在這個圍牆區裡面。

貝耶華先生稱：他到公安局去解釋說，李小姐住在他的公寓

裡是合法的，公安局拒不接見他。這位外交官說，李爽離開圍牆住區，想去看望她的姐妹，就被抓走了。中國人必須持有特別通行證，或在外國人陪伴下，才能獲准進入這個圍牆住區。

附錄三　小題大做 **
—— 評白天祥等人在所謂「李爽案件」上的喧嚷

近日來，法國一些報刊和電臺、電視臺就所謂「李爽案件」大做文章。法國前駐華使館外交官埃馬紐埃爾・貝勒弗魯瓦[32]（中文名叫白天祥）接二連三地對法國報紙和電臺、電視臺發表談話，歪曲事實真相，攻擊中國的政策。中國輿論界注意到，這樣大規模的宣傳攻勢，是自一九六四年中法兩國建立外交關係以來所罕見的。

所謂「李爽案件」是怎麼一回事呢？原來，這個被白天祥稱作是他的「未婚妻」的李爽，是中國一個女公民。今年七月起，她被白天祥利用其外交官身份窩藏在北京他的寓所達兩個月之久。李爽由於觸犯中國法律，九月間被拘留，最近根據國務院《關於勞動教養問題的決定》第一條，決定對她進行勞動教養兩年。

這本來是中國政府挽救、教育失足青年的措施，純屬中國內部事務。它同中法兩國關係毫無關係。但令人遺憾的是，白天祥和法國某些人士卻小題大做，歪曲事實，搞得滿城風雨。他們把事情說成是中國阻撓了白天祥和李爽的婚姻，「嘲弄了人權」；還說什麼「中國改變了政策」「壓制自由化」，甚至揚言李爽案

件「損害了中法兩國關係」。

李爽的被決定勞教，根本不是什麼「婚姻」問題。我們決不排外，也不反對中國人同外國人正常的接觸。但李爽的行為表明，在中國確有極個別的人，不顧國家和民族的尊嚴，喪失國格與人格，從事出賣自己靈魂的活動；也確實有極個別的外國人在各種外衣掩護下，從事欺負中國人甚至是別有用心、干涉中國內政的活動。

白天祥攻擊中國政府對李爽的處理「粗暴」。這位曾經擔任過駐中國的外交官，對中國「勞動教養」這一改造、挽救失足青年的有成效的制度居然這樣無知，是令人吃驚的。參觀過中國勞教所的許多國際法學界知名人士都知道，勞動教養不是判刑，這種制度所體現的人道主義精神，使許多失足青年轉變成有用之才。

尤其奇怪的是，白天祥等人攻擊中國對李爽的處理是「鎮壓」「制服」知識份子，攻擊「中國改變了政策」。中國執行什麼樣的政策完全是中國的內政，是用不著外國人來指手畫腳的。中國堅持四項原則，也堅持對外開放的方針，是前後一貫的。「中國改變政策」「壓制自由化」的喧嚷，完全是無的放矢，有意製造混亂。為什麼白天祥硬要把處理一個犯有罪行的女青年這樣一件事，說成是中國「政策的改變」呢？他這樣做是不是要掩蓋他的那些不合外交官身份的活動，轉移人們的視線呢？

中國政府和人民十分珍視中法人民之間的友誼和中法兩國之間的友好關係。中國人是照顧大局的。正是出於這樣的原因，我們對於幹了與外交官身份不相容的事情的白天祥本人並未採取嚴厲措施，也沒有公布他的那些活動事實。我們希望不出現需要公

布這些材料的情況。正因為這樣，我們對於今年九月以來法國一些報刊、電臺就所謂「李爽案件」進行的歪曲宣傳，迄今未予理會。但是，令人遺憾的是，白天祥等人反而變本加厲，利用這件小事，掀起新的軒然大波，這是違背中法兩國人民的意願的。

附錄四　The Li Shuang Case: A Wet Blanket over Romantic Love?*

A news paper special report, writen by Mr. Christopher S. Wren and entitled "China Jails Woman for Affair with Frenchman"[33] has been duplicated, together with another short report[34] and distributed to he students of Harvard Law School this January as reference materials for a course in Contemporary Chinese Law. It seems that both of these reports, especialy the first, are now considered to be important materials for researching current Chinese law.

Since I have recently arrived at Harvard Law School from he People's Republic of China (PRC), a lot of American friends and students here put many questions to me regarding this case, such as: Who is Li Shuang? What is the background of her case? What laws did she violate, what crimes did she commit? Why did the Chinese government interfere with her freedom to marry, throwing a wet blanket over romantic love and disrespecting human rights? Confronted so often with so many questions, I feel obligated to discuss this case with any who are interested. I should like, therefore, to present my personal view of Chinese law in order that the truth and essence of this case might be as clear as possible, for the aforesaid newspaper reports contain many unclear, incorrect or self-contradictory points.

Who Is Li and What Is the Background of Her Case?

Mr. Wren's special report stated:

Li Shuang, a 24-year-old avant garde artist, fell in love with Emmanuel Bellefroid, a 33-year-old French Embassy attache, and they became engaged. Friends here say that the couple was promised by the Chinese that they could get married... On Tuesday the authorities disclosed that Miss Li had been sentenced to two years of "re-education through labor" in a penal institution... Mr. Bellefroid was separated from his wife...

This account contains much misunderstanding, misstatement and inexactitude.

Who is Li? As Chinese reports say, she was originaly an art designer for the China Youth Arts Theater. After resigning in January 1981, she became an unemployed vagrant and woman hoodlum. She had no regular employment for a long time, and instead engaged in indecent activities, offensive to public morals, thus affecting social order. It is especialy necessary to point out that she refused to mend her ways in spite of the repeated admonitions of authorities. Heedless of the consequences, she moved flagrantly into Bellefroid's apartment and lived with him for two months, taking advantage of his diplomatic privileges to protect herself. As aresult, in accordance with the provisions of

Chinese law, she was detained and subjected to two years of rehabilitation through labor (RHTL) by a Chinese judicial organ and according to correct judicial procedure. Since then, Bellefroid has incited a large-scale outcry about this case, distorting the facts and attacking the perfectly correct actions of the Chinese authorities.

Here, a word about the strict distinction between illegal sexual relationships and lawful love and marriage may be quite necessary. As we know, first of all, the People's Republic of China is a socialist country. The state requires each citizen to live by his own work, so long as he is able to work, and to observe public order and social morals. The Constitution of the PRC confirms many kinds of freedom, such as, inter alia, freedom of speech, correspondence, the press, assembly, association, and even freedom of demonstration and freedom to strike. But it has never provided for so-caled "individual freedom" for immoral and unlawful corruption of sex. Quite to the contrary, all immoral and unlawful sexual activities are condemned by the public and, if the circumstances are serious, are punishable by law. Undoubtedly, all honest and upright persons in the world, including all fair-minded humanitarians and human rights advocates should never consider "freedom" of adultery or of prostitution as a proper kind of freedom to individuals or as a proper part of human rights to citizens, because it is universally acknowledged that these activities offend public morals, and harm and endanger national health.

Second, since the smashing of the "Gang of Four", contacts

between the peoples of China and other countries have increased. Most foreigners are true friends of the Chinese people. They continue to work hard to accelerate the cultural and economic exchanges between China and other countries. But a few foreigners inherit the insulting attitude of old colonialists and mistakenly consider the new China to be still the old China a semi-colony, a paradise for the foreign adventurers where sexual enjoyment and dissoluteness can be obtained at will. They go in for bullying the Chinese under the cover of various garbs.

Unfortunately, a few Chinese girls, dazzled by the display of wealth of some foreigners, disregard national dignity and forfeit national character and their own personality, by selling their own souls and bodies. In other words, they engage in prostitution, or prostitution in disguised form. As everyone knows, prostitution, strictly banned since 1949, has disappeared from the Chinese mainland. Its recrudescence in a very few cities, especially that which occurs under the flagrant protection of foreigner's powerful position or certain privileges of a foreigner and thus despises andmocks the sanctity of Chinese Law, seriously injures the national self-respect of the Chinese people and enrages them, because it has brought back the painful memories of the colonial humiliations that they suffered for more than one hundred years before 1949. They do wish to prohibit sternly this phenomenon in its re-sprouting stage as soon as possible.

This is an important part of the background of Li's case. If we view this case against such a background, together with other factors, we can easily understand why the Chinese authorities handled this casein such a serious manner. This strictness accurately reflects the common will of the Chinese people and meets with their full support.

Of course, it is not difficult to imagine that the same situation would probably be viewed quite differently insome Western countries because of the difference in history, culture, social system and concepts of morality. But I am sure that all foreign friends can understand that the Chinese have had to review their biter experiences of the past, which are full of untold tribulations, tramplings, violations and insults imposed on the Chinese people by colonialists and imperialists. They must also, therefore, fuly understand and wilingly respect the proper national feelings of the Chinese people.

What Laws Did Li Violate and What Crime Did Li Commit?

Since Li is a citizen of China and her illegal activities occurred in China, it is entirely proper for China, a sovereign state, to handle the violation of law by Li according to Chinese law, treating it as a purely internal affair. This common sense choice of law seems to have been forgotten by many, so we must re-emphasize it as a prerequisite to analyzing this case.

My own speculation is that Li may have violated the following laws of China: First, she may have violated the Security Administration Punishment Act of PRC. [35] Article 5 provides: "A person who commits any one of the following acts disrupting pubic order shall be punished by detention, fine or warning." One of the acts listed in section 8 is "engaging in prostitution or having sexual relations with a woman secretly engaged in prostitution in violation of the government order repressing prostitutes" [36]. As an important addition, Article 30 further provides: "After their punishment has been completed, persons who are habitual loafers, do not engage in proper employment and repeatedly violate security administration may be sent to organs of RHTL if they require such rehabilitation." [37]

Second, she violated the Decision of the State Council of the PRC on Rehabilitation Through Labor. [38] Article 1 of this decree provides: "The following kinds of persons shall be taken in and their RHTL shall be carried out: (1) Those who do not engage in proper employment, behave like hoodlums,... violate security administration and refuse to mend their ways despite repeated admonitions." [39] In 1979, a Supplementary Regulation was promulgated, in which Article 3 added, "The time period for RHTL is from one to three years... Holidays and Sundays shall be days of rest" [40]

Mr. Wren's report said that the statement issued by the Chinese Embassy in France on November 12 last year "did not say what crime Miss Li had committed." Of course not The Embassy's statement was not a written verdict or judgment, and so it did not need to list, one by one, the details of the chargesand to cite the relevant laws. But the commentary issued by Xinhua reporter on November 14 last year had already clearly pointed out that Li was sent to RHTL for two years in accordance with Article 1 of the State Council's "Decision on

Rehabilitation Through Labor." [41]

Then, did Li violate the current Criminal Law of the PRC? To answer this question it is necessary to point out both of the folowing: 1) In the light of reports that I have read, the Chinese government did not consider Li's behavior a crime violating the Criminal Law and therefore did not punish her according to that law, but disposed of this case pursuant to the Decisionon RHTL. This point has been mentioned previously and will be developed further in Part Three of the present article. 2) Whether Li's activities violated the Criminal Law depends upon the marital status of Bellefroid: when he was living with Li, was he single, married, widowed, divorced, or only separated? Mr. Wren reported: "Bellefroid was separated from his wife." But at the beginning of the same report, he said that Bellefroid and Li "became engaged... [and] were promised by the Chinese that they could get married" [42]. Isn't this contradictory? As everyone knows, "separated" is a marital status substantialy different from "divorced." Even in the legal provisions and official documents of the United States, the former has always been strictly distinguished from the latter. [43] It is obvious that "divorced" means the death of the legal marital relationship, while "separated" means the legal marital relationship is still alive, but that each spouse lives apart from the other. How could a husband, then, having a lawful wife, legally "become engaged" to another woman and call the latter his "fiancee"? How could they be "promised by the Chinese that they could get married" legally? Thus, if Mr. Wren's version is correct, Bellefroid and Li were committing the crime of bigamy. [44]

One might argue that Li didn't marry Bellefroid, but merely lived together with him for two months, therefore, she didn't commit bigamy. True, according to the Marriage Lawof the PRC (1980), a marriage, to be legal, must be registered at the marriage registration office and a marriage certificate must be issued. [45] But there are many cases in which a man or a woman having a legal spouse, lives with an other person of the opposite sex, not only secretly commiting adultery, but openly treating each other as husband and wife without a second marriage registration. In judicial practice, these cases have always been considered de facto bigamy and have been punished as bigamy, so as to control this crime more effectively. These practices have already been summed up in a generaly recognized principle accepted in the recently published *The Legal Dictionary* [46] and also adopted by the authoritative weekly, *Zhongguo Fazhi Bao (Chinese Legal System Reports)*. [47]

Contrasted with these practices, we may say that Li's openly living together with Bellefroid inside the diplomatic compound for two months (had Mr. Wren's narration about Bellefroid's marital status at that time been correct) would have already constituted a crime of bigamy in fact.

Certainly, I should add that if Bellefroid had actualy gone through the formalities of divorce with his French wife before Li publicly lived together with him, Li would not have been commiting bigamy in fact, but her relationship with Bellefroid, as a whole, would still have been considered hoodlumish and meretricious. [48]

A Wet Blanket, a Big Stick or a Life Buoy?

Mr. Wren reported that in China, "the authorities have warned Chinese citizens against mixing with foreigners. ... While she (Li) was obviously used as an example for other couples, it is uncertain whether the case represents a more significant crackdown against the intelectual nonconformity". These ambiguous comments confusethe normal, legal contacts betweenthe Chinese and foreigners with the abnormal, illegal ones. They also confuse problems of law with those of politics, and mistake an atempt to rehabilitate for persecution and intimidation.

It is common knowledge that Chinese are never blindly xenophobic, never indiscriminately opposed to things and persons foreign, and have never objected to normal and legal contacts, including normal and legitimate marriages between Chinese and foreigners. We can cite many examples to ilustrate this. There is no need to list the couples who have been married throughout the years. The recent happy mariage between another diplomat of the very same French Embassy in Beijing, Christian Galiano, anda Chinese woman, Zhao Jiang, last October, speaks suficiently for Chinese allowance of the matrimony between the Chinese and foreigners. This marriage, I am glad to say, has been reported objectively in Mr. Wren's article.

Regrettably, Bellefroid's case was quite different from Galliano's. Taking advantage of his diplomatic privileges, including the immunity of judicial jurisdiction, [49] Bellefroid paid no heed to the statutes and codes of the host country to which he was accredited, and behaved in a way incompatible with his diplomatic status. Together with Li Shuang, he transgressed the above-mentioned Chinese laws and abused his diplomatic privilege of residence inviolability[50] to harbor and shield Li. Why do I say"abused"? Because the Vienna Conventionon Diplomatic Relations expressly provides: "Without prejudice to their privileges and immunities, it is the duty of all persons enjoying such privileges and immunities to respect the laws and regulations of the receiving State. They also have a duty not to interfere in the internal affairs of that Sate." [51] And, of course, the private residence of a diplomat as well as the premises of the mission "must not be used in any manner incompatible with the functions of the mission as laid down in the present Convention or by other rules of general international law." [52]

In the event a diplomat abuses his diplomatic privileges and there by violates the law of the receiving State, the host sovereign State is entitled, according to the principles ofinternational law, to take harsh action against the law-violating diplomat such as making public all facts concerning his (such as Bellefroid's) disreputable behavior, pronouncing him a persona non grata and deporting him. [53] But the Chinese government refrained from doing this out of respect for the Sino-French friendship.This is why the Chinese authorities limited themselves only to punishing a law-violating citizen of their own, in accordance with their internal law.

Bellefroid, however, requited kindness with ingratitude. He and his friends wantonly attacked China's handing of the Li Shuang caseas a "cracking down" on intelectuals, "suppressing liberalization" and as an indication of "a change of policy in China". This hulabaloo of slander and fabrication, of entirely random accusations, is obviously intended to create confusion, so as to cover up Bellefroid's activities, which were extremely incompatible with his diplomatic status, and to divert public attention. In a word, Bellefroid tried hard to whitewash and prettify himself by confusing legal problems with politics: embellishing and beautifying Li's indecent law-violating behavior as so-called "political liberalization", and calumniating a proper legal punishment of Li as so-called political "cracking down" on intellectuals.

This is nothing but a smoke-screen! Those with discerning eyes can see the essence of it at first sight. Someone ignorant of the real facts, but without prejudices, perhaps even Mr. Wren, would gradualy come to see the truth clearly, even through Bellefroid's smoke-screen.

I must also say a few words about the procedure and nature of the RHTL that Li has been subjected to. Many may assume that no procedure for RHTL existed before the decision was made against Li because they didn't find it in the narration of the said report. But, as the statement issued by the Chinese Embassy in France noted, Li was subjected to two years of RHTL "by a Chinese judicial organ according to judicial procedure" [54], In accordance with the Supplementary Regulations on RHTL promulgated in 1979, when a person is to be subjected to RHTL, the mater shall be considered and approved (on the basis of a full investigation, of course) by the"Administrative Commitees for Rehabilitation Through Labor". These Committees are established in the provinces, as well as the large and medium cities, and are composed of responsible persons of the civil administration, public security and labor departments. All activities of RHTL organs must be "supervised" by the peoples procuracies. [55]

Certainly, no one should criticize Mr. Wren too harshly for his failure to outline the RHTL procedure in his report. We understand that it is impossible to include everything in a short special report and that he might not have been familiar with the procedure involving RHTL. Even if he were, he had not been accorded the opportunity to be present at the interrogation proceedings.

As to the last point, according to the Criminal Procedure Law of the PRC, though all cases shall, in general, be publicly tried by people's court, those "cases involving state secrets or the shameful secrets of individuals shall not be tried and heard in public" [56] .On such occasions, i. e. , in cases where the state secrets, personal reputation, or public morality and the fresh air of the community are felt to be at stake, attendance is denied to both ordinary Chinese and foreigners (including foreign newsmen and reporters). These persons are neither interested parties to the action, nor witnesses, nor are they persons who are ordinarily allowed entry into the courtroom: close relatives and friends of the actual parties, legal counsels, jurors, judges and court officers and other persons having business with the court in the case.

Indeed, Li's case was not considered a criminal one and therefore was not tried strictly according to the Criminal Procedure Law; nevertheless, it is obvious that the fundamental spirit of the aforesaid provision should be applicable since it would have been applied to a case such as Li's.

In this regard, some American friends have raised important questions: Even though those cases that are not heard and tried in public are exceptional and may be few in number, don't they nonetheless infringe upon and injure freedom of the press? And even more important, do not such exceptions pose the threat that defendants may be treated unjustly when the court's actions are not subject to public scrutiny?

These are very interesting and significant questions, worthy of further discussion. And, as people are well aware, these issues themselves are not only debatable, but have been debated in legal circles in the United States too. The exceptions to public trial are a subject that requires in-depth research and analysis, and can comprise many treatises in itself. Here we may only point out that in the United States there exist principles and exceptions with regard to public trials that are considerably similar to those of China.

For example, as a general principle, the United States Constitution providesin its First Amendment that the "Congress shall make no law abridging freedom of the press". Furthermore, the Sixth Amendment provides: "In all criminal prosecutions, the accused shall enjoy the right to a speedy and public trial"; and section 1 of the Fourteenth Amendment provides that no state shall deprive any person of life, liberty, orproperty without "due process of law". In short, freedom of the press and the defendant's right to a public trial both are generally protected by the Constitution against deprivation by federal and state authorities. [57]

On the other hand, however, the judicial practices of the United States show that neither freedom of the press nor the defendant's right to a public trial is absolute, but that each must be balanced against other interests that might justify closing the courtroom to the public and the press. Various state interests have been held to be suficiently compelling to justify the total or partial exclusion of the public and the press even over the defendant's objections. Such interests have included protecting young victims and complaining witnesses in rape cases [58]; preventing the revelation of an undercover agent's identity [59]; avoiding disclosure of a corporation's trade secrets [60]; and preserving the confidentiality of anti-skyjacking procedures [61], etc. Moreover, according to these cases, total or partial exclusion of the public and the press is not without constitutional foundation.

Additionaly, the defendant often prefers to waive his right to a public trial and even on his own initiative asks for a closed or partially closed one in order to protect himself from sensationalism in the press, public favor, and any possibility of an unfair trial that may result therefrom.

Surely the right of access of the public or the press to judicial proceedings is of no greater constitutional moment than the defendant's right to a public trial. Thus, the former right might similarly be overridden in circumstances like those listed above.

Reviewing these legal provisions and judicial precedents, we may geta preliminary impression that with regard to the problem of public trials, the legislature orjudiciary must carefuly assess and balance the different competing interests in general, or in each particular case, attentively consider the advantages and disadvantages, so as to precisely carve out the properly principled exception that will be fair and equitable for the society, the state and the individuals concerned.

Finaly, in addition to the closed trial issue, it is essential to further explain the nature and features of RHTL, to which Li has been subjected.

RHTL is not a penalty in the propers ense, but rather a form of education by compulsion. As everyone knows, the PRC is a socialist state. Its Constitution provides: "Work is an honorable duty for every citizenable to work"; the state applies the socialist principle: "He who does not work, neither shall he eat." Citizens must "observe labor discipline, observe public order, respect social ethics" [62] . On the basis of this constitutional spirit, the RHTL system was established in order to reform those persons who have the capacity to work, but who loaf, violate law and discipline, and do not engage in proper employment. RHTL transforms them into new persons who support themselves by their own labor. Further, RHTL preserves public order and benefits socialist construction. In accordance with the express provisions of the relevant decree, the RHTL is "a measure of a coercive nature for carrying out the education and reform of persons receiving it. It is also a method of arranging their getting employment". Persons who receive RHTL shall "study labor and production skills and cultivate the habit of loving labor", so as to "have the conditions of getting employment". During the period of RHTL, they "shall be paid appropriate wages in accordance with the results of their labor". Moreover, consideration may be given to deducting a part of their wages in order to "provide for the maintenance expenses of their family members or to serve as a reserve fund that will enable them to have a family and an occupation" [63]

These provisions show that the RHTL quite differs from the "reform through labor" of Criminal Law in two main aspects: 1) The latter is an important part of fixed-term imprisonment, a kind of criminal punishment—penalty; and the former is not a simple penalty in its proper sense, but a coercive educational and professional training measure; 2) The latter forced labor is without any pay, whereas the former enjoys appropriate wages.

This long-held practicein China has proved that the system of RHTL is especialy effective in remolding and redeeming delinquent and sinking youths into people useful to the society. Both the active, and beneficial role played by this system and the revolutionary humanitarian spirit embodied in it have been recognized by many noted international jurists and scholars who have visited RHTL centers in China.

Thus, anyone without prejudice and bias would certainly come to the conclusion that what the Chinese authorities have done to Li is neither a wet blanket over romantic love, nor a big stick on intellectual nonconformity, but a life buoy for the sinking person!

附錄五　《紐約時報》報導英文原文

N.Y. Times, Nov. 13, 1981, at 36, Col. 1.

China Jails Woman for Affair with Frenchman*

By Christopher S. Wren

Specialto *N. Y. Times*

Peking, Nov. 12-The Chinese Government has been trying to justify to the West the sentence it imposed on a Chinese woman who was arrested, after she began living with a French diplomat in a compound for foreigners here.

Li Shuang, a 24-year-old avant garde artist, fell in love with Emmanuel Bellefroid, a 33-year-old French Embassy attache, and they became engaged. Friends here say that the couple was promised by the Chinese that they could get married.

But on Sept. 9, after living for two months in Mr. Bellefroid's apartment, she was seized and taken away by plainclothes policemen at the entrance to the San Li Tun diplomatic compound while Mr. Bellefroid was in Hong Kong. He has since returned to France.

On Tuesday the authorities disclosed that Miss Li, who had not been heard from for two months, had been sentenced to two years of "re-education through labor" in a penal institution.

French Official Angered

The case took on wider implications because France's Foreign Trade Minister, Michel Jobert, was meeting officials in Peking when the two-year sentence was disclosed. Mr. Jobert reportedly tried to intervene for the couple with senior officials, including Deng Xiaoping and Prime Minister Zhao Ziyang, but was told that the mater was China's internal affair.

According to French sources here, an angry Mr. Jobert canceled a news conference and the last two technical meetings on his schedule and left Peking the same evening. One source reported that Mr. Deng called it a "regretable coincidence" that Miss Li's sentence was disclosed while the French official was visiting Peking.

Today the official New China News Agency issued a statement prepared for Chinese embassies in Paris and elsewhere giving Peking's version of the affair.

"The problem is not a problem of marriage between Li Shuang and Emmanuel Bellefroid, as someone said, but her violation of the Chinese law", according to the statement, which was also provided here by the Foreign Ministry to some Western reporters.

Exact Crime Not Specified

The statement did not say what crime Miss Li had commited. But the authorities have warned Chinese citizens against mixing with foreigners. In Peking, foreign residents are assigned to walled off, segregated apartment that are guarded by soldiers. At public restaurants, foreigners are usually steered to separate dining rooms away from other customers.

But while such contacts, and marriages, are discouraged, they are not impossible. Today's statement took note of another staff member at the French Embassy, Christian Galiano, who last month was alowed to marry a Chinese woman, Zhao Jiang. In an earlier case this year, a Canadian was alowed to mary a dancer.

Some foreign residents here familiar with Miss Li's case believe that she outraged Chinese officials, who in general hold puritanical views, by moving into Mr. Bellefroid's apartment, thereby flouting Communist strictures against fraternization and extramarital sex. Mr. Bellefroid was separated from his wife, who returned to France.

Moreover, Miss Li was prominent in an avant garde group of Peking artists who had flirted with political dissidence. While she was obviously used as an example for other couples, it is uncertain whether the case represents a more significant crackdown against the intellectual nonconformity.

The New China News Agency statement indicated that the Chinese are discomfited by the uproar that the incident has created in France, where Mr. Bellefroidis living.

"It is entirely proper for China, a sovereign state, to handle the violation of law by Li Shuang according to Chinese law," the statement said. "It has nothing to do with the relations between China and France.

We are sure that our French friends will and can understand China's handling of this purely internal affair."

N. Y. Times, Sept 13, 1981, at 5, Col. 6.

French Diplomat Says China Holds His Fiancee*

Peking, Sept. 12 (AP) A French Diplomat said today that the police were holding his Chinese fiancée.

Emmanuel Bellefroid, 33 years old, an attache at the French Embassy, said he returned from abroad Thursday and learned that Li Shuang, had been seized Wednesday outside the foreigners' compound in which they live.

Mr. Bellefroid said the police refused to see him when he went to explain that Miss Li had been in his apartment legally.She was seized as she was leaving the compound to meet her sister, the diplomat said. Chinese are alowed inside the compound only with special passes or in the company of a foreigner.

注釋

* 本文根據一九八二年初筆者在哈佛大學所作的一次專題演講整理而成，原文刊載於美國紐約法學院《國際法與比較法學刊》第3卷第1期（1982年初出版）。原文見本文附錄四。文中所援引和評析的法律法規，均以一九八一年當時有效者為準。閱讀時請注意查對和比較一九八一年以來有關法律法規的發展情況，以明其歷史發展脈絡，並獲得最新信息。

〔4〕 原文載於《紐約時報》1981年11月13日第36版第1欄。談文中譯本見附錄一。

〔5〕 題為《法國外交官説中國拘留了他的未婚妻》，載於《紐約時報》1981年9月13日第5版第6欄。談文中譯本見附錄二。

〔6〕 即哈佛大學法學院前副院長、東亞法律研究中心主任柯恩（Jerome Cohen）教授，他是美國法學界知名的「中國通」。當時修習柯恩教授主講的「當代中國法律」這門課的博士生，除來自美國外，還有許多來自英、法、德、日、澳等國的留學人員。

〔7〕 該案例於一九五七年十月二十二日第一屆全國人民代表大會常務委員會第八十一次會議通過，同日公布施行。收輯於《中華人民共和國公安法規選編》（1950-1979），法律出版社1982年版，第73、79-80頁。該條例於一九八六年九月五日修訂，原第5條和第30條的規定合併改列為第30條，並有重要補充。一九九四年五月十二日，該條例再次修訂，其中第30條規定未作更動。二〇〇五年八月二十八日，第十屆全國人民代表大會常務委員會第十七次會議通過《中華人民共和國治安管理處罰法》，自二〇〇六年三月一日起施行。一九九四年五月十二日修訂公布的《中華人民共和國治安管理處罰條例》同時廢止。

〔8〕 該決定於一九五七年八月一日第一屆全國人民代表大會常務委員會第七十八次會議批准，一九五七年八月三日國務院公布施行。

〔9〕 該規定於一九七九年十一月二十九日第五屆全國人民代表大會常務委員會第十二次會議批准，同日國務院公布施行。

〔10〕 參見新華社記者評論：《小題大做》，載《光明日報》一九八一年十一月十五日。詳見本文附錄三。

〔11〕 見本文附錄一。雷恩先生在一九八一年九月十三日發表的另一篇報導中，也説到李爽是貝耶華的「未婚妻」。

〔12〕 例如，在美國駐華大使館頒發的非移民簽證申請書中，其第十九欄就對「分居」與「離婚」作了明顯的區分。

〔13〕 一九七九年七月一日通過的《中華人民共和國刑法》第180條規定：「有配偶而重婚的，或者明知他人有配偶而與之結婚的，處二年以下有期徒刑或者拘役。」（按：該法已於1997年3月14日修訂，原第180條有關重婚罪的規定改為第258條。文字未作改動。）

〔14〕 參見一九八〇年九月十日公布的《中華人民共和國婚姻法》第7條。（按：該法已於2001年4月28日修訂，原第7條改列為第8條。文字內容稍有增補。）

〔15〕「重婚：已有配偶的男女未辦理離婚手續又與他人結婚，或雖未登記而實際上與他人以夫妻關係相對待而共同生活。是破壞一夫一妻制的違法行為。……凡以重婚論處的，應解除其非法的重婚關係，追究其刑事。」參見《法學詞典》，上海辭書出版社1980年版，第521-522頁。

〔16〕參見《他犯有重婚罪嗎？》，載《中國法制報》1981年10月2日。文章以「本報法律顧問組」解答諮詢的形式指出：所謂重婚……是指已有配偶的男女，在其配偶沒有死亡，或者其婚姻關係沒有依法解除之前，又同他人登記結婚，或者雖未進行結婚登記，但與他人在事實上以夫妻關係同居生活，構成了事實婚姻。」

〔17〕據另外一篇報導說：一九八〇年九月間，法國外交官貝耶華與李爽在北京一次美術展覽中相遇。按貝耶華的描述，兩人「一見鍾情」當時，貝耶華的妻子在法新社駐北京辦事處工作。到了一九八一年五月，貝耶華向中國有關當局申請，要求與李爽結婚，並且出具了與法國妻子離婚的證明。但是，在此之前好幾個月裡，李爽仰仗洋人外交特權公開從事變相賣淫的下流放蕩行為已經嚴重地影響了社會秩序，並激起當地群眾的憤怒。由於當時李爽的流氓阿飛行為問題正在處理之中，尚懸而未決，在此種情況下，中國有關當局暫且不能批准李爽與貝耶華結婚。於是，李爽不顧有關當局的一再勸誡，明目張膽地搬入北京使館區貝耶華居住的外交官員住所，公開同居兩個月，並且利用貝耶華的外交官特權庇護自己，因為中國治安人員不能隨意進入使館區外交官住所。其後，一九八一年九月間，在李爽離開使館區外交官住所外出時，被中國有關當局依法拘留，接著又在一九八一年十一月間被送交「勞動教養」。參見中國新聞社特寫稿，載美國商務部：《FBIS每日報導》（中國專輯）1981年11月16日，第G2頁。

〔18〕一九六一年四月十八日簽訂的《維也納外交關係公約》第29條規定：外交代表人身不得侵犯。外交代表不受任何方式之逮捕或拘禁。接受國對外交代表應特示尊重，並應採取一切適當步驟以防止其人身、自由或尊嚴受到任何侵犯。「第31條進一步規定：外交代表對接受國之刑事管轄享有豁免權。」參見王鐵崖、田如萱編：《國際法資料選編》，法律出版社1982年版，第606頁。

〔19〕《維也納外交關係公約》第30條第1款規定：外交代表之私人寓所一

如使館館舍，應享有同樣的不可侵犯權和同等的保護。」第22條第1款進一步明確規定：「使館館捨不得侵犯。接受國官員非經使館館長許可，不得進入使館館舍。」參見王鐵崖、田如萱編：《國際法資料選編》，法律出版社1982年版，第606頁。

〔20〕《維也納外交關係公約》第41條第1款。參見王鐵崖、田如萱編：《國際法資料選編》，法律出版社1982年版，第610頁。

〔21〕《維也納外交關係公約》第41條第3款。參見王鐵崖、田如萱編：《國際法資料選編》，法律出版社1982年版，第610頁。

〔22〕《維也納外交關係公約》第9條第1款規定：「接受國可以隨時在不必解釋決策理由的條件下，通知派遣國，宣告使館館長或使館任何外交職員為不受歡迎人員，或使館任何其他職員為不能接受人員。遇此情形，派遣國應斟酌情況召回該有關人員或解除其在使館中之職務。」參見王鐵崖、田如萱編：《國際法資料選編》，法律出版社1982年版，第601頁。

〔23〕參見《中國駐巴黎大使館澄清對李爽的勞教處罰》，載美國商務部：《FBIS每日報導》（中國專輯）1981年11月13日，第G1頁。

〔24〕參見《關於勞動教養問題的決定》第2條、第3條，《關於勞動教養的補充規定》第1條、第5條。

〔25〕參見1979年7月1日通過的《中華人民共和國刑事訴訟法》第8條、第111條第1款。該法已於1996年3月17日修訂，原第8條改列為第11條，原第111條改列為第152條，同時在文字上將「國家機密」更改為「國家秘密」，「個人陰私」更改為「個人隱私」。

〔26〕See Geise v. United States, 262 F. 2d 151, 151-157(9h Cir. 1958), cert, denied. 361 U. S. 842(1959).

〔27〕See United States ex. rel. Lloyd v. Vincent, 520 F. 2d 1272, 1272-1276 (2d Cir. 1975). cert, denied. 423 U.

〔28〕See Stamicarbon v. American Cyanamid Co., 506 F. 2d 532. 532-542 (2d Cir. 1974).

〔29〕See United States v. Bell, 464 F. 2d 667, 667-676 (2d Cir. 1972), cert, denied. 409 U. S. 991(1972).

〔30〕參見一九七八年三月五日通過的《憲法》第10條、第57條。中國現行憲法制定於一九八二年，其後又經過一九八八年、一九九三年、一九九九年、二〇〇四年以及二〇一八年五次修正。一九七八年

《憲法》第10條和第57條的基本精神，已分別被吸收於一九八二年《憲法》的第6、42、53條。

〔31〕參見國務院《關於勞動教養問題的決定》，小引言，第2條第2款、第3款。

* 原文載於《紐約時報》1981年11月13日第36版第1欄。

* 原文載於《紐約時報》1981年9月13日第5版第6欄。

**原文載於《光明日報》1981年11月15日。

〔32〕法文原名為Emmanuel Bellfid，前文譯為昂瑪努・貝耶華，係參照商務印書館1973年出版的《譯音表》所列法語標準譯音而改譯的。
　　——摘錄者注

* This Article was first published in the New York Law School *Jounal of Intenainal and Comparative Law* (U. S. A.), Vol. 3, No. 1, 1982. This article was written in January, 1982 on the basis of a speech made by the authorat Harvard Law School.

〔33〕*N. Y. Times*, Nov. 13, 1981. at 36, Cl. 1. See App.1.

〔34〕French Diplomat Says China Holds His Fiancee, N.Y. Times, Sept.13, 1981, at 5, Col. 6. See App. 2.

〔35〕Passed at the 81st Meeting of Standing Committee of the National People's Congress, Oct. 22, 1957; promulgated on the same day.

〔36〕The Policy and Law Research Section of the Public Security Ministry of the People's Republic of China: A Corpus of Public Security Laws and Regulations (1950-1979)114, Mass Press, Beijing (1980)[hereinafter cited as Public Security Laws]. See also 22 *Xinhua Banyuekan* 82 (1957).

〔37〕Public Security Laws, art. 121.

〔38〕Approved at the 78th Meeting of the Standing Committee of the First Session of the NPC, Aug. 1, 1957; promulgated by the State Council, Aug. 3, 1957.

〔39〕Public Security Laws, art. 391. See also 17 *Xinhua Banyuekan* 195 (1957).

〔40〕Supplementary Regulations of the State Council on RHTL. Approved at the 12th Meeting of the Fifth Session of the NPC, Nov.29, 1979; promulgated by the State Councilon the same day.See Public Security Laws, art. 393. See also 11 Xinhua Yuebao 12-13 (documents ed. 1979).

〔41〕Commentary by Xinhua reporter, A Big Fuss over a Trifle, *Guangmig*

Daily, Nov. 15, 1981.

〔42〕 *N. Y. Timss*, Nov. 13. 1981. at 36, Col. 1. See App. 1. The other report, published Sept. 13. 1981 also stated that Li was Bellefroid's "fiancee." See French Diplomat Says China Holds His Fiancee, *N. Y. Times*, Sept 13, 1981 at 5, Col. 6. See App. 2.

〔43〕 For instance, such a distinction also appears in the 19th column of the Non-immigrant Visa Application issued by the U. S. Embassy in China.

〔44〕 Article 180 of the Criminal Law of the PRC provides: "Whoever has a spouse and commits bigamy or whoever marries another person clearly knowing the other has a spouse shall be sentenced to not more than two years of fixed-term imprisonment or to criminal detention. " See *Renmin Ribao (People's Daily)*, July 7, 1979. See also 6 *Xinhua Yiubao* 77 (documents ed. 1979).

〔45〕 See article 7 of the Marriage Law of the PRC (1980), *Renmin Ribao*, Sept. 16, 1980. See also 9 *Xinhua Yuebao* 61 (documentsed.1980).

〔46〕 "Bigamy: A man or a woman who already has a spouse and does not go through formalities of divorce, marries another person via marriage registration; or although not via such a registration yet lives together with the other, factualy treating each other in the relationship of husband and wife." See *The Legal Dictionary*, Shanghai Dictionaries Press, 1980, p. 521。

〔47〕 See Did He Commit a Bigamy? *Zhongguo Fazhi Bao*, Oct. 2, 1981, at 3: Concretely to say, bigamy means that a man or a woman who already has a spouse, registeredly marries another person again before his/her spouse has died or before their marriage relationship has been legally terminated; or, although (he or she) has not yet initiated any marriage registration again, yet lives together with the other factualy in the status of husband-and-wife relationship, it thus constitutes a factual marriage. Ibid.

〔48〕 Another source said, Bellefroid met Li Shuang at an art exhibition in Beijing in September 1980. As Bellefroid put it, "It was love at firsts ight". At the time Bellefroid's wife was working in the AFP office in Beijing. Up to May,1981 Bellefroid applied to the Chinese authorities concerning his intention to marry Li Shuang and produced a certificate of his divorce. At the time, Li Shuang's indecent behavior for several months had already seriously interfered with social order, and had made the masses extremely angry.The departments concerned obviously could not approve the marriage of Li Shuang to Bellefroid while her hoodlum case was pending. Then, in spite of repeated admonitions, she flagrantly moved into Bellefroid's apartment and lived with him for two months, taking advantage of his diplomatic privileges to protect herself. Hence, in accordance with Chinese law, Li was detained in September 1981, and was sent to RHTL in November 1981. See Zhongguo Xinwen She, Feature, U. S. Department of Commerce: FBIS, Daily Report—China, Nov.16, 1981, G2.

〔49〕Vienna Convention on Diplomatic Relations, done at Vienna April 18, 1961, 23 U. S. T. 3227, T. I. A. S. No. 7502, 500 U. N. T. S. 95 [hereinafter cited as Vienna Convention]. "The person of a diplomatic agent shall be inviolable. He shall not be liable to any form of arrest or detention." Ibid., art. 29. "A diplomatic agent shall enjoy immunity from the criminal jurisdiction of the receiving State." Ibid., art. 31. As of January1, 1981, one hundred and forty-eight nations including the People's Republic of China, France, United Kingdom, United States and the U. S. S. R. were pariestothe Convention. See Treaties in Force—A List of Treaties and Other International Agreements of the United States in Force on January1, 1981.

〔50〕Section 1 of article 30 of Vienna Convention provides: "The private residence of a diplomatic agent shall enjoy the same inviolability and protection as the premises of the mission."Section1of article 22 of Vienna Convention provides in advance that: "The premises of the mission shall be inviolable. The agents of the receiving State may not enter them, except with the consent of the head of the mission."

〔51〕Ibid., art. 41, sec.1.

〔52〕Ibid., art.41, sec. 3.

〔53〕Article 9 of Vienna Convention provides: "The receiving State may at any time and without having to explain its decision, notify the sending

State that the head of the mission or any member of the diplomatic staff of the mission is persona non grata or that any other member of the staff of the mission is not acceptable. In any such case, the sending State shall, as appropriate, either recall the person concerned or terminate his functions with the mission."

〔54〕See PRC Paris Embassy Clarifies Li's Reeducation, U. S. Department of Commerce: FBIS, Daily Report—China, Nov. 13, 1981, G1.

〔55〕See Supplementary Regulations of the State Council on RHTL, arts. 1, 2, and 5. Article 5 provides: "the people's procuracies shall exercise supervision over the activities of the organs of rehabilitation through labor."See also 11 Xinhua Yuebao 13 (documentsed. 1979).

〔56〕See *Renmin Ribao* , July 8, 1979, and 6 *Xinhua Yuebao* 79, 88 (documents ed.1979). Article 8 of the Criminal Procedure Law of the PRC provides: "the people's courts shall try and adjudicate all cases in public unless otherwise provided by this law. Defendants have a right to obtain defense, and the people's courts have a duty to guarantee that defendant's obtain defense. "Article III of the Criminal Procedure Law of the PRC provides: "the people's courts shall try and adjudicate cases of the first instance in public. However, cases involving state secrets or the shameful secrets of individuals shall not be tried and heard in public."

〔57〕See In Re Oliver, 333 U. S. 257, 272-273 (1948).

〔58〕See Geise v. United States, 262 F. 2d 151, 151-157 (9th Cir. 1958), cert. denied, 361 U. S. 842 (1959)

〔59〕See United States ex. rel. Lloyd v. Vincent, 520 F. 2d 1272, 1272-1276 (2d Cir. 1975). cert. denied, 423 U. S. 937 (1975)

〔60〕See Stamicarbon v. American Cyanamid Co , 506 F. 2d 532, 532-542 (2d Cir. 1974).

〔61〕See United States v. Bell, 464 F. 2d 667 , 667-676 (2d Cir. 1972), cert. denied, 409 U. S. 991 (1972).

〔62〕Arts. 10, and 57. See *Remnin Ribao* , March 8 , 1978.

〔63〕Public Security Laws, art. 392. See also 17 *Xinhua Banyuekan* 195 (1957).

*1981 by The New York Times Company. Reprinted by permission.

*1981 by The New York Times Company. Reprinted by permission.

小議對外學術交流的「大忌」*

中華文明，博大精深；中外文明平等交流，源遠流長。數千年來，其間充滿無數互相碰撞、激盪和揚棄，更充滿無數互相借鑑、滲透、吸收和交融。後者是中外文明交流的主流，促進了世界文明的繁榮絢麗，但也時時出現一些逆流，對於中外文明交流起了損害的作用，不容小覷。為了弘揚主流，抑制逆流，特以國際經濟法為例，就對外學術交流中需要防止的三種「大忌」，小議一番。

第一，忌閉目塞聽，夜郎自大。歷史上，中國有許多明君宣導向域外先進文明虛心學習，汲取精華，相容並蓄，但也有不少昏庸顢頇的統治者慣於夜郎自大，對域外先進文明閉目塞聽，視為異端邪說，一律貶斥。他們自命為「奉天承運」的「天子」，並以「天朝大國」自居，在對待周邊國家的態度上，存在著一定的自大與輕狂。直到鴉片戰爭的大炮轟開「天朝大國」的國門，才猛然醒悟：不向域外先進文明虛心學習，勢必導致落後，落後必然挨打！

第二，忌囫圇吞棗，盲目附和。就人文社科而言，來自外國的思潮和理論，其中多有精神食糧，但也有不少是精神鴉片。鑒此，在國際學術交流中，我們切忌言必稱希臘羅馬、哈佛耶魯、

劍橋牛津，而對自己祖宗留下的深厚文明積澱和豐富思想瑰寶則「不曉得」或「忘記了」。我們既要謙虛謹慎，認真學習和吸收外來的一切有益新知，切忌閉目塞聽，妄自尊大；又要對外來的種種「權威」理論，結合國情和世情，深入探討，獨立思考，加以鑒別，切忌妄自菲薄，盲目附和。為此，要刻苦學習中外歷史，鑽研理論，善於史論結合，擺出事實，講清道理，有理有據地闡明自己的見解，平等而又自信地參加國際熱點難點問題的討論和爭鳴，不渝不懈，追求客觀真理和社會公平。

第三，忌屁股坐歪，脊梁缺鈣。在國際學術交流中，身為中國人，應時刻不忘祖國，踐行「知識報國，兼濟天下」的使命。試剖一例，舉一反三：WTO組織成立至今已經二十餘年，許多事實證明，WTO法制為全球各國或地區提供了多邊貿易平臺，功不可沒，值得讚揚。但WTO法並非全是「良法」，其中既有「良法」，也有「劣法」，不應全盤肯定，更不能頂禮膜拜；WTO／DSB（WTO爭端解決實體）的執法實踐也非全盤「善治」，其中也有偏袒強權成員和欺凌弱勢成員的不公裁決，不容漠視和掩蓋。

特別是，二〇一二至二〇一四年在WTO「稀土案」中，「被告」中國在專家組和上訴機構兩審中連續敗訴，舉世矚目，全國譁然。按照裁決，中國出口的稀土，雖屬全球稀缺、極其珍貴的精尖工業「維生素」，但就是必須只賣「白菜價」，既不許限制出口，也不許出口加稅。對此蠻橫裁決，眾多中國學者深感「切膚之痛」，依法據理，撰文揭露和批判其執法不公，努力訴諸國際公正輿論，討回公道；也有高明專家，呼籲WTO及時糾正失

誤，建立判例糾錯制度，亡羊補牢，以免失去公信。但是，人們也遺憾地看到，竟有一些宣講文稿和相關出版物，三年多來在國內多個論壇反覆宣講散發，極力讚頌「WTO是模範國際法」，是「良法善治的典型」，甚至把《WTO協議》和《入世議定書》吹捧為「聖經」。對於上述「稀土案」中WTO的兩審裁決，只津津樂道一審裁決思路是如何之「嚴謹縝密」，二審裁決思路是如何之「技高一籌」；而對於中國橫遭兩審裁決沉重打擊之特大冤屈和深遠禍害，卻三緘其口，不置一詞。難怪有人提出異議和質疑：此種視角和做派，是否有些「屁股坐歪，脊梁缺鈣」？是否略欠赤子之心，家國情懷？

注釋

* 本文發表於《光明日報》2015年7月31日第2版「文化評析‧講好中國故事」。

向世界展現中國理念*

　　在二戰後七十多年的全球治理中，一直存在兩種理念。一種理念由以美國為首的強權發達國家所主導，傾向於強權政治，由強國壟斷國際話語權；另一種理念由包括中國在內的眾多發展中國家所宣導，強調各國不論大小強弱，在國際事務中均應平等相待、互利共贏。

　　中國一貫主張確立公正合理的全球治理理念和全球治理體制。一九七四年，鄧小平同志在聯合國大會第六屆特別會議上闡述了毛澤東同志提出的「三個世界」理論，並莊嚴聲明：中國是一個社會主義國家，也是一個發展中的國家，屬於第三世界；中國堅決反對任何形式的霸權主義，自己也決不搞霸權主義。二十一世紀以來，中國的綜合國力持續增強，中國積極與新興經濟體和廣大發展中國家合作，在國際社會形成日益強勁的新興力量。特別是黨的十八大以來，以習近平同志為總書記的黨中央提出打造人類命運共同體的主張和弘揚共商共建共用的全球治理理念，並積極努力踐行，突出顯示了敢於和善於提出中國方案、貢獻中國智慧的膽略和氣魄。當前，順應歷史潮流和時代呼喚，中國正在大力宣導國家主權、民族自決、和平共處、睦鄰友好、聯合自強等觀念，得到了世界上越來越多國家和人民的認同；積極推進

「一帶一路」建設、發起成立亞洲基礎設施投資銀行等實踐，推動全球治理體制向著更加公正合理的方向發展。當今世界，各國相互依存、休戚與共。推進世界和平穩定與發展繁榮，必須構建以合作共贏為核心的新型國際關係，打造人類命運共同體。中國將為此做出自己的貢獻。

中國提出的共商共建共用的全球治理理念，是中華傳統文化中積極處世之道的繼承、發展與創新。中國傳統文化中有構建「大同世界」的理想。早在春秋戰國時代，以孔子為代表的儒家先賢就針對當時社會的不公不義和戰亂頻仍，提出了構建美好和諧社會的理念和追求。儒家學者還提出兼善天下、四海之內皆兄弟等理念，認為人與人之間不分強弱、貧富，都可以親如兄弟、平等相待。儒家宣導「和為貴」，同時強調君子應和而不同，既能與他人和睦相處，但又不苟同其錯誤見解。在條件不具備的時候，至少應做到獨善其身；在條件具備的時候，就應勇於承擔、兼善天下，參與治國平天下的大業。中國堅持奉行的和平外交政策、共商共建共用理念，均可以從上述思想理念中找到歷史淵源。

中國主張和宣導的打造人類命運共同體的主張和弘揚共商共建共用的全球治理理念，符合時代潮流，符合全人類的根本利益。中國的大國外交、周邊外交協調推進、豐富多彩，突出展現了全方位外交的創新活力和蓬勃生機，也證明了中國特色全球治理理念具有引領作用。當今時代國際舞臺上的競爭，很大程度上是思想理念的較量。不同的全球治理理念對於國際話語權的分配和全球治理體制的確立發揮著很大的能動作用。對於中國來說，

要向世界傳播中國觀念、闡明中國價值，就要堅持道路自信、理論自信、制度自信，並將其轉化為行動自覺。一方面，苦練「內功」，增強自己的綜合國力，以實力增強理念的說服力；另一方面，弘揚新的全球治理理念不能單靠一己之力，而需要致力於國際合作，形成強大合力，促使現存治理秩序不斷棄舊圖新，走向公正合理。中國在努力宣揚「和為貴」「化干戈為玉帛」等思想的同時，也應警惕一些國家破壞國際安寧與世界和平秩序的企圖和行動，做好各方面周全準備，安而不忘危，治而不忘亂。

注釋

* 本文發表於《人民日報》2016年6月5日第5版。

朝著合作共贏方向發展推動國際經濟法理念變革*

第二次世界大戰結束後七十餘年來，全球治理中有兩種理念及其相應體制一直在矛盾中不斷碰撞嬗變，一種是以美國為首的西方若干發達國家所主導的全球治理理念和體制，另一種是眾多發展中國家參與的全球治理理念和體制。這兩大理念和體制的分歧或差異在於：由誰來主導實施全球治理？如何實施全球治理？前者主張僅由少數幾個發達強國來治理，壟斷和操縱國際事務話語權和決策權；後者則主張世界事務應秉持合作共贏原則，由世界各國包括發展中國家平等參與治理。這兩種針鋒相對的治理理念對許多世界事務的解決產生了影響。與之相對應，當代全球治理體系變革也對國際經濟法理念產生著影響。

在傳統國際經濟法律格局中，磋商和決策過程只在七八個最發達國家內部進行，它們定出基調或基本框架之後，交由十幾個或二十幾個發達國家組成的經濟性組織或區域性組織協調各方利害關係，定出共同主張和一致步調，然後才提交全球性的經貿大會或國際經濟組織進行討論。這種做法，從一開始就排除、剝奪了眾多發展中國家的知情權、參與權、話語權、決策權，從而使它們在磋商過程中處於弱勢地位。另外，在全球性國際經濟組織

規章中，幾個發達國家也定出不公平、不合理的表決制度，實行表決權力大小不一甚至極端懸殊的投票安排，從而使寥寥幾個西方發達大國加在一起，就可以操縱全球重大經濟事務的決策。有的超級大國享有的特多投票權或特大表決權，往往可以在很大程度上左右重大決策，甚至可以在一定條件下實現其獨家否決的特權。西方大國在這種磋商和決策過程中，憑藉其經濟實力上的優勢操縱世界經濟貿易合作走向，甚至隨時根據自己的需要，拒不遵守或完全背棄自己依國際條約應承擔的義務。眾多發展中國家在這種決策體制下，往往難以實現和保護自己的經濟權益。這樣不公平不合理的局面，在經濟全球化、各國經濟互相緊密依存的現實情勢下，不僅會損害發展中國家的經濟主權和各種經濟權益，而且不利於全球經濟持續健康發展。

要改變這種局面，就必須從根本上改變世界經濟貿易決策權力分配不公的格局，強調一切國家應當對世界經濟貿易享有平等的參與權、話語權和決策權。這就要以公正、公平、合理為原則，對當今現存的國際經濟貿易規則予以分析，凡是達到公正、公平、合理標準，符合建立國際經濟新秩序需要的，就可加以沿用、重申；凡是不符合這種需要，只是「口惠而實不至」的空頭支票，就要積極加以改善；凡是直接與這一標準背道而馳的，就努力廢棄和破除。

變革現存國際經濟秩序的要求，並非單純是一種政治口號或政治理念。它在實踐中也推動了國際經濟秩序和國際經濟法走上吐故納新的道路，使廣大發展中國家在一定程度上逐步改變完全無權、聽憑強權國家任意擺布的處境。實際上，二戰結束後，國

際社會中改變國際經濟法制的爭鬥就時起時伏。比如，二○○一年十一月開啟的多哈回合談判，就體現出新舊兩種觀念的較量。現存國際經濟法律規範中蘊含各種不公平規則是一種客觀現實。在這種情況下，如果學者還吹捧國際經濟規則全都是良法、模範法，對它應俯首貼耳，是不符合正直學者應有的法律理念和法律職責的。

改變當今國際經濟法律規則的制定格局任重而道遠。面對當代國際社會「南弱北強」、實力分化的戰略態勢，發展中國家要變法圖強，既不可能一蹴而就，也不能無所作為，而應動員和凝聚實力，堅持不懈建立國際經濟新秩序，一步一個腳印地向前邁進。

全球治理體系變革源於國際力量對比變化，全球治理的新格局取決於國際力量的新對比。在中國的積極引領下，眾多發展中國家變革全球治理體系的合理要求、吶喊和努力，其強度和力度都有較大的提升。當前，加強全球治理、推動全球治理體系變革乃是大勢所趨。中國要抓住機遇、順勢而為，推動國際經濟秩序朝著更加公正合理的方向發展，聯合眾多發展中國家以及願意順應歷史潮流的發達國家，共同構建合作共贏的全球治理體系，為促進人類福祉做出更大貢獻。

注釋

* 本文發表於《人民日報》2016年11月7日第16版。

第八章
建構中國特色國際法學理論[*]

當代中國正走在實現中華民族偉大復興的歷史征程上。中國綜合國力的持續增長，引起許多國家的關注和讚許，但也遭到西方一些國家及人士的誤讀。在新的歷史條件下，中國日益廣泛深入地融入經濟全球化進程，需要承擔更大的國際責任，這就相應地需要擴大在全球治理中的話語權。世界也期待中國在全球事務的治理和決策中、在實現國際公平正義方面發揮更大作用。

從法律視角看，中國擴大和增強在全球治理中的話語權，就是要在制定國際法律規範中擁有更大的參與權和決策權。不可否認，迄今通行的國際法律規範及其相應的理論學說，主要是在特定歷史條件下，以美國為首的西方發達國家主持制定並主導推動的，其中含有不少蔑視國際秩序的「惡法」。這些「惡法」損害了發展中國家應有的公平合理權益。在這種情況下，中國的國際法學者理應順應時代呼聲，致力於建構具有中國特色的國際法學理論新體系，增強中國參與全球治理的話語權，追求國際公平正義。

關注國際秩序的除舊布新。從發展中國家的視角看，當代的國際政治經濟秩序既有基本公平合理、符合《聯合國憲章》的部分，也存在不公平不合理的部分。相應地，現存的國際法律規

範，既有基本公平合理、符合《聯合國憲章》和發展中國家權益的「良法」，也存在不公平不合理、損害發展中國家權益的「惡法」。因此，國際法學研究應當對國際法律規範進行分析整理，推動破舊立新、開拓創新。創建具有中國特色的國際法學理論新體系，是時代賦予中國國際法學人的歷史使命，責無旁貸。

　　研究治理變革的相關主張。隨著時代發展，現行全球治理體系與時代潮流不適應的地方越來越多，國際社會對全球治理體系變革的呼聲越來越高。努力推動全球治理體系變革日益成為國際社會密切關注的新焦點，也理應成為中國國際法學者的關注點。推動全球治理體系變革是國際社會共同的事業，應堅持共商共建共用原則，使全球治理體系變革的相關主張轉化為各方共識，形成一致行動。中國要引導利益不同、見解相異的各方形成共識，共同推動全球治理體系變革，確實需要下很大的力氣。這就需要國際法學者貢獻力量，繼續向國際社會闡釋我們關於推動全球治理體系變革的理念，讓全球各方聆聽到清晰、堅定的中國話語，從而凝聚人心，共同將這種體系變革由理念變為現實。

　　立足中國實際。中國改革開放以來，學習引進了不少西方發達國家的國際法學理論。這些理論往往立足於那些國家各自的實際，以其國家利益為核心。因此，其中難免蘊含著維護發達國家既得權益、維護國際舊秩序的內容，不符合中國實際，在實踐中可能侵犯眾多發展中國家的應有權益。因此，中國學者很有必要在學習、借鑑有關國際法學新知識的基礎上，密切聯繫中國實際，從中國的角度和人類命運共同體的立場來研究和評析當代國際法，敢於和善於開拓創新，逐步確立起以馬克思主義為指導、

具有中國特色的國際法學理論新體系。

學會自主鑒別。在國際學術舞臺上，中國學者既要謙虛謹慎，認真學習和吸收有益的知識，切忌閉目塞聽、妄自尊大；又要敢於和善於對外來的種種所謂權威理論或時髦學說加以鑒別，切忌妄自菲薄、盲目附和。應平等地參加國際熱點難點問題的討論，有理有據地闡明自己的見解，發出中國的正義之聲，為全球治理貢獻中國智慧。

注釋

* 本文發表於《人民日報》2017年5月8日第15版。

第九章
「左公柳」、中國魂與新絲路
——「七七事變」七十週年隨筆*

　　「七七」傍晚散步，口哼童年老歌自娛，見微風輕拂道柳，浮想聯翩，憶起抗日戰爭當年流行一時的《玉門出塞》，如今六十歲以下的青壯年大眾恐怕多半不知道、不會唱。此曲乃一九一九年五四運動闖將、北京學生領袖羅家倫[64]作詞，李惟寧譜曲，不但詞句優美，寥寥數語，便將偉大祖國西部邊陲——遼闊新疆的美景、歷史、地理高度概括，栩栩如生地盡顯紙上，跳躍在流暢悅耳的音樂中，讀來、唱來均朗朗上口，充滿詩情畫意；更重要的是，其中凝聚著濃濃的「中華魂」和強烈的家國情懷，被人們推崇為羅氏一生的最佳詩作，[65]很值得後人溫故知新，大力弘揚。茲特抄錄如下，並根據歷史記載和個人理解，略加詮釋，提供大眾共用。羅家倫原詞是：

　　左公柳拂玉門曉，塞上春光好！天山融雪灌田疇，大漠飛沙旋落照，沙中水草堆，好似仙人島；過瓜田碧玉叢叢，望馬群白浪滔滔。想乘槎張騫，定遠班超，漢唐先烈經營早，當年是匈奴右臂，將來更是歐亞孔道，經營趁早！經營趁早！莫讓碧眼兒（木屐兒），射西域盤雕！

李惟寧把羅家倫詞譜曲如下：

1=bE　4/4　　　　　**玉門出塞**　　　　罗家伦 词　李惟宁曲

1·2 | 3·5 6⁵⁶53 | 2- 02·5 | 3²³2110 | 1111 636 3- |
左 公 柳 排 玉 门　 晓，　塞 上 春 光 好！　天山溶雪 灌田 畴，

6666 535 2- | 02 126 61 50 | 53 ²⁵²2- ⁻165 | i--0 |
大漠飞沙 旋落　 照，　沙 中水草 堆，　好 似 仙人 岛，

1·6 66 660 660 | 2·1 11 ²21 ²21 | 61 5 ⁶536 | 32 |
过 瓜田 碧玉 丛丛，　望 马群 白浪 滔滔，想乘槎 张 骞，定远

¹²16 1·2 | 3·5 6⁵⁶53 | 2-0 255 | 2²³2110 | 1111 636
班超，汉帝 先 热 经营 早，当年是 匈 奴右臂，将来更是 欧亚孔

3- | 6666 1111 3·1 61 | 63 6 52 22 | i--‖
道， 经营趁早，经营趁早，莫 让 木屐儿 射西域盘 踞。

　　歌詞作者羅家倫（1897-1969）既是五四運動時期的學生領
袖和革命闖將，後來又成長為我國著名的教育家、思想家、社會
活動家。他一九一七年入北京大學，頗受蔡元培校長薰陶和器
重；曾與傅斯年等創辦《新潮》雜誌，積極投身五四新文化運動
和愛國學生運動。「**內懲國賊，外抗強權**」的口號就是他在學運
傳單中率先提出的。一九二〇年獲蔡元培選拔，赴歐美留學。一
九二六年回國後，歷任國立清華大學、國立中央大學校長。他把
「創造有機體的民族文化」作為中央大學的使命。一九三七年
「七七事變」後，日軍大舉侵華，國難當頭，他主持該校西遷重
慶，在日機狂轟濫炸中堅持弦歌不輟，改革辦學體制，建樹頗
多。一九四三年，國民黨政府積極建設西北地方，以增強抗戰能
力，特派羅家倫為「監察使」，兼西北考察團長，從事陝西、甘
肅、寧夏、新疆等五省國防建設的考察與設計。據此推斷，這首
謳歌新疆「塞上春光好」、激勵抗日鬥志的名曲，當係一九四三

年他率團考察新疆時觸景生情、弘揚中華國魂的一大傑作。

　　「左公柳」[66]是晚清重臣和著名儒將**左宗棠**在一八七七年帶領數萬湘軍西進收復新疆時一路所植**道柳**。左宗棠當年來到西北大漠地區，深感氣候乾燥，了無生氣，而又水土不服，遂命令部隊在進軍大道沿途、宜林地帶和近城道旁遍栽楊樹、柳樹，綿延千里。其用意在於，一是鞏固路基，二是防風固沙，三是暫歇戎馬之足，四是利行人遮涼。凡他所到之處，都要動員軍民植樹造林。後來人們便將左宗棠及其部屬所植造福百姓的柳樹，尊稱為「左公柳」。左公此舉，體現了樸素的改善生態環境、民生福祉至上意識。

　　眾所周知，自從一八四○年英帝國主義發動侵略中國的鴉片戰爭以來，西方帝國主義列強頻頻發動侵華戰爭，迫使清政府簽訂大量喪權辱國的不平等條約。十九世紀下半期，晚清政府面臨嚴重的內憂外患危機，當時身為陝甘總督的左宗棠，面對外寇入侵，國土淪喪，挺身而出，同朝廷投降派抗爭，力排「眾議」，贏得朝野廣泛支持，接受重任，**掛帥西征**，指揮清軍剿滅了在俄英列強支持下大舉入侵新疆的阿古柏匪徒，並堅持鬥爭抗拒了沙俄的侵略，以實力為後盾與沙俄談判，終於**使大片淪陷的國土重新回到祖國懷抱，為維護祖國的統一，做出了不可磨滅的貢獻**。

　　在這同時左宗棠挾軍事勝利之威，掀起了一股新政的狂飆，掃蕩著那經年累世的污泥濁水。左宗棠在西北開創的政治新風有幾個鮮明特點。第一，強化國家主權，力主新疆建省。他痛斥朝中那些放棄西北的謬論，「周、秦、漢、唐之盛，奄有西北。及其衰也，先捐西北，以保東南，國勢浸弱，以底滅亡」。強調一

旦放棄西北，勢必導致國家滅亡。從漢至清，新疆只設軍事機構而無行省郡縣。左公前後五次上書籲請建省，終得批准，從此西北版圖歸於一統。第二，反貪倡廉。清晚期的官場已成糜爛之局，貪腐成性。他嚴懲了幾起地方官和軍官貪污、吃空餉的典型，嚴立新規。而他自己高風亮節，以身作則，陝甘軍費，每年過手一千二百四十萬兩白銀，無一毫進入私囊。西北主政十年，沒有安排一個親朋，堅持「欲肅政風先嚴家風」。第三，懲治尸位素餐不作為。他最恨那些對貪污、失職、營私等事「官官相護」，身居要位卻怕事、躲事、不幹事的懶官、庸官，常駁回其文，令其重辦，「如有一字含糊，定惟該道（主官）是問！」

　　羅家倫歌詞中「過瓜田碧玉叢叢，望馬群白浪滔滔」一句，形象地描繪了新疆哈密瓜田綠色碩果纍纍，猶如叢叢碧玉；草原放牧的白色馬群，猶如滔滔白浪。歌詞中「想乘槎張騫，定遠班超」一句，乃回想歷史，頌揚漢代張騫、班超的歷史功勛。張騫（西元前164年至西元前114年）是中國西漢時期傑出的外交家和政治家，多次出使西域。他開闢「絲綢之路」的卓越貢獻，至今彪炳史冊，舉世敬仰。「張騫乘槎」是民間傳說：漢武帝指令張騫窮溯河源，張騫乘槎（小舟）而去。經月至一處，見城郭如官府，室內有一織女，又見一丈夫（男人）牽牛飲河。後還至蜀中（四川），方知已至「牛郎，織女」二星座。[67]

　　班超（西元32-102）是東漢時期著名軍事家、外交家。他在中國西域促進民族融合和開拓鎮邊長達三十一年之久，在擔任西域都護主官期間，平定內亂，外禦強敵，為保護西域的安全、「絲綢之路」的暢通，以及促進中外文化的交流做出了巨大貢

獻。班超以三十六人出西域為始,以西域五十餘國全部歸附而終,實現了當初「投筆從戎」的願望,顯示了他傑出的軍事才能。後世尊稱他為「班定遠」,緣於他歷經數十年艱苦奮鬥,貢獻了自己畢生的心血,終於完成了促進民族融合、維護祖國統一的大業,被授予「定遠侯」封號,實至名歸。[68]

「漢唐先烈經營早」句中的「先烈」是多義詞,一般指當代為革命而捐軀犧牲的烈士,此處特指漢唐歷代建功立業的先驅和先賢。[69]

歌詞末尾大聲疾呼「**經營趁早!經營趁早!莫讓碧眼兒(木屐兒),射西域盤雕!**」,是整首歌的創作主旨和核心,也是畫龍點睛之「睛」,更是歌唱的最強音。其中,「碧眼兒(木屐兒)」[70]顯然隱指沙俄、英國、日本等侵華奪疆的帝國主義勢力;「西域盤雕」[71]則泛指中國新疆的所有資源和一切財富,絕不許帝國主義列強肆意掠奪。

羅家倫這首名曲強烈體現了「中華國魂」和「中華脊梁」,卻又獨具一格,與當年傳唱大江南北的抗日救亡歌曲,互相媲美,互相補充。如今,六七十年過去了,中華大地飽經滄桑,斗換星移,已成為和平崛起的復興大國。國家主席習近平同志提出的「一帶一路」倡議及其實踐,近年來正在日益廣泛地獲得國際社會的普遍認同和積極參與,越來越多的周邊國家和遠方友邦正在參與共建共用,新的陸上「絲綢之路」和歐亞交通孔道,[72]正在大踏步地向西拓展延伸。現實表明:「中國智慧」「中華國魂」和「中華脊梁」,不但正在華夏代代傳承發展和不斷創新,而且正在引領全人類利益共同體不斷走向普遍繁榮。

二〇一七年七月七日初草，二〇一八年三月第七稿改定

※　　　※　　　※

以下摘錄秦翰才《左文襄公在西北》一書「結論」數點附在本文末尾，諒必有助於有心的讀者進一步理解左宗棠當年的個人抱負、自律修身、愛國情懷、「中華國魂」和「中華脊梁」與當今中國人應有的個人抱負、自律修身、愛國情懷、「中華國魂」和「中華脊梁」之間的代代傳承發展和不斷砥礪創新。[73]

結束這一本書，我想不嫌重複，再把文襄公經營西北的所有成就，就以前所說，歸納為下面幾點：

第一，文襄公從《天下郡國利病書》《讀史方輿紀要》，研究到《新疆識略》《海國圖志》，於西北險要厄塞、風土人情和西北境外情形，瞭如指掌。文襄公又從漢武帝以後的追擊匈奴和羌，唐太宗以後的應付突厥、回紇和吐番，研究到清聖祖、世宗、高宗三朝的平定準、回兩部和青海，同治朝楊嶽斌輩在陝、甘、新用兵的情形，於他們政略和戰略的得失成敗，了然於胸。文襄公根據研究所得，消化了前人的良法美意，同時注意儘量避免重蹈前人的覆轍。這樣，才成立了他自己的經營西北的方案，文襄公在西北的成就，就是這一種對於西北大勢健全的、準確的和實際的認識在起作用。

第二，文襄公是一個忠貞的人：「可以托七尺之孤，可以寄百里之命。」所以，他既奉命西征，便自誓「與西事相終始」。文襄公是一個剛強的人：「富貴不能淫，貧賤不能移，威武不能屈。」所以，他能敢作敢為，排除了當地一般驕兵悍將，貪官污

吏，土豪劣紳，乃至國外強鄰所給予他種種困難。文襄公是一個
謹慎的人：「臨事而懼，好謀而成」。所以，雖說「每一出兵，
鬚髮為白」，到底算無遺策，戰無不勝；而在政治上的一切措
施，經他深思熟慮的結果，也絕不搞亂子。文襄公又是一個清廉
的人：「一介不取，一塵不染。」布衣蔬食，度他淡泊的生活；
所以雖經費支絀萬分，時鬧饑荒，而仍能號召朋儕部屬，收群策
群力、一心一德之效。文襄公在西北的成就，是這一種吾國向來
所貴重的士大夫的素養在起作用。

　　第三，文襄公在上海設一個採辦轉運局，採運槍炮彈藥和機
械，籌措華洋商借款，探報中外重要消息。文襄公在漢口設一個
後路糧臺，採運土產器材，照料新募和過境的勇丁，轉運上海軍
需，籌措華商借款。文襄公在西北設一個總糧臺和一個軍需局，
催收和轉解各省協款，接運和分配滬鄂軍需，照料新募和遣散的
過境勇丁，籌措華商借款。文襄公在用兵關外時，更設幫辦一
織，坐鎮蘭州。而從老河口以上，一路還有絡繹不斷的運輸的機
構，供應的設備，防護的部隊。文襄公本人先以平涼為大本營，
嗣以宿州為大本營，最後以哈密為大本營，居中指揮前敵，照顧
方兵。兵事一了，更跟著趕辦善後，於是當大軍直搗新疆南路西
四城時，從上海而漢口，而西安，而蘭州，而肅州，而喀什噶
爾，數千萬裡綿綿一線，宛如常山之蛇，節節呼應，文襄公自己
闡發這一個「一氣卷舒」的局勢說：「如琴瑟然，手與弦調，心
與手調，乃能成聲，此理易曉。」這好比如今所說的「工作配
合」。文襄公在西北的成就，就是這一種前後方圓滿的配合在起
作用。

　　第四，當然還要說到清政府，他們能信任文襄公，給他完全的權力；撤回了景廉、袁保恒和穆圖善輩和文襄公不能合作的人；容納了劉典、周開錫、劉松山劉錦棠、張曜、王加敏和沈應奎輩文襄公所引重的人，他們能採納文襄公眼光遠大的主張，摒棄了李鴻章輩反對的議論，拒絕和修正了英俄兩國的無理的要求文襄公的成功，也就是一種內外一致的局面在起作用。

　　於是吾們可採三國演義中「後人有詩贊曰」的方式，引下面一首宋伯魯的七律來歌詠文襄公，懷念文襄公，並作為本書的尾聲：

　　「左侯崛起中興日，誓掃天驕擴帝仁。萬里車書通絕域，三湘子弟盡功臣。鳳林魚海春風遠，玉色金城柳色新。今日西陲需保障，九原誰為起斯人！」

注釋

〔64〕參見鄭笛：《羅家倫情繫邊塞》，載《世紀》2005年第1期；張昌華：《大學校長羅家倫》，載《讀書文摘》2007年第6期。另參見朱磊：《每棵左公柳都有檔案》，戴嵐：《為古柳創造更好生存空間》，兩篇文章均載於《人民日報》2014年9月13日第10版，其電子版本見於人民網：http://nx. people. com. cn/ n/2014/0913/c192150- 22295544. html。

〔65〕參見陳一萍：《唱起〈玉門出塞〉這首歌》，載《世紀》2005年第4期；王濤：《憶〈玉門出塞歌〉》，載《晚霞》2006年第3期。

〔66〕參見秦翰才：《左文襄公在西北》，嶽麓書社一九八四年版。此書是作者秦翰才先生長期研究中國晚清重臣左宗棠抗擊帝國主義侵華、收復中國新疆的力作，商務印書館一九四五年初版於重慶，一九四六年再版於上海。新中國建立前後，開國大將王震率領中國人民解放軍挺進新疆、解放新疆、屯墾開發新疆和保衛中國西陲（戍邊）

過程中，立下重大功勛，他深知當年左宗棠率軍抗擊帝國主義侵華、收復中國新疆的歷史偉績對後世的教育意義和啟迪作用，故特建議左宗棠祖籍湖南省嶽麓書社於一九八四年重印秦翰才《左文襄公在西北》一書，其提倡以史為師、弘揚中國國魂和家國情懷的深刻寓意，是不言而喻的。參見甘肅老姜：《「左公柳」與左公柳檔案》，載《蘭州日報》2010年6月2日第11版，其電子版本見於蘭州新聞網：http://rb. lzbs. com. cn/html/2010-06/02/content_55463. htm。

〔67〕參見周妍、任繼昉：《「張騫乘槎」典故研究》，載《長春師範大學學報（人文社會科學版）》2014年第3期。

〔68〕參見泰衛星：《班超與西域》，載《新疆大學學報（哲學‧社會科學版）》1983年第1期；莫任南：《班超對中西交通的貢獻》，載《湖南師院學報（哲學社會科學版）》1980年第2期；張永輝：《從班超經略西域看東漢絲綢之路上的民族政策》，載《中國民族博覽》2018年第1期。

〔69〕參見《現代漢語詞典》（第7版）「烈士」詞條，商務印書館2016年版，第823頁。

〔70〕「碧眼」是白種人的特徵之一。「碧眼兒」是當年中國文人對西方列強侵華白種人的貶稱。「木屐（ji）」是日本人過去常用的木制拖鞋。「木屐兒」是當年中國文人對侵華日本人的貶稱。「莫讓碧眼兒（木屐兒），射西域盤雕」一句後來被普遍修改為「莫讓木屐兒射西域盤雕」。

〔71〕「盤雕」指大型猛禽，體型粗壯，翅及尾羽長而寬闊，扇翅較慢，常在近山區的高空盤旋翱翔，能捕食野兔、蛇、幼畜等大型動物，也嗜食鼠類。我國常見的種類有金雕和烏雕。

〔72〕「孔道」指交通往來必經之道路。羅家倫所撰《玉門出塞》中「將來更是歐亞孔道「一語，在當年是中國人的預見和期盼，如今在中國牽頭引領和積極推動的」一帶一路」國際實踐中，正在加速轉化為現實，為中國、為歐亞兩洲和全球大眾造福。

〔73〕參見秦翰才：《左文襄公在西北》，嶽麓書社1984年版，第282-284頁。

第六編——有關陳安學術論著和學術觀點的書評等

本書第六編所輯書評薈萃數十篇，並非本書作者所撰，但均是對本書作者近四十年來的學術理念和學術追求的積極呼應和同氣相求，形成了對國際經濟法學領域「中國特色話語」的共鳴強音，在國際論壇上對共同構建「中國特色國際經濟法學理論新體系」發揮了積極的推動作用。

由《詩經·伐木》佳句「嚶其鳴矣，求其友聲」衍生的古諺古訓「同聲相求，同氣相投」，源自《易經·乾卦》的「同聲相應，同氣相求」，先後措辭略異，其含義基本相同，都是提倡匯合社會正能量的理念、話語，聚集形成大聲的理論吶喊，加以弘揚，促其轉化為造福社會的物質力量。這些古諺古訓迄今已在中華大地內外廣泛流傳了數千年。當代中國人對這些傳承數千年的精闢古諺古訓和先進實踐，自應賦以新的時代意義，更加自覺地積極踐行。

正是秉持和自覺踐行這些精闢的古諺古訓，本書作者特地把國內外高端同行學者所撰數十篇書評，薈萃一起，輯入本書，以饗讀者，冀能從一個側面，證明國際經濟法學領域的「中國特色話語」，確實是「友聲四起，吾道不孤」[1]同時，也殷切期待從更多的國內外學者和讀者中獲得「中國特色話語」更大的共鳴強音，共同參與構建「中國特色國際經濟法學理論新體系」的理論長征，共同推動國際經濟秩序和全球治理體系與時俱進的變革和創新。

《陳安論國際經濟法學》書評薈萃

　　復旦大學出版社於二〇〇八年出版《陳安論國際經濟法學》（五卷本）之後，曾經邀請中國國際經濟法學界知名學者撰文針對這部多卷本專著加以評論，進行「筆談」，先後收到六篇書評，相繼發表於不同報刊。其中一篇同時發表於《中華讀書報》和光明網（2009年8月15日）四篇發表於《西南政法大學學報》（2012年第2期），另一篇言簡意賅的短評，發表於《國際經濟法學刊》二〇〇九年第十六卷第三期。現在把六篇全部收錄於此，以存完璧，並向各位書評作者謹致衷心謝忱。

一、陳安：知識報國，壯心不已

張永彬*

　　二〇〇九年五月，新中國國際經濟法學的奠基人、廈門大學法學教授陳安先生迎來了自己的八十歲生日。雖然年已耄耋，先生依然壯心不已，彙集自己自改革開放以來、三十年研究國際經濟法學主要成果的五卷本《陳安論國際經濟法學》，幾乎在同時，由復旦大學出版社推出。「趕在『老年癡呆症』光臨之前，多做些力所能及的『知識報國』點滴小事，匯入振興中華的大

潮，才能對此生有個起碼交代。」先生如是言道。而作為中國改革開放三十年來首次以獨撰多卷本形式推出的當代法學家的個人研究成果合集，《陳安論國際經濟法學》被認為是中國學者構建中國特色國際經濟法學派的奠基之作和代表性成果，引起了中外法學界的極大關注。

老驥伏櫪，志在千里

回憶往事，歷歷在目，五十一歲重返法學領域，在別人衝刺的年齡起跑，陳安稱這「是我們這一代法學工作者特殊的遭遇」。一九五〇年七月，陳安從廈大法律系畢業後，服從組織分配，歷經法院、法律系、馬列主義教研室（哲學、政治經濟學、政治學）、教育系、歷史系等單位，多次奉命「轉行」直到一九七八年底撥亂反正、改革開放後，一九八〇年廈大復辦法律系，陳安才奉命「歸隊」重操已經荒疏了二十七年的舊業——法律，開始關注「久違」了的國際法。這半世紀光陰流轉，陳安只用「彈指之間」來形容，「前五十年，蹉跎歲月，虛擲韶華；後三十年，欣逢鄧小平路線指引下的太平盛世，來日無多，產生了緊迫感：必須急起直追，才能努力『搶回』一點失去的時間」。近二十年來，陳安先生先後取得了十一項國家級、省部級科研成果一等獎七項國家級、省部級科研成果二等獎，其獲獎等級之高、數量之多，在中國人文社會科學學者中是罕見的，而在上述十一項一等獎成果中，八項是在他七十歲退休以後取得的。

可以說，中國認真恢復法學特別是國際法的教學和研究，和中國實行改革開放基本國策幾乎是同步的。對外開放首先遇到的

是大量的國際經濟法律問題。多年來，陳安一直注意有的放矢，針對外國媒體、政壇和法學界對中國的各種誤解和非難，撰寫多篇雙語專論，予以澄清和批駁；通過學術論證，努力維護中國的國家尊嚴、國際信譽和民族自尊，他提出的著名的「6C軌跡」論獲得了國際法學界的公認，這也是陳安先生依據大量史實，探索建立國際經濟新秩序的規律和路徑得出的初步結論。陳安先生說，總結歷史，以史為師，國際弱勢群體爭取和維護平權地位和公平權益，舍韌性的「南南聯合自強」，別無他途可循。在這條路上，既不能盲目「樂觀」，期待「畢其功於一役」；也不能盲目「悲觀」，遇到挫折就灰心喪志；更不能奢望只憑孤軍奮鬥，即可克敵制勝。

作為中國國際經濟法學的奠基人之一，一九九三年至今，陳安先生連選連任中國國際經濟法學會會長，在國際權威期刊上發表了十八篇長篇英文版專題論文，其中《南南聯合自強五十年的國際經濟立法反思》一文被長期擔任發展中國家政府間組織「南方中心」秘書長的國際知名人士Branislav Gosovic先生評價為「對第三世界思想體系的重大創新來自中國」，為中國國際經濟法贏得了極大聲譽。

就中國的人文社會科學如何在世界學術論壇上獲得自己的位置，先生自有獨到見解：「在國際學術論壇上，中國人既要謙虛謹慎，認真學習和吸收有益的新知，切忌閉目塞聽，妄自尊大；又要敢於對外來的種種『權威』理論，衡諸國情和世情，深入探討，獨立思考，加以鑒別，乃至質疑，切忌妄自菲薄，盲目附和。簡言之，要認真刻苦地學歷史，鑽理論，擺事實，講道理，

有據有理地闡明自己的見解，敢於發出中華之聲和弱勢群體之聲，平等地參加國際熱點難點問題的討論和爭鳴，追求客觀真理和社會公平。」

經濟主權上的「攻防戰」

而他自己，便是如此踐行的。早在一九八〇年底，陳安先生便和在美國享有「中國通」美譽的哈佛大學法學院的柯恩教授在有關徵收外資的問題上有過一場針鋒相對、事關國家經濟主權的辯論。其時，柯恩教授來訪廈門，在一場演講中批評新中國政府不尊重私有財產，隨意沒收（confiscate）外國人資產；主張為了吸引外商來華投資，應當在立法中規定絕對不侵犯外國人一切財產。在場的學者回憶，陳安先生當面坦率指出，他的批評不符合中國的實際情況，並列舉中國的有關法律規定逐一予以反駁，同時援引美國的相關法律和國際慣例，辨析「沒收」（confiscation）與「徵收」（expropriation）的區別。柯恩教授當即表示：「你的知識補充了我的不足」並邀請陳安先生前往哈佛訪問和講學。後來，以此次辯論為基礎，陳安撰寫了相關的中英雙語論文《我國涉外經濟立法中可否規定對外資絕不實行國有化》，其中有關觀點被後來的修訂立法所吸收。

二〇〇四年，柯恩教授應邀來廈參加國際學術會議，老友重逢，聚敘甚歡，「但我們之間又在美國單邊主義與WTO多邊主義之間矛盾衝突問題上，各持己見，激烈爭辯」陳安先生說，可以說，他們是「不打不相識」的「諍友」，在互相尊重對方的基礎上，通過國際性前沿問題的學術爭鳴，實行知識互補，達到共同

提高。

在《陳安論國際經濟法學》第一卷第一編第一篇論文「論國際經濟法學科的邊緣性、綜合性和獨立性》一文中，陳安先生對美國著名的洛文費爾德（Andreas F. Lowenfeld）教授所撰、流行全美、宣揚「美國立場」的《國際經濟法》通用教材中的若干觀點提出了尖銳的批評。先生回憶，那是數年前在海牙的一次國際學術會議上。」洛文費爾德教授在國際經濟法學領域建樹頗多，享有國際盛譽。但是，他的某些學術觀點卻彌漫著或殘留著殖民主義、擴張主義、霸權主義氣息。這是國際弱勢群體發展中國家不能苟同的。作為發展中國家一員的中國，其學人固然可以而且應當從洛文費爾德教授的著作中學習國際經濟法前沿知識的精華，卻不能不加認真思考、鑒別和必要的剔除，以致連同其中包含的糟粕，囫圇吞下。」「我認為，這既是國際弱勢群體即發展中國家的學者們的權利，也是這些學者們義不容辭的職責。」陳安先生表示。

創建中國的國際經濟法學派

除個人的學術努力外，陳安先生還不負國內同行所托，在志士仁人的鼎力支持下，使中國國際經濟法學會獲得中華人民共和國民政部批准，正式登記成為國家一級的民間學術社團。通過這個學術平臺，更有效地積極開展國際經濟法領域的國內外學術交流，逐漸形成和確立了「以文會友，以友輔仁，知識報國，兼濟天下」的學會宗旨和共識。陳安先生初創和主編的《國際經濟法學刊》，在全國同行、先進的積極參與下，定位為全國性、開放

性的國際經濟法領域優秀學術著述的集刊，現由北京大學出版社出版。十年來，已連續出版十五卷。其學術水準和社會影響受到國內外理論界和實務界的普遍肯定和讚譽，並已入選「中文社會科學引文索引」（CSSCI）學術資料來源集刊。

「『創建中國的國際經濟法學派』此議最初是一九九三年在中國國際經濟法珠海年會期間由中國社科院法學所李澤銳教授和復旦大學法學院董世忠教授提出來的。我認為，這項創新建議符合於中國的國情，也符合於時代的需要。中國人當然不能妄自尊大，但也不必妄自菲薄。『創建中國的國際經濟法學派』，當然不可能一蹴而就，也不可能期待在三五年、一二十年之中由幾個人完全實現。要完全實現，並獲得廣泛的國際認同，需要幾代中國學人群體的連續努力和不懈追求。中國人應當有這種志氣和抱負，從現在就起步，朝這個方向邁步前進。」先生平和地說。

筆者發現，《陳安論國際經濟法學》這部五卷本專著的書名也參照國際上著名法學著作常用的「××論××法」的慣例命名，先生解釋說，「以人名冠於書名，確有不少先例，諸如《奧本海國際法》（*Oppenheim's International Law*）、《戲西和莫里斯論衝突法》（*Dicey & Morris on the Conflict of Laws*）等等。我以自己的姓名冠於五卷本，主要是表示這部書中所論，均屬個入學習和研究心得體會，文責自負。」因此，把此舉理解為「是當代中國人排除百年來形成的民族自卑殘餘、努力樹立應有的『躋身國際前驅』自信自強之心願與追求，似也非絕對不可」。他俏皮地反問：「閣下以為然否？」

二、中國國際經濟法學的基石之作

——評陳安教授的《論國際經濟法學》

張玉卿*

　　擺在面前的五卷本《陳安論國際經濟法學》是廈門大學陳安教授的力作，由復旦大學出版社出版，其內容涵蓋國際經濟法基本理論、國際貿易法、國際投資法、國際仲裁法以及世貿組織（WTO）法等內容。本書第二、三卷包括對一系列經典國際投資、國際仲裁或國際貿易案件的解析與評論，第四、五卷還包括陳安教授多年來在國內外英文期刊上發表的十八篇英文長篇專論文章。

　　探究學科的前沿問題是這套著作的一大特點。《陳安論國際經濟法學》並不是一部四平八穩、面面俱到的教科書式著作，而是篇篇都在研究、探討和論述當前國際經濟法非常尖銳、極為複雜、最需要關注與解決的問題。從南北矛盾到南南合作，從國際投資到投資爭端解決，從OPIC、MIGA、ICSID到GATT／WTO，從美國貿易法到開展國際貿易的原則與慣例，從國際商事法律到國際仲裁，這套著作涵蓋了當前中國國際經濟法的前沿和熱門的課題，既有廣度，又有深度，值得我們認真研讀。

　　觀點鮮明、論據堅實充分是本書的另一個特點。例如，陳安教授力主建立國際經濟新秩序，堅持經濟主權原則、公平互利原則、全球合作原則以及有約必守原則，反對貿然拆除《華盛頓公約》賦予發展中國家的四個「安全閥」，並主張公正、公平的國際仲裁與嚴格的監督體制。這些問題都緊扣中國國際經濟法領域

的實際與需要，立論務實、清晰，論述旁徵博引，有理有據，落地有聲，分析深入細緻，條理邏輯嚴密，可謂持之有故，言之有理，堪稱法學專業著作中的精品。

陳安教授是中國國際經濟法學的創始人與領軍人之一，他通過撰寫和主編一系列著作建立了比較完善的中國國際經濟法學學科體系，這些著作包括：《國際貿易法學》《國際投資法學》《國際金融法學》《國際稅法學》《國際海事法學》以及《國際經濟組織法》等。另外，他還撰寫了一系列有關介評MIGA、ICSID以及其中與中國相關問題的專論，撰寫了大量的投資與國際貿易方面的案例分析文章以及中國涉外仲裁的監督機制方面的評論與立法建議，可謂學富五車，著作等身。這些著作與專論所體現的思想充滿中國特色，獨具創新之見，不落窠臼，體現了陳安教授勇於開拓、治學嚴謹、孜孜不倦、勤於筆耕的學者風範。讀陳安教授的著作，我們還會體會到他赤誠的愛國情懷，他以自己的知識和身體力行諄諄教誨後學，服務於社會實踐，服務於國家的改革開放，是我們學人的典範。

我與陳安教授相識近三十年，他一直是我的良師益友。陳安教授待人謙虛誠懇，樂於助人，是一位可親可敬的長者。為人、為學我都從他那裡受益良多。

我為本套專著的出版，向陳安教授致以衷心的祝賀。

三、試論秉持第三世界共同立場的中國特色國際經濟法學派的形成及其代表性成果

張永彬*

在國際上，作為一門新興邊緣學科，國際經濟法學較之國際公法學、國際私法學的獨立突出不免落後「晚成」；而在中國，國際經濟法學研究與教學的正式啟動則更顯姍姍來遲，其啟動和發展幾乎和一九七八年中國實行改革開放基本國策同步俱進。究其主要緣因，在於閉關鎖國、積貧積弱之時似乎「無須」國際經濟法，而對外開放首先遇到的恰是大量的國際經濟法律問題。國際經濟法學遂因緣際會，在改革開放後的中國應運而生，並迅速成長。隨著國力的強盛，秉持第三世界共同立場的中國國際經濟法學者的聲音日益受到全世界的關注。這其中，不能不提到，中國國際經濟法學的開拓者和奠基人之一、國際知名的中國學者、一九九三年至今連選連任中國國際經濟法學會會長的廈門大學法學院陳安教授及其代表性成果——五卷本《陳安論國際經濟法學》。

老驥伏櫪，志在千里

回首三十多年前，經濟面臨崩潰邊緣的中國，結束了「十年浩劫」，撥亂反正，開始實行改革開放的基本國策。[2]時已五十一歲的陳安重返法學領域，「在應當衝刺的年齡才起跑」[3]陳安稱「這是我們這一代法學工作者特殊的遭遇」[4]。陳安重返法學生涯於改革開放之始，他的學術生命從此與改革開放緊密相連。

[5] 早在一九五〇年七月，陳安即從廈門大學法律系畢業，嗣後，他服從組織分配，相繼在地方法院、廈大法律系、廈大馬列主義教研室（哲學、政治經濟學、政治學）、下放農村鍛煉、廈大教育系及歷史系等單位工作，多次奉命「轉行」，直到一九八〇年廈大復辦法律系，陳安才奉命「歸隊」重操已經荒疏了二十七年的舊業——法律，再次關注「久違」了的國際法。前半世紀的光陰流轉，他用「蹉跎歲月」來自我形容，後三十多年則是急起直追，只為「挽回」失去的寶貴時光。正是這樣的人生境遇和不懈努力，陳安先生三十多年來先後取得十三項國家級、省部級科研成果一等獎，八項國家級、省部級科研成果二等獎，[6] 其獲獎等級之高、數量之多，在中國人文社會科學學者中罕有其匹，而在上述十三項一等獎成果中，十項是在他七十歲退休以後取得的，[7] 而最新的一項一等獎[8] 更是在他八十二歲之際摘取的。新近，他又針對當代霸權主義者橫加於中國的誣衊——「中國威脅」論，撰寫中英雙語論文，史論結合，揭露真相，痛加撻伐，以正國際視聽，引起國內外人士的高度重視。[9] 概言之，其學術生命之旺盛之長久，愛國情懷之強烈，行文筆鋒之犀利，三者如此緊密融合，且均臻上乘，堪稱學界一奇。

中國特色國際經濟法學派的創建軌跡

回顧三十年來以陳安為代表的中國國際經濟法學者在國際經濟法領域走過的曆程，其軌跡清晰可尋，歷歷在目。

（一）一九八七年「國際經濟法學系列專著」的出版，開創
　　　了中國特色國際經濟法學理論體系的先河，此後二十
　　　多年又相繼推出多部高校教材、專題專著和多篇雙語
　　　學術論文，使這一特色理論體系逐步走向成熟

　　一九八七年由鷺江出版社出版、陳安教授主編的「國際經濟
法學系列專著」，包括了《國際投資法》《國際貿易法》《國際貨
幣金融法》《國際稅法》和《國際海事法》五部著作，這是中國
第一套國際經濟法學系列專著。出版後次年（1988年）即榮獲福
建省人民政府社科優秀成果一等獎，這也是陳安教授學術生涯中
榮獲的第一個省部級一等獎。

　　當時國內外學者對國際經濟法的概念、性質、範圍解釋不
一，尚無定論。具代表性的有兩種觀點：一種觀點認為，國際經
濟法屬於國際公法的範疇，是經濟領域的國際公法，屬於國際公
法的一個分支，各國國內的涉外經濟法規範，應排除在國際經濟
法之外。學界通常稱此種觀點為「狹義國際經濟法學說」。另一
種觀點認為，國際經濟法不限於、不等於經濟領域的國際公法，
而應綜合調整國際經濟關係的國內法規範和調整國際經濟關係的
國際法規範，成為一門新的獨立的法學部門。學界通常稱此種觀
點為「廣義國際經濟法學說」。一九八二年前後，美國紐約大學
法學院洛文費爾德教授編寫的一套以「國際經濟法」命名的六卷
本叢書，持「廣義國際經濟法」觀點，被世界國際經濟法學界認
為是具有重大影響的著作。但其立足於美國的實際，以美國的利
益為核心來分析美國涉外經濟法以及國際經濟法的各種問題，闡
述和論證西方發達國家對這些問題的基本觀點。

　　陳安教授一九八七年主編的上述國際經濟法學系列專著，首次在中國以系列專著的形式闡述了國際經濟法學是一門新的獨立的邊緣性法學部門，同時密切聯繫中國實際，注意從中國的立場來研究和評析國際交往中的有關法律問題，同時注意闡述和論證第三世界發展中國家對有關法律問題的共同立場。與洛文費爾德教授的前述六卷本叢書相比，雖然同樣主張國際經濟法是獨立的法學部門，但卻站在不同的立場上，與前者形成鮮明的對照，在國際經濟法這個引人關注的國際學術舞臺上，發出了中國國際經濟法學者獨立自主的聲音。學界認為這開創了中國特色國際經濟法學科體系和理論體系的先河。[10] 雖然今日來看，二十多年前的研究難言完備，但依然不掩其當年初創時期的學術光芒和思辨鋒芒。例如，在輯入《陳安論國際經濟法學》五卷本的開宗明義第一篇《論國際經濟法學科的邊緣性、綜合性和獨立性》一文中，陳安先生早在二十年前就對美國著名的洛文費爾德教授所撰、流行全美、宣揚「美國立場」的《國際經濟法》通用教材中的若干觀點，提出了尖銳的批評。[11] 陳安先生認為，洛文費爾德教授在國際經濟法學領域建樹頗多，享有國際盛譽。但是，他的某些學術觀點卻彌漫著或殘留著殖民主義、擴張主義、霸權主義氣息。這是國際弱勢群體即發展中國家不能苟同的。作為發展中國家一員的中國，其學人固然可以而且應當從洛文費爾德教授的著作中學習國際經濟法前沿知識的精華，卻不能不加認真思考、仔細鑒別和必要剔除，以致連同其中包含的糟粕囫圇吞下。他認為，這既是國際弱勢群體即發展中國家的學者們的權利，也是這些學者們義不容辭的職責。

就中國的人文社會科學如何在世界學術論壇上獲得自己的位置，先生自有獨到見解：「在國際學術論壇上，中國人既要謙虛謹慎，認真學習和吸收有益的新知，切忌閉目塞聽，妄自尊大；又要敢於對外來的種種『權威』理論，衡諸國情和世情，深入探討，獨立思考，加以鑒別，乃至質疑，切忌妄自菲薄，盲目附和。簡言之，要認真刻苦地學歷史，鑽理論，擺事實，講道理，有據有理地闡明自己的見解，敢於發出中華之聲和弱勢群體之聲，平等地參加國際熱點難點問題的討論和爭鳴，追求客觀真理和社會公平。」[12]

秉持這種學術理念和學術追求，陳安先生率領他的學術團隊批判地學習和研究外來新鮮知識，取其精華，棄其糟粕，並在此基礎上，敢於和善於不斷開拓創新，相繼推出《國際經濟法總論》[13]《國際經濟法學》《國際經濟法學概論》《國際經濟法學專論》（兩卷本）[14]、「國際經濟法學系列專著」（五卷本，北京大學出版社1999-2001年版）、《國際經濟法學芻言》（兩卷本）等教材和教學參考書，供全國不同層次和不同專業的高校學員學習之需。同時，又瞄準國際經濟法學領域前沿的最新動態和熱點難點問題，帶領團隊集體攻關，先後推出《美國對海外投資的法律保護及典型案例分析》[15]《「解決投資爭端國際中心」述評》[16]《MIGA與中國：《多邊投資擔保機構述評》[17]《國際投資爭端仲裁「解決投資爭端國際中心機制」研究》[18]《國際投資法的新發展與中國雙邊投資條約的新實踐》[19]等專著。此外，他個人還針對上述熱點難點問題撰寫中英雙語論文，[20]積極參加國際學術爭鳴，有理有據地闡述獨到觀點，提出國策建言。通過

上述團隊和個人研究成果的不斷積累，具有中國特色的國際經濟法學科體系和理論體系初步成形，並正在逐步走向成熟。

　　一份有分量的長篇調查報告，客觀地反映和記錄了中國國際經濟法學研究在陳安等中國學者群體多年努力開拓下欣欣向榮的現狀和發展趨勢，明確總結出：正是對外開放的國策推動了中國國際經濟法學的迅速發展，充分肯定了中國國際經濟法學作為獨立法律學科地位的確立和學科體系的初步建立。同時指出：目前，中國各政法院校、大學的法學院和法律系一般都將國際經濟法學作為一門主要的專業課程，一些大學的國際金融、世界經濟專業也將國際經濟法學列為必修課程。「國際經濟法學所取得的豐碩成果及其對我國國際經濟法律實踐所產生的積極影響，初步證明了廣義國際經濟法學說的科學性，也展示了廣義國際經濟法學廣闊的發展前景和強大的生命力。」[21]

（二）創建「中國特色國際經濟法學派」之首議（1993 年）

　　創建「中國特色國際經濟法學派」此議最初可溯及至一九九三年在中國國際經濟法珠海年會期間，由中國社科院法學所李澤銳教授和復旦大學法學院董世忠教授提出。此項創新建議得到陳安先生的高度認同。陳安先生認為：「這既符合於中國的國情，也符合於時代的需要。中國人當然不能妄自尊大，但也不必妄自菲薄。」「創建中國的國際經濟法學派，當然不能一蹴而就，也不可能期待在三五年、一二十年之中由幾個人完全實現。要完全實現，並獲得廣泛的國際認同，需要幾代中國學人群體的連續努力和不懈追求。中國人應當有這種志氣和抱負，從現在就起步，

朝這個方向邁步前進。」[22]正是在這樣的遠見卓識下，以陳安為代表的中國國際經濟法學界，篳路藍縷，一步一個腳印，配合國家的改革開放國策，經過三十餘年的努力，秉持和代表第三世界共同立場和聲音的中國國際經濟法學者已然崛起。以陳安為代表的中國國際經濟法學派，以其創新、務實、豐碩的學術成果以及日益完備的理論體系，正在形成自己的獨立風格和鮮明特色，為建立國際經濟新秩序發出時代的強音。

（三）一九九三年始，長期執掌作為全國性一級學術社團的中國國際經濟法學會及其會刊《國際經濟法學刊》

除了個人的學術努力外，陳安先生還不負國內同行所托，在眾多志士仁人的鼎力支援下，使中國國際經濟法學會獲得了中華人民共和國民政部批准，正式登記成為國家一級的民間學術社團，陳安先生也自一九九三年以來連選連任中國國際經濟法學會會長，並通過這一學術平臺，更有效地積極開展國際經濟法領域的國內外學術交流，逐漸形成和確立了「以文會友，以友輔仁，知識報國，兼濟天下」的學會宗旨和共識。陳安先生初創和主編的學會會刊《國際經濟法學刊》，在全國同行、先進的積極參與下，已成為全國性、開放性的國際經濟法領域優秀學術著述的集刊，由北京大學出版社出版，已連續出版十八卷，每卷四期，先後發表了大量代表中國水準的高水準的國際經濟法論文，其學術水準和社會影響受到國內外理論界和實務界的普遍肯定和讚譽，並已入選「中文社會科學引文索引」（CSSCI）學術資料來源集刊，成為國際學術交往和展示中國學者國際經濟法學研究成果的

交流平臺。

（四）銳意培養青年才俊，致力學術團隊的建設與傳承

一九八四年三至四月，陳安教授應聯合國教科文組織邀請，作為中國派出的「國際法教育考察組」成員之一，由北京大學國際法研究所所長王鐵崖教授率領，一行三人，出訪西歐和北美五國二十個城市，對西方發達國家的法學教育進行調研、考察，並與一百多位法學界有關人士進行交流。回國後，陳安教授依據此次考察見聞，結合中國國情，就國際法專業人才培養等方面的問題撰寫「萬言書」，[23] 提出許多具體的改進建議。諸如：（1）派人員出國深造應考慮門類、品種和國別的多樣化；（2）應積極參加國際性的學術會議或學術團體；（3）國際法課程的教學應注重培養學生解決實際問題的能力，強調大量的課前預習和活躍的課堂對話，開設類比法庭課（Moot Court）、法律門診課（Clinical Program in Legal Aid）或學生法律援助服務專案（Student Legal Aid Service）；（4）提倡由優秀研究生主辦專業學刊，作為法學拔尖人才的搖籃；（5）注重開發利用外籍華人和港臺留學生中的法學人才資源；（6）建立全國性的國際法資料中心，資源分享，互通有無；（7）組織和推動全國國際法專業力量的合作，協同致力研究國家面臨的外交、外貿問題，提供國策建言，實行「知識報國」。如今這些建議有的已被有關部門採納，並行之有效；有的則尚待借鑑他山之石，付諸實踐，俾使中國的國際法人才培養事業與時俱進，更上層樓。

陳安教授以廈大法學院為基地，在人才培養方面開創出了

「寓教學於科研，溶科研於教學，使出人才與出成果並舉」的研究生培養方法，強調「從難從嚴訓練，成果人才並出」。[24] 他指出，培養研究生的目的是為國家輸送高層次的專業人才，為了快出人才，出好人才，很有必要把出成果作為培養人才的手段。從研究生入學伊始，就從難從嚴出發，狠抓基本功訓練，力爭實現成果與人才同時並出。其基本訓練方式包括：實行「大運動量」訓練，敢於堅持嚴格要求，力排某些學生的怕苦「眾議」和畏難「惰性」，要求儘早過好法學專業英語關；提倡多學科交叉滲透，兼修相關相鄰課程，建立合理的知識結構；強調理論聯繫實際，參加各類實踐，提高實務工作能力；充分信賴，及時「壓」擔，嚴密組織，嚴格把關；賦予新設專業較大「成才自留權」，加速形成「人才生產基地」，提高人才生產力。

陳安教授主要負責博士生培養方案的設計，抓研究生師資隊伍的學風和教風建設，帶領有關教師和研究生申請承擔國家有關科研課題，指導他們進行科研攻關，指導教師與研究生編輯《國際經濟法學刊》，並積極指導年輕一代研究生導師的成長。多年來，陳安教授率頭採用這種方法，培養了數十名學有專長的碩士和博士，他們知識結構合理，綜合能力較強，大多已成為各教學、科研單位的教學和科研骨幹。以陳安教授為帶頭人的廈門大學國際經濟法專業學術團隊，經過二十多年的集體努力，在科研和教學方面均取得了突出的成果，在全國同一專業學科中居於領先地位，其所屬的「廈門大學國際法學科」於二〇〇二年被評為國家重點學科。十年以來經數度中期審核、重評，均完全合格，一直保持學術青春和全國領先地位至今。

畢業後留校堅持與陳安教授在廈門大學合作共事、協力開拓的優秀研究生，如今均已成長為國內知名的中青年教授和新一代的博士生導師。其中成就突出的有曾華群教授（博士生導師）、廖益新教授（博士生導師）、徐崇利教授（博士生導師）、李國安教授（博士生導師）等。在其他高校執教的知名學者，如西安交通大學的單文華教授（院長）、西北政法大學的李萬強教授（院長），當年都曾在廈大法學院師從陳安教授，積極參與團隊科研，成績優異，脫穎而出。當年在廈大攻讀國際法學博士學位後投身實務界的執業人士，如趙德銘律師、林忠律師、傅明律師、謝嵐律師等，如今也都在中國涉外法律事務和國際法律事務中，善於運用專業知識，折衝樽俎，創業有成，成為同行中的佼佼者。

中國特色國際經濟法學派的標誌性成果

前述五卷本《陳安論國際經濟法學》的問世，是中國特色國際經濟法學派的標誌性成果，標誌著中國特色國際經濟法學派的初步形成。

在五卷本《陳安論國際經濟法學》問世之前，陳安教授所著兩卷本《國際經濟法學芻言》（北京大學出版社2005年版）首次整理彙集了陳安教授自改革開放以來二十餘年間在國際經濟法領域耕耘所開拓和收穫的豐碩成果，並榮獲第五屆「吳玉章人文社會科學獎」一等獎。五卷本《陳安論國際經濟法學》的推出，則更加系統地梳理了陳安教授在國際經濟法學領域的學術追求和學術思想，更加突出顯示了陳安教授在當代國際經濟法前沿的新成

果及其對該領域理論和實踐中出現的新熱點問題和難點問題的新探索。特別是，伴隨著中國在「入世」後迅速崛起，面對各國對中國崛起所發出的不同聲音，陳安教授站在建立國際經濟新秩序的高度，旗幟鮮明地代表廣大發展中國家依法仗義執言，力圖為包括中國在內的當代第三世界爭取國際經濟公平權益和平等地位提供法學理論武器，提出了一系列具有鮮明中國特色的國際經濟法學派的學術觀點和主張，[25] 從而初步形成了有獨特風格、有獨到見解的中國國際經濟法學派。因此，五卷本《陳安論國際經濟法學》堪稱中國特色國際經濟法學派的標誌性成果。其最為突出之處在於：

（一）致力構建中國特色國際經濟法學理論體系

《陳安論國際經濟法學》全書約三百一十萬字，薈萃了陳安教授在中國實行對外開放基本國策三十年來，研究國際經濟法學這一新興邊緣學科所獲的主要成果，系統、集中地展示了陳安教授三十年來為創建中國特色國際經濟法學所作的開創性學術建樹。全書共分五卷八編，即國際經濟法基本理論（一）、國際經濟法基本理論（二）、國際投資法、國際貿易法、涉臺經濟法、國際法教育、英文版論文選輯以及有關本書作者論著和學術觀點的報導、評論和函件等。其中有關國際經濟法基本理論的研究就占了全部五卷中整整兩卷的篇幅，於此可以看出作者為構建中國國際經濟法學科體系和基本理論體系傾注了大量心血，努力嘗試開拓創新。全書雖為鴻篇巨制，但體系和脈絡相當清晰。這些文字忠實地記錄了自二十世紀七〇年代末以來，陳安教授三十年如

一日，不懈探索、辛勤耕耘，牽頭引領同行學者們，共同將國際經濟法這一當年很少人承認的法律部門，逐步開拓和發展成為對中國改革開放做出重大貢獻的獨立的法律部門。[26]

（二）代表廣大發展中國家力主建立國際經濟新秩序（NIEO）

當代國際社會中時常流行形形色色力圖阻撓或扭曲建立國際經濟新秩序（NIEO）歷史潮流的各種學說，諸如「新自由主義經濟秩序」論、「WTO憲政秩序」論、「WTO體制有法必守、執法必嚴、違法危險、變法徒勞」論、「經濟民族主義擾亂全球化秩序」論、「中國應當完成『角色轉變』：從現存國際經濟秩序的革命者轉變為維護者」論、「中國應當全盤接受美國領導的現存國際經濟秩序，安分守己，才能從中獲取更大利益」論等等。這類學說發源和流行於西方強權國家，而近年來「西風東漸」，在中國國內不乏附和呼應之聲，形成一種「時髦」，甚至有教授對這類說教捧之為「精深而獨到的見解」，足以「開闊中國學者的眼界」，不惜濃墨重彩，加以美化和拔高。這些似是而非的「時髦」理論確實造成了一系列新的思想混亂。陳安教授以敏銳的眼光、獨立的思考和嚴謹的論證，對此類「時髦」理論逐一地、連續地加以批評剖析，力求澄清是非，排除誤導，避免實踐錯誤。[27]陳安教授強調：建立NIEO乃是二十世紀五〇年代以來全球弱勢群體數十億人口爭取國際經濟平權地位的共同奮鬥目標，也是鄧小平一九七四年在聯合國莊嚴講臺上向全球鄭重宣布的中國戰略目標。當代中國人應當秉持「科學的發展觀」，與時俱進、全面、完整、準確地加深理解鄧小平的「韜光養晦、有所作為」

方針，將中國在構建NIEO歷史進程中的戰略座標和基本角色，定位為旗幟鮮明、言行一致的積極推動者。中國理應進一步發揚傳統的具有獨特內涵的中華民族愛國主義，通過BRICSM類型的「南南聯合」群體，堅定不移地成為建立NIEO的積極推手和中流砥柱之一。中國理應致力推動國際經濟新秩序和國際經濟法制逐步實現新舊更替、吐故納新和棄舊圖新，在「變法圖強」、南北平等、和諧合作的前提下，謀求世界的共同繁榮。

（三）抓住國際經濟法的首要關鍵，深入剖析當代經濟主權上的「攻防戰」

早在一九八一年初，陳安先生便和在美國享有「中國通」美譽的哈佛大學法學院的柯恩教授在有關徵收外資的問題上有過一場針鋒相對的辯論。其時，柯恩教授來訪廈門，在一場演講中批評新中國政府不尊重私有財產，隨意沒收（cofiiscae）外國人資產；他認為，為了吸引外商來華投資，應當在立法中規定絕對不侵犯外國人一切財產。陳安先生當場指出，他的批評不符合中國的實際情況，並列舉中國的有關法律規定逐一予以反駁，同時援引美國的相關法律和國際慣例，辨析「沒收」（confiscation）與「徵收」（exprpriation）的區別。陳安先生認為，中國在涉外經濟立法中，不宜、不必、不應、不容明文規定對外資絕對不實行徵收或國有化。東道國在必要時有權依法徵收境內外資並給予補償，乃是當代國家經濟主權權利之一，而且已是國際通行的立法慣例，中國不應通過立法自行「棄權」。相反，務必留權在手，但決不任意濫用。

柯恩教授當即表示：「你的知識補充了我的不足」，並邀請陳安先生前往哈佛訪問和講學。後來，以此次辯論為基礎，陳安撰寫了相關的中英雙語論文《我國涉外經濟立法中可否規定對外資絕不實行國有化》[28]其中有關觀點被後來的修訂立法所吸收。[29]

二〇〇四年，柯恩教授應邀來廈門參加國際學術會議，老友重逢，聚敘甚歡。「但我們之間又在美國單邊主義與WTO多邊主義之間矛盾衝突問題上，各持己見，激烈爭辯」。陳安先生說，可以說，他們是「不打不相識」的「諍友」，在互相尊重對方的基礎上，通過國際性前沿問題的學術爭鳴，實行知識互補，達到共同提高。

在經濟全球化加速發展的條件下，各國經濟主權的原則和觀念是否應當弱化和淡化？這是當代國際論壇上頗有爭議的一大理論問題和實踐問題。如何看待各國經濟主權，素來是國際經濟法中首屈一指的關鍵所在，也是一大熱點難點問題。長期以來，以曾經擔任美國國際法學會會長的權威教授路易士・漢金（Louis Henkin）為首的學者極力鼓吹弱國「主權過時」論、「主權有害」論；另一位被西方學界推崇為「WTO之父」的美國權威國際法教授約翰・傑克遜（John H. Jackson）則牽頭極力倡導「美國主權（實為霸權）優先」論。針對美國權威教授們在國家經濟主權這個關鍵問題上的似是而非、流行全球的理論觀點，陳安先生作了針鋒相對、有理有據的批評和剖析。他以WTO體制運作十年來美國單邊主義與WTO多邊主義交鋒的三大回合作為中心，撰寫中英雙語的長篇學術論文，[30]綜合評析美國「1994年主權大辯論」一九九八至二〇〇〇年「301條款」爭端案以及二〇〇二

至二〇〇三年「201條款」爭端案的前因後果和來龍去脈，指出這三次交鋒的實質都是美國經濟「主權」（經濟霸權）與各國群體經濟主權之間限制與反限制的爭鬥，都是植根於美國在一九九四年「入世」之初就已確立的既定方針：力圖在「入世」之後仍然推行其單邊主義政策，以維護和擴大其既得的經濟霸權，可以隨時背棄其在WTO體制中承擔的多邊主義義務。

上述既定方針，是美國「1994年主權大辯論」得出的結論，它標誌著在這第一回合大交鋒中美國單邊主義的勝利和WTO多邊主義的敗北。其後，在第二回合的大交鋒中，審理「301條款」爭端案的專家組執法不公，以模棱兩可、「小罵大幫忙」的方式偏袒美國，實際上導致美國單邊主義的再度獲勝和WTO多邊主義的再度敗北。在第三回合的大交鋒中，經過兩審結案，美國終於在二〇〇三年十一月敗訴，這雖然標誌著美國單邊主義的初步敗北，固屬可喜，但是充其量，只能把它視為十年來WTO多邊主義此前兩次事實上敗北之後的「初度小勝」，對其發展前景，實不宜過度樂觀。因為，美國總統在「201條款」爭端案中敗訴之後發表聲明，對上述既定方針毫無改弦易轍之意，足見禍根未除，「病根」仍在，故其單邊主義的霸權頑症可能隨時複發，WTO多邊主義仍然前途多艱，可謂「慶父不去，魯難未已」鑒此，善良的人們不能不經常保持清醒，增強憂患意識，隨時謹防美國單邊主義大棒之捲土重來和再度肆虐。

另外，「201條款」爭端案中WTO多邊主義之初度小勝，端賴與美國對壘的二十二個主權國家（包括中國在內），敢於和善於運用掌握在自己手中的經濟主權，與經濟霸權開展針鋒相對的

鬥爭。可見，所謂WTO正式運轉之後，有關國家經濟主權的原則和概念應當日益「淡化」「弱化」云云，此類說辭，至少是不符合現實、不夠清醒的，也是很不可取的；至於美國權威學者鼓吹經濟主權「過時」論云云，則顯然是居心叵測的理論陷阱，對此，不能不倍加警惕！

（四）突出顯示鮮明的中國特色

當今的國際經濟法，其學科發展水準在某種程度上可以說是與一國在國際經濟舞臺上的實力相關聯的。由於廣大發展中國家在經濟上的弱勢，長期以來，以美國為首的西方國家的權威學者的某些學術觀點流行全球，彌漫著或殘留著濃烈的殖民主義、擴張主義、霸權主義的氣息。作為發展中國家一員的中國的學者，陳安教授的論著立足於中國國情和國際弱勢群體即廣大發展中國家的共同立場，致力於探索和開拓具有中國特色的國際經濟法學，提出諸多開創性見解，為國際社會弱勢群體「依法仗義執言」，提供維護其應有平等權益的法學理論武器，這是貫穿全書的學術理念和追求，也是該書的基本學術主張和論述主線。如書中提出的著名的「6C軌跡」論，依據大量史實，探索建立國際經濟新秩序的規律和路徑；通過史論結合，有理有據地揭示近代史上的「殖民十惡」，論證全球弱小民族堅持愛國主義，要求改變國際經濟舊秩序和更新國際經濟立法的正當性；強調當代國際經濟秩序和國際經濟法律規範的破舊立新，勢必循著螺旋式上升的「6C軌跡」曲折而又不斷地向前發展；排除「速勝」論、「坦途」論和「瓦解」論的影響，令人信服地指出：要逐步更新國際經濟立

法，建立起國際經濟新秩序，舍韌性的南南聯合自強，別無他途可循。[31] 書中類似的開創性見解還有很多。[32] 可以說，這些成果突出地顯示了中國國際經濟法學派的鮮明特色和理論水準。

（五）躋身國際前驅

作為國際知名的中國學者，五卷本專著中有近兩卷的篇幅是陳安教授相繼發表在國際權威期刊上的長篇英文版專題論文。[33] 中國國際法學界前輩權威學者郭壽康教授認為：這些用英語發表的作品，投身國際爭鳴，弘揚中華學術，在國際上影響很大，既體現出發展中國家的主張與立場，也擴大了中國的國際影響，為中國國際經濟法學贏得了國際聲譽。[34]

國際知名人士B. 戈索維奇（Branislav Gosovic）先生（曾長期擔任發展中國家政府間組織「南方中心」秘書長），對陳安教授所撰《南南聯合自強五十年的國際經濟立法反思：從萬隆、多哈、坎昆到香港》長篇專題論文給予很高評價，認為它標誌著「對第三世界思想體系的重大創新來自中國」[35]，在世界上特別是第三世界產生了重大影響。

陳安教授在進行學術研究的同時，作為中國政府依據《華盛頓公約》於一九九三年、二〇〇四年，二〇一〇年三度遴選向「解決投資爭端中心」（ICSID）指派的國際仲裁員，作為國際知名的商務仲裁員，還積極參與國際經濟司法的實踐。書中收錄的其研析涉外或涉華經貿爭端仲裁的典型案例，或深入探討相關法理問題，提出創新見解；或依法據理，剖析批判，匡謬驅邪，伸張正義，留下了他在國際經濟司法舞臺上鮮明的剛正不阿的印

跡。

　　另值得一提的是，全書文辭優美流暢，尤其是用英文撰寫的文章如同用母語寫出的文章一樣生動，實為難得，充分顯示出老一輩學者深厚的學養和扎實的功力。

　　概言之，五卷本《陳安論國際經濟法學》積三十年之功而匯成鴻篇巨制，具有鮮明的中國特色，堪稱「獨樹中華一幟，躋身國際前驅」。正如中國國際法學界前輩權威學者、一百歲高齡的朱學山教授所言：這部新著既是創建中國特色國際經濟法學理論的奠基之作和扛鼎之作，也是學術報國和經世致用之作。全書秉持陳安教授「三十年來一貫的學術追求，即體察當代南北矛盾的現實，依據和提煉第一手資料，運用當代國際法理論，通過學術論證，致力為發展中國家弱勢群體『依法仗義執言』，為當代第三世界爭取國際經濟平權地位提供法學理論武器，三十年如一日，不懈不渝，可謂『一劍悴礪三十年』」〔36〕。

　　此外，五卷本《陳安論國際經濟法學》的書名同樣引人關注。這也是中國改革開放以來首次參照國際慣例以學者姓名命名的多卷本法學專著。在國際法學界，以學者個人姓名命名「××論××法」，是國際上不少著名法學著作的命名慣例，如《奧本海國際法》（*Oppenhein's International Law*）《戴西和莫里斯論衝突法》（*Dicey & Morris on the Conflict of Laws*）等等。五卷本《陳安論國際經濟法學》的問世，未嘗不是當代中國學者排除百年來形成的民族自卑殘餘，努力樹立應有的「躋身國際前驅」的自信自強心志與正當追求。如此，具有鮮明特色的中國國際經濟法學派的形成和存在，當在不遠的將來為世所公認，並必將為世所重。

四、從陳安教授辛勤探索的結晶中感悟其治學之道

朱欖葉*

《陳安論國際經濟法學》簡介

《陳安論國際經濟法學》一書（以下簡稱「五卷本」）分列八編，含中、英雙語專論七十八章，共約三百一十萬字，二〇〇八年由復旦大學出版社推出。其篇章結構和主要內容如下：

第一編，國際經濟法基本理論（一）。含十六章專論，分別從國際經濟法學科的性質、基本原則、其產生和發展、國際經濟法幾種理論的批判、南北關係、南南合作等方面探討了國際經濟法基本理論問題。

第二編，國際經濟法基本理論（二）。含十三章專論，分別對中國國內國際經濟法學界的不同觀點展開了分析和評論，還包括對一些具體案件的評析。

第三編，國際投資法。含十五章專論，探討了多邊投資擔保制度、美國海外私人投資保護制度、中國吸引外資和對外投資制度，分析了涉及國際投資的幾個具體案例。

第四編，國際貿易法。含七章專論，通過具體案例分析了國際貿易法中的一些具體問題，如合同無效、抵押及其爭端管轄權、匯票承兌爭端管轄權、商檢結論等。

第五編，涉臺經濟法。含五章專論，對《臺商大陸投資權益保障協定》《多邊投資擔保機構公約》對中國臺灣地區的適用問題、中國「入世」後海峽兩岸經貿問題「政治化」之防治等問題

提出了作者的獨到見解。

第六編，國際法教育。含四章專論，以作者從事法學教育半個多世紀的感悟，剖析了法學教育中一些發人深省的問題。

第七編，英文版論文選輯。這一部分包括了陳安教授原先發表於國外學術刊物上的十八篇英文長篇專論。

第八編，附錄。含有關本書作者論著和學術觀點的報導、評論和函件等。

五卷本給讀者的啟示

面對厚厚的五卷本，雖當時一口答應復旦大學出版社參加筆談，但真的坐下來，卻覺得有些惶恐。要寫一篇簡扼的「書評」，評介蘊含在這五卷本中的陳安教授的學術思想、學術理念和學術追求，談何容易！筆者作為國際經濟法學界的晚輩，早就聽說了陳安教授的大名，也曾在許多會議上聆聽過老師的高論，但有緣當面請教，還是十二年前的事。自那以後，在每年的國際經濟法學會年會或其他學術會議期間，都有幸聽到老師的發言。看著手頭這五卷書，筆者在思考著：我們從陳安教授辛勤探索的結晶中可以學到什麼？

（一）秉持鮮明立場，獨樹中華一幟

只要是讀過陳安教授論文的人，都可以從中感受到他論述問題的鮮明立場。不管是他對國際經濟新秩序「6C軌跡」的分析〔37〕，還是「南南聯合自強」的觀點〔38〕都是鮮明地從發展中國家特別是中國的立場出發。陳安教授的觀點並不一定每個人都能接

受，但是他論述問題的堅定不移的出發點，卻是我們很多學者所忽視，或至少不夠重視的。這樣的出發點，不是像時下有些人那樣，在某篇論文的最後簡單加上一個「我國的對策」，而是貫穿於他研究和分析的全過程。陳安教授並不輕易否定國外的各種理論，但也絕不盲從。例如，陳安教授對美國國際法學權威學者傑塞普、洛文費爾德、漢金、傑克遜等人的某些關鍵性理論觀點和學術主張，都秉持虛心學習、嚴肅對待的態度，通過獨立思考、剖析批評，取其精華、去其糟粕。〔39〕對任何一個問題，不是從表面現象看，而是作深層次的分析。比如《世紀之交在經濟主權上的新爭議與「攻防戰」綜合評析十年來美國單邊主義與WTO多邊主義交鋒的三大回合》一文〔40〕將美國加入WTO之前的「主權大辯論」、美國「301條款」案（歐共體提出）美國「301條款」案（歐共體、韓國、日本、中國、巴西、墨西哥、紐西蘭等提出的鋼鐵保障措施案），置放在美國一貫的經濟霸權主義宏觀背景下作了深刻分析。他指出，當代來自超級大國的國家經濟主權「淡化」「弱化」之類的時髦說法，既不符合現實，也是很不可取的；也提醒全球弱勢群體國家，切忌輕信盲從，墮入理論陷阱。〔41〕有了大量的事實和引證，這樣的分析讓人口服心服。何謂「獨樹中華一幟」？〔42〕這就是一大典範。

（二）力求查證原始資料，養成嚴謹治學習慣

流覽陳安教授的每篇論文，看到大量的注釋，其中不但有馬列著作，有中國的歷史古籍，還有各個年代外國學者的著述，更有大量的第一手原始資料。〔43〕但是，我們卻較少看到也引用近

期其也學者的論述。這並不是陳安教授不了解近期學術動向，更不是也不看別人的文章，而是也力求運用最直接的原始「證據」來支持自己的觀點。筆者想起了最早和陳安教授探討問題的一件事。二〇〇〇年，筆者出版了第一本《世界貿易組織國際貿易糾紛案例評析》，其中就論及美國與歐共體之間關於「301條款」的案件。在評析該案時，筆者把它誤認作了歐共體「荷爾蒙」案的續篇，在書中說：一九九八年二月，DSB通過了荷爾蒙案專家組和上訴機構的報告，確認歐共體的某些措施不符合《實施衛生與植物衛生措施協定》，要求歐共體修改這些措施。此後，美國就曾經揚言要根據301條款對歐共體實施報復。歐共體的申訴就是在這一背景下出臺的」〔44〕。此後，陳安教授就不止一次打電話來，要筆者告訴他美國是在什麼時候如何「揚言」的。在寫此案的案件評析時，筆者原先僅僅憑著自己對一篇報導的記憶寫出了上述的話。等到陳安教授細究，筆者找遍了所有材料，都無法找到美國何時、何地、如何揚言要報復歐共體「荷爾蒙」案的原始出處。後來筆者繼續尋找，才搞清其實是美國對歐共體「香蕉案」的執行情況不滿而要求報復，導致了歐共體的申訴。反觀陳安教授的《世紀之交在經濟主權上的新爭議與「攻防戰」：綜合評析十年來美國單邊主義與WTO多邊主義交鋒的三大回合》一文，對這個同一案件的來龍去脈和前因後果卻寫得清清楚楚。〔45〕從這件事可以看出，陳安教授在研究中，每一個細節都要努力搞清楚，這可能已經形成了習慣，但卻是許多學人所不及的。

（三）緊密關注當代國際事件，善於進行多維角度分析

緊密關注當代國際事件，並以法學理論加以分析，指出對待這些事件的正確態度，這是陳安教授的書給我們的又一啟示。從一九八〇年對蘇聯「有限主權論」的剖析[46]到多哈回合談判[47]，從不同仲裁案件的裁決[48]到中國臺灣地區的WTO成員地位[49]，再到對「黃禍」論「中國威脅」論的批判[50]，書中都不是就事論事的表面介紹，而都是理論結合實際的深入分析。陳安教授善於從歷史淵源、國際政治、世界經濟和國際法的多維角度，廣徵博引，由此得出的綜合結論不僅令人信服，而且所提出的相應對策也有理有據，成為政府有關部門決策的重要參考。[51]

結　論

近年以來，學術界真是奇聞不斷，層出不窮，抄襲、造假「蔚然成風」，陰暗角落的諸般「潛規則」似乎就要公然登堂「轉正」，一時間純潔的、學術的校園氛圍似乎已經凋零而不復存在。但是，細細揣摩陳安教授五卷本的論文，再看看周圍的同事們辛勤刻苦的工作狀態，筆者的心情頓時平靜了許多：任憑亂雲飛渡，人間學術正氣，仍自巋然兀立，常在長青！聯想到近年來與陳安教授接觸過程中的一些感悟，筆者深深感到，像陳安教授這樣的人才是中國一代知識份子的楷模。

五、中國特色國際經濟法學的理念與追求

—— 《陳安論國際經濟法學》的學術創新與特色貢獻

曾華群*

　　陳安老師積三十年之功蔚為大觀的《陳安論國際經濟法學》（五卷本）以馬克思主義為指導，以南北問題為主線，站在中國和廣大發展中國家的立場，堅持建立國際經濟新秩序的目標，深刻論證國際經濟法的基本原則，充分反映了作者創建中國特色國際經濟法學的理念和追求。

以馬克思主義為指導論述國際經濟法學的基本問題

　　如所周知，中國特色法學理論是中國特色社會主義理論的重要組成部分之一，其指導思想和理論基礎是馬克思主義。作為中國特色法學理論的重要組成部分之一，中國特色國際經濟法學儘管具有「國際性」，其指導思想和理論基礎同樣是馬克思主義。

　　早在二十世紀四〇年代，作者在廈門大學求學時就開始接受馬克思主義的啟蒙和薰陶，五〇至七〇年代，曾專門從事馬克思主義教學和研究。對馬克思主義特別是民族殖民地及主權理論學養深厚，是其致力創建中國特色國際經濟法學的重要思想和理論優勢。在八〇年代以來的國際經濟法學研究中，作者援引馬克思主義原著的精闢論述，分析國際經濟關係的發展，以殖民掠奪史揭示南北問題的根源和實質及闡釋馬克思主義主權觀。

（一）分析國際經濟關係的發展

國際經濟關係既是國際經濟法藉以產生和發展的主要依據，又是國際經濟法調整的主要對象。作者以辯證唯物主義和歷史唯物主義詳細分析國際經濟關係發展的三大主要階段（即早期的國際經濟交往與國際經濟關係的初步形成，資本主義世界市場的形成與國際經濟關係的重大發展，社會主義國家的出現、眾多弱小民族的獨立與國際經濟關係的本質變化），深刻指出，歷史唯物主義的基本原理「是對人類社會長期發展進程客觀事實的科學總結」，「是對各國社會進行解剖的利器，也是對國際社會實行科學分析的指南」[52]。

（二）以殖民掠奪史揭示南北問題的根源和實質

基於歷史事實，作者以激揚文字歷數十五世紀以來列強在亞非拉地區推行殖民主義的十大罪惡行徑，稱為「殖民十惡」（即「欺蒙詐騙，以賤易貴」「明火執仗，殺人越貨」「踐踏主權，霸占領土」「橫徵暴斂，榨取脂膏」「強制勞役，敲骨吸髓」「獵取活人，販賣奴隸」「壟斷貿易，單一經濟」「種毒販毒，戕民攫利」「毀滅文化，精神侵略」和「血腥屠殺，種族滅絕」[53]進而總結：「漫漫數百年，一部殖民史，就是一部弱肉強食史，也就是歐美列強和全世界眾多弱小民族之間的國際經濟關係史的主要內容。」[54]「十五世紀以來的數百年間，歐洲列強在亞、非、美廣大地區實行殖民掠奪的歷史，是一部火與劍的歷史，也是一部血與淚的歷史。」[55]

在中外國際經濟法學論著中，居於道義制高點，以如此犀利

筆觸歷數殖民之惡，似為僅見。或許有人會認為這是政治學或史學的內容，但筆者以為，殖民掠奪史在西方國際經濟法學論著中諱莫如深，卻是中國特色國際經濟法學應有的立論根基。正本清源，溫故知新。只有回顧和銘記歷史，才能深刻理解南北問題的根源和實質，認清西方列強罄竹難書的罪惡「發家史」及其對廣大發展中國家所欠下的巨大「歷史債務」，也才能深刻理解建立國際經濟新秩序的正當性、必要性和緊迫性，正確認識社會發展規律和國際經濟關係的發展趨勢和方向。在法理上，殖民掠奪史是經濟主權、公平互利和全球合作等國際經濟法基本原則的必要鋪陳。

（三）闡釋馬克思主義主權觀

作者對馬克思主義主權觀的研究和論述，重點強調民族自決權和批判民族虛無主義。兩者相輔相成，構成了作者研討馬克思主義主權觀的核心主張，即十分強調尊重和維護廣大發展中國家的主權，堅決反對社會帝國主義等形形色色的霸權主義。

在專著《列寧對民族殖民地革命學說的重大發展》（1981年）中，作者系統深入研究馬克思、恩格斯關於民族殖民地問題的基本理論，列寧一八九五至一九二四年期間在弱小民族國家主權問題上的學說，重點探討國際共產主義運動史上有關「民族自決」問題的長期論戰，研究國際公法上有關弱小民族國家主權學說的爭鳴辯論，側重論述殖民地、半殖民地弱小民族國家主權——民族自決權問題在國際共產主義運動隊伍中的論戰過程及其發展歷史。[56]

在專論《論社會帝國主義主權觀的一大思想淵源：民族虛無主義的今昔》（1981年）中，作者回顧和縷述當年馬克思、恩格斯和列寧與偽裝成「國際主義者」的形形色色的民族虛無主義者多次論戰的歷史事實，追本溯源，探討曾經猖獗一時的社會帝國主義主權觀的理論基礎和思想淵源，揭露它既是對國際法主權原則的粗暴踐踏，又是對馬克思主義主權觀的徹底背離。[57]

應當指出，馬克思主義主權觀具有重要的現實意義。研究國際共產主義運動中的民族殖民地學說和國際法上的弱小民族國家主權學說，有助於理解當代發展中國家的歷史來由、現實地位和發展趨向及南北問題的根源和實質。研究近代以來西方列強和社會帝國主義的霸權行徑及相關學說，有助於認清當前全球化趨勢下美國推行的霸權主義及西方學者否定或淡化主權的「理論先導」與前者的一脈相承或異曲同工。不難看出，作者在國際經濟法基本理論研究中強調經濟主權原則，深刻批判美國經濟霸權及西方學者否定或淡化主權的謬論，源於對馬克思主義主權觀的深刻理解和研究積澱。

站在中國和其他發展中國家的立場提出南北矛盾發展的「6C律」

不容否認，作為法學學科之一，國際經濟法學具有普世價值，各國國際經濟法學者當有共同的立場、價值取向和追求。基於此，各國國際經濟法學者需要加強學術交流，增強共識，求同存異，共同促進世界性國際經濟法學的發展和繁榮。

同樣不容否認，作為法律規範之一，國際經濟法既是發達國家鞏固國際經濟舊秩序的重要工具，也是發展中國家改革國際經

濟舊秩序、建立國際經濟新秩序的重要工具。換言之，國際經濟法規範體現了新舊法律規則並存、衝突的狀況。在國際經濟法的發展過程中，始終貫穿維護國際經濟舊秩序與建立國際經濟新秩序的鬥爭。相應地，各國國際經濟法學者並非居於同一的、純粹的、超脫的法的立場。在全球化背景下，由於國家利益、歷史傳統、意識形態、宗教信仰、文化等因素，各國特別是南北國家的國際經濟法學者各有其不同的立場、價值取向和追求。西方國家國際經濟法學者對其立場，或直言不諱，或猶抱琵琶。在國際經濟法學研究中，作者一向旗幟鮮明地站在中國和其他發展中國家的立場，堅持和發展「三個世界」理論，堅持建立國際經濟新秩序的目標，體現了「知識報國，兼濟天下」的志向和胸懷。

（一）堅持和發展「三個世界」理論

二十世紀八〇年代末九〇年代初蘇東劇變、冷戰結束後，世界格局發生了重大變化。作者堅持和發展「三個世界」理論，明確指出：現在的世界實際上存在著互相聯繫又互相矛盾著的三個方面，從而使全球劃分為三個世界：首先，美國、蘇聯是第一世界，蘇聯在一九九一年瓦解之後，美國遂成為第一世界中唯一的超級大國；亞、非、拉美發展中國家和其他地區的發展中國家，是第三世界；處在這兩者之間的發達國家是第二世界。中國是一個社會主義國家，也是一個發展中國家，它和其他發展中國家，曾經有過共同的經歷，當前又面臨著共同的鬥爭。過去、現在和將來長時間共同的處境和共同的利害，決定了中國屬於第三世界。[58]作者進一步分析，世紀之交，國際經濟秩序破舊立新的

爭鬥進入新的回合。其主要特點有三：一是冷戰已告結束，和平與發展成為當代世界主題；二是霸權主義和強權政治在各種新「包裝」下有新的發展，「新干涉主義」和「新炮艦政策」不時肆虐；三是經濟全球化趨勢加速發展，南北矛盾日益突出，廣大發展中國家的經濟主權面臨嚴峻挑戰。[59]

對當前國際經濟秩序，西方學界有不同的解讀，諸如「新自由主義經濟秩序」論、「WTO憲政秩序」論和「經濟民族主義擾亂全球化秩序」論等，總體上是不提「三個世界」、南北問題和新舊國際經濟秩序，另闢蹊徑，以所謂「經濟全球化」「法律全球化」理論淡化或否定國家主權。作者針對上述各說，逐一辨析，言簡意賅，切中肯綮。

針對「新自由主義經濟秩序」論，作者指出，「宣揚全面自由化、市場化和私有化的新自由主義和『華盛頓共識』的本質是為國際壟斷資本在全球擴張服務的」；「『新自由主義經濟秩序』的說教及其實踐，實質上乃是殖民主義、資本主義、帝國主義三位一體的國際經濟舊秩序在當代的更新和翻版，充其量只不過是『新瓶裝舊酒』或『換湯不換藥』罷了」。

針對「WTO憲政秩序」論，作者指出，「WTO憲政秩序」論的先天性缺陷和致命性弱點在於，它忽略了當代WTO體制及其規則缺乏堅實的、真正的民主基礎；WTO體制雖然素來被稱為擺脫了「權力導向」，轉而實行「規則導向」，但其「立法」完全是「權力導向」之下的產物，帶著先天的不公胎記，其「司法」和「執法」實踐也出現過「財大者力大氣粗」、霸權或強權國家不受約束或規避制裁的弊端，實際上體現了「規則導向」向

「權力導向」的異化、轉化；「WTO憲政秩序」論要求將貿易自由憲法化、最高化、絕對化的主張是不可取的。[60]

針對「經濟民族主義擾亂全球化秩序」論，作者指出，其實質是以莫須有的「罪名」，力圖迫使國際弱勢群體離開原定的建立國際經濟新秩序的奮鬥目標。他認為，把「經濟民族主義」理解為全球各民族特別是各弱小民族堅持在經濟上獨立自主，堅持國際經濟主權，是基本正確的。[61]

筆者以為，堅持和發展「三個世界」理論，是正確認識新時期中國在國際經濟關系和國際體制的「立場」和「戰略定位」問題的必要前提。基於「三個世界」理論，才能深入分析當前西方強勢主導的形形色色的「國際經濟秩序新論」，也才能堅持和發展建立國際經濟新秩序的理論。鑒於南北問題仍然是當前國際經濟發展的重大問題，尋求建立公正的「國際秩序」和真正的「全球治理體系」[62]不能回避南北問題，更不能回避改革國際經濟舊秩序、建立國際經濟新秩序這一根本性問題。

（二）提出南北矛盾發展的「6C律」

早在《國際經濟法總論》（1991年）中，作者即以馬克思主義為指導，指出：在國際經濟和國際經濟法的發展過程中，始終貫穿著強權國家保持和擴大既得經濟利益、維護國際經濟舊秩序與貧弱國家爭取和確保經濟平權地位、建立國際經濟新秩序的鬥爭。這些鬥爭，往往以雙方的妥協和合作而告終，妥協合作之後又因新的利害矛盾和利益衝突而產生新的爭鬥，如此循環往復不已，每一次循環往復，均是螺旋式上升，都把國際經濟秩序以及

和它相適應的國際經濟法規範，推進到一個新的水平或一個新的發展階段。」[63]

在專論《南南聯合自強五十年的國際經濟立法反思：從萬隆、多哈、坎昆到香港》（2006年）和專著《國際經濟法學專論》（2007年）中，作者總結萬隆會議以來的南北鬥爭史，進一步提出了南北矛盾發展的「6C律」及其特點，強調南南聯合自強對建立國際經濟新秩序的重大意義。其主要觀點可概要如下：

國際經濟秩序的新舊更替和國際經濟法的破舊立新是在南北矛盾發展進程中產生的。南北國家之間既有互相矛盾、互相鬥爭的一面，又有互相依存、互相合作的一面。因此，南北矛盾鬥爭的每一個回合，往往以雙方的妥協和國際經濟秩序在某種程度上的除舊布新而告終。妥協之後經過一段時間，又在新的歷史條件下產生新的矛盾鬥爭。南北矛盾上述規律性的發展進程，可概括稱為螺旋式的「6C軌跡」或「6C律」即Contradiction（矛盾）→ Conflict（衝突或交鋒）→ Consultation（磋商）→ Compromise（妥協）→ Cooperation（合作）→ Coordination（協調）→ Contradiction New（新的矛盾）。當代國際經濟秩序和國際經濟法正是在此種「6C律」的基礎上和支配下，不斷經歷著新舊交替、吐故納新、棄舊圖新和破舊立新的進程。[64] 南北問題的根本解決取決於國際經濟新秩序的建立，取決於南北國家基於經濟主權、公平互利和全球合作等國際經濟法基本原則的真誠合作。發展中國家要在南北經濟關係中獲得真正平等的地位，只有依靠獨立自主和自力更生，提高本國的經濟實力，才能提高和增強在南北合作中的談判地位和能力。與此同時，要大力加強南南合

作，以求聯合自強和共同發展。[65]

「6C律」的提出具有重要的理論和實踐意義。首先，指明發展中國家「鬥爭中求生存，合作中求發展」的必由之路。南北國家之間矛盾、衝突之後是磋商、妥協、合作和協調，張弛有度，循環往復，反映了南北雙方既相互矛盾、衝突又相互依存、合作的客觀現實和南北矛盾運動的發展規律。第二，揭示發展中國家的持續鬥爭是促進國際經濟秩序的新舊更替和國際經濟法的破舊立新的原動力。發達國家為保持和發展其在國際經濟交往中的優勢地位，自然成為固守和維護國際經濟舊秩序的守護神。而發展中國家為改變其在國際經濟交往中的劣勢地位，必然成為要求改革國際經濟舊秩序、建立國際經濟新秩序的主力軍。第三，強調建立國際經濟新秩序和國際經濟法新規範的長期性和艱巨性。長遠看來，在上述「6C律」的發展過程中，國際經濟秩序的新舊更替和國際經濟法的破舊立新總體上處於上升態勢。但在特定歷史時期，由於南北國家在矛盾、鬥爭中此強彼弱，此消彼長，在發達國家占上風的情況下，則可能出現下行態勢。對發展中國家而言，如同逆水行舟，每一個進步，都需要艱辛的鬥爭和努力，稍有懈怠，已取得的成果可能得而復失或名存實亡。對於建立國際經濟新秩序和國際經濟法新規範的長期性和艱巨性，發展中國家應有戰略的眼光和充分的準備。

（三）新時期中國在國際經濟關係和國際體制中的立場和戰略定位

關於新時期中國在國際經濟關係和國際體制中的立場和戰略

定位，特別是中國在建立國際經濟新秩序中的地位與作用，中外學者見仁見智。近年來，隨著中國經濟的發展和國際影響力的提升，某些西方學者熱衷於強調中國的「領導作用」和「大國責任」，甚至提出「中國威脅」論，其用意發人深思。[66]中國是現存國際經濟秩序的最大受惠者、維護者、改良者、改革者，抑或革命者？眾說紛紜。作者在國際經濟法理論研究中的相關視角和論述富有啟迪。

首先，是作者研究國際經濟法問題的角度。在論述「我國涉外經濟立法中可否規定對外資絕不實行國有化」問題時，作者指出：「從中國國情與國際輿情的結合上來考慮問題，從南北矛盾的歷史與現實的結合上來考慮問題，從新、舊兩種國際經濟秩序的更迭興替上來考慮問題，作為在世界上具有舉足輕重地位的社會主義國家和發展中國家，作為第三世界的一個中堅成員，中國在本國關於經濟特區和沿海開放城市的涉外經濟立法中，顯然不宜、不必、不應、不容明文規定對外資絕對不實行徵用或國有化。」[67]由此可見，作者所主張的研究國際經濟法問題的三個角度分別是中國國情與國際輿情的結合、南北矛盾的歷史與現實的結合以及新、舊兩種國際經濟秩序的更迭興替，對中國的明確定位是「第三世界中堅成員」。

其次，鑒於新時期中國在國際經濟關係和國際體制中的立場和戰略定位是新中國成立以來的延續，有必要考察新中國對外交往的一貫立場。作者指出：「獨立自主和平等互利，乃是新中國對外經濟交往中一貫堅持的最基本的法理原則和行為規範，也是中國對外經濟交往健康發展的兩大基石。」[68]

關於新時期中國在國際經濟關係和國際體制中的立場和戰略定位，作者在論述古代中國的自我定位和近現代中國歷史形成的「中華民族愛國主義」獨特內涵的基礎上明確指出，中國應成為建立國際經濟新秩序的積極推手，應致力於成為南南聯合自強的中流砥柱之一，中國與全球弱勢群體共同參與建立國際經濟新秩序的戰略目標，應當堅定不移，韌性鬥爭，百折不撓，即應當堅持戰略原則的堅定性，又堅持策略戰術的靈活性。[69]

概言之，歷史已然成就了中國作為「第三世界中堅成員」的地位。作為「第三世界中堅成員」，中國的基本立場理應是，奉行獨立自主和平等互利原則，成為建立國際經濟新秩序的積極推手，致力於成為南南聯合自強的中流砥柱之一，堅持建立國際經濟新秩序的戰略目標。無論將來中國國際經濟地位發生怎樣的改變，應該有始終如一的、堅定的立場和目標。以國際投資關係為例，中國必須堅持和強調經濟主權、公平互利和全球合作原則，不能因為居於資本輸出國地位就片面強調資本輸出國的權益，要求資本輸入國限制其主權。中國一向反對發達國家「以鄰為壑」「損人利己」的做法，同樣也要引以為戒，嚴格自律。隨著中國國際經濟地位的改變，對外經濟政策可以根據形勢的變化而調整，但立場要堅定，不因經濟地位的轉變而變化，不因利益的誘導而變化。中國國際經濟法學者進行學術研究應有「第三世界中堅成員」的「立場」意識，政府主管部門在國際經濟實踐中也應有「第三世界中堅成員」的堅定立場。

論證南北矛盾中形成的國際經濟法基本原則

一般而言，國際經濟法的基本原則指國際社會普遍接受的調整國際經濟關係的最基本的法律原則。作者認為：「國際經濟法的基本原則，指的是貫穿於調整國際經濟關係的各類法律規範之中的主要精神和指導思想，指的是這些法律規範的基礎和核心」[70]；「在當代國際經濟法基本規範或基本原則更新發展的全過程中，始終貫穿著強權國家保護既得利益、維護國際經濟舊秩序與貧弱國家爭取平權地位、建立國際經濟新秩序的矛盾和鬥爭。這種矛盾鬥爭，乃是當代世界性『南北矛盾』鬥爭的主要內容。」[71]作者強調國際經濟法基本原則是在南北矛盾中形成的，旨在強調其「發展性」和「動態性」，強調發展中國家建立國際經濟新秩序的目標，反映了中國國際經濟法學的特色。以下概述作者有關經濟主權原則、公平互利原則和全球合作原則的部分重要觀點。

（一）經濟主權原則

如所周知，主權是國際法的基石。當前，為推進經濟全球化，西方國家以理論為先導，提出了否定或淡化主權的種種理論。[72]對於廣大發展中國家而言，面臨的首要任務是堅持和維護《聯合國憲章》確立的國家主權原則。[73]

關於經濟主權原則，作者重點研究了經濟主權原則的形成原因及其基本內容、世紀之交經濟主權「攻防戰」及中國堅持經濟主權原則的實踐。

1. 經濟主權原則的形成原因及其基本內容

作者指出，發展中國家強調和堅持經濟主權有其特定的歷史原因和現實原因。從歷史上看，大多數發展中國家在二戰結束之前都處在殖民地、半殖民地地位；二戰結束後，殖民地、半殖民地弱小民族相繼掙脫殖民枷鎖，取得政治獨立，但經濟上仍然遭受原宗主國的控制，不同程度地處於從屬或附庸的地位。政治主權是經濟主權的前提，經濟主權是政治主權的保障。發展中國家強調經濟主權實質上是全世界弱小民族反殖民主義鬥爭的必要繼續和必然發展。[74]

根據一九七四年《各國經濟權利和義務憲章》的規定，作者概括國家經濟主權的主要內容，包括：各國對本國內部以及本國涉外的一切經濟事務享有完全、充分的獨立自主權利，不受任何外來干涉；各國對境內一切自然資源享有永久主權；各國對境內的外國投資以及跨國公司的活動享有管理監督權；各國對境內的外國資產有權收歸國有或徵用；各國對世界性經貿大政享有平等的參與權和決策權。[75]

2. 世紀之交經濟主權「攻防戰」

近年來，作者以馬克思主義主權觀為指導，針對當前全球化趨勢下西方國家否定或淡化「主權」的理論和實踐，進行了深入的專題研究。作者以WTO體制運作十年來美國單邊主義與WTO多邊主義交鋒的三大回合作為中心，綜合評析美國一九九四年「主權大辯論」、一九九八至二〇〇〇年「301條款」爭端案及二〇〇二至二〇〇三年「201條款」爭端案的前因後果和來龍去脈，指出這三次交鋒的實質，都是美國經濟「主權」（經濟霸權）

與各國群體經濟主權之間限制與反限制的爭鬥，植根於美國早在一九九四年「入世」之初確立的其單邊主義政策高於其WTO義務的既定方針；提出這場以經濟主權問題為核心的激烈論戰對發展中國家的重要啟迪是：增強憂患意識，珍惜經濟主權；力爭對全球經貿大政決策權實行公平的國際再分配；善用經濟主權保護民族權益，抵禦霸權欺凌和其他風險；警惕理論陷阱，摒除經濟主權「淡化」論。[76]

作者深刻指出：「主權『過時』論、主權『廢棄』論的主旨在於徹底解除弱小民族的思想武裝，好讓當代霸權主義在全球通行無阻；『淡化』論和『弱化』論的『發展方向』，正是歸宿於『過時』論和『廢棄』論。這種歸宿，絕不是弱小民族之福，而是善良的人們不能預見其後果的理論陷阱」。[77]

3. 中國堅持經濟主權原則的實踐

不言而喻，作為發展中大國，中國理應與廣大發展中國家站在一起，堅持經濟主權原則。作者主張，無論是在國內立法實踐方面，或是國際條約實踐方面，中國都要堅持經濟主權原則。

針對中國涉外經濟立法中可否規定對外資絕不實行國有化問題，作者主張，在中國經濟特區和沿海開放城市的涉外經濟立法中，不應明文規定在任何情況下都不對外資實行徵用或國有化。其主要理由是，從外資國有化問題的論戰史、中外簽訂的雙邊投資保護協定、西方國家對「國有化」的理解及中國的憲法精神和現有政策等方面看，不適宜、不必要、不應當、不容許作此規定。其結論是：「鑒於東道國在必要時有權依法徵收境內外資，並且給予適當補償，乃是當代國家經濟主權權利之一，而且已經

成為國際通行的立法慣例，中國不應通過立法自行『棄權』」；「務必留權在手，但決不任意濫用！」[78]

　　在國際實踐方面，作者主張，中國在「入世」談判中應堅持經濟主權原則，指出：「中國是主權牢牢在握的獨立國家，中國人民十分珍惜自己經過長期奮鬥得來不易的主權權利……儘管『復關』和加『入世』貿組織的談判曠日持久，難關重重，中國堅持經濟主權原則，有關加入多邊貿易體制的基本立場和方針不變。」[79]

　　當前，國際投資法發展迅速，其趨向值得密切關注。傳統國際投資法本來就是發達國家為保護其海外投資者的產物，帶有與生俱來的片面維護資本輸出國權益的烙印，其新近發展並未起到平衡發達國家與發展中國家之間、東道國與外國投資者之間的權利和利益關係，而是更加片面強調保護發達國家和外國投資者的權益，進一步限制東道國的主權。通過此類規範的不斷強化，發達國家推動投資自由化，以實現其國家利益。近來，雙邊投資條約普遍規定接受「解決投資爭端國際中心」（ICSID）的管轄，甚至規定投資者可以單方面啟動ICSID程式。在經濟全球化趨勢下，中國的某些國際實踐順應了西方國家主導和推波助瀾的所謂「時代潮流」。針對二十世紀九〇年代以來中外雙邊投資協定的「爭端解決」條款的新發展，作者明確提出，中外雙邊投資協定實踐中的「逐案審批同意」「當地救濟優先」「東道國法律適用」和「重大安全例外」四大「安全閥」不宜貿然拆除；[80]進而主張，區分南、北兩類國家，實行差別互惠，明文排除最惠國條款對爭端程式的普遍適用，切實維護中國的應有權益。[81]

（二）公平互利原則

公平互利原則是在「公平」這一傳統法律概念基礎上結合「互利」概念發展起來的國際經濟法基本原則，強調實質上的平等，進一步明確了平等互利的含義，是平等互利原則的新發展。

關於公平互利原則，作者重點研究公平互利原則是平等互利原則的發展及公平互利原則的主旨。

1. 公平互利原則是平等互利原則的發展

作者在分析公平互利原則的形成過程中指出，在國際交往實踐中，發展中國家認識到，僅僅從或主要從政治角度強調主權平等原則，往往只能做到形式上的平等，難以實現實質上的平等。在某些場合，發達國家往往以形式上的平等掩蓋實質上的不平等。因此，應從經濟角度、從實質上重新審視傳統意義上的主權平等原則，賦予其新的時代內容，互利原則由此產生。國家之間的關系，只有建立在平等的基礎上，才能做到互利；只有真正地實行互利，才算是貫徹了平等的原則，才能實現實質上的平等。[82]

把傳統的國際法上分立的平等原則與互利原則結合成調整國際政治、經濟關系的一項基本原則，標誌著國際法上平等原則的新發展。[83] 作者特別指出了中國有關平等互利原則的實踐對公平互利原則形成的貢獻。在國內法實踐方面，中國人民政治協商會議在一九四九年九月二十九日通過的《共同綱領》中，明確把平等互利規定為與外國建立外交關系的前提條件及對外經濟交往、調整國際經濟關系的基本準則。在國際法實踐方面，一九五四年四到六月，中國與印度、緬甸一起，率先把平等互利原則與互相尊重主權和領土完整、互不侵犯、互不干涉內政、和平共處

等五項原則作為指導當代國際關係的基本準則，逐漸獲得了國際社會的普遍認同。[84]

2. 公平互利原則的主旨

作者指出：「在國際經濟交往中強調公平互利，究其主要宗旨，端在於樹立和貫徹新的平等觀。對於經濟實力相當、實際地位基本平等的同類國家說來，公平互利落實於原有平等關係的維持；對於經濟實力懸殊、實際地位不平等的不同類國家說來，公平互利落實於原有形式平等關係或虛假平等關係的糾正以及新的實質平等關系的創設。[85]

在論證公平互利原則時，作者進一步指出：「這種新的平等觀，是切合客觀實際需要的，是科學的，也是符合馬克思主義基本觀點的。早在百餘年前，馬克思在剖析平等權利時，就曾經指出：用同一尺度去衡量和要求先天稟賦各異、後天負擔不同的勞動者，勢必造成各種不平等的弊病，並且斷言：『要避免所有這些弊病，權利就不應當是平等的，而應當是不平等的。』馬克思的這種精闢見解，對於我們深入理解當代發展中國家提出的關於貫徹公平互利原則、實行非互惠普惠制等正義要求，具有現實的指導意義。」[86] 作者形象的結論是，對經濟實力懸殊的國家，「平等」地用同一尺度去衡量，用同一標準去要求，實行絕對的、無差別的「平等待遇」的實際效果，「有如要求先天不足、大病初愈的弱女與體魄強健、訓練有素的壯漢，在同一起跑點上『平等』地賽跑，從而以『平等』的假像掩蓋不平等的實質」。[87]

（三）全球合作原則

全球合作原則是一九七四年《建立國際經濟新秩序宣言》和《各國經濟權利和義務憲章》宣導的一項富有時代特點的國際經濟法基本原則。基於南北問題的認識，要實現建立國際經濟新秩序的目標，必須進一步強調、堅持和實踐全球合作原則。

關於全球合作原則，作者重點論證南北合作是全球合作原則的中心環節和南南聯合自強是建立國際經濟新秩序的唯一路徑。

1. 南北合作是全球合作原則的中心環節

作者指出，南北合作是全球合作原則的中心環節，是國際經濟關係上眾多弱者與少數強者之間在不同階段的互相妥協和互相讓步；就其內在實質而言，是國際經濟關係中剝削者與被剝削者、強者與弱者之間的妥協，也是對弱肉強食規則緩慢的逐步否定。[88]

南北合作的依據是發達國家與發展中國家在現實經濟生活中存在極其密切的互相依存和互相補益關係。這決定了南北國家「合則兩利，離則兩傷」，促使南北國家在不同發展階段的鬥爭中終究要相互妥協，作出「南北合作」的選擇，從而解決各個相應階段的南北矛盾。

南北合作的阻力來自發達國家，特別是來自第一世界的美國。相對而言，第二世界的政界、法界中，出現了一些能較冷靜正視南北互相依存現實的明智人士。

關於南北合作的成效，基於對《洛美協定》和《科托努協定》的研究，作者在肯定南北合作生命力之後，深刻指出：「《洛美協定》式的南北合作，仍然遠未能從根本上改變南北雙方之間

很不平等、很不公平的經濟關係」；「距離實現徹底公平互利的南北合作從而建立起國際經濟新秩序的總目標，還有相當漫長、艱辛的路程」。〔89〕

2. 南南聯合自強是建立國際經濟新秩序的唯一路徑

作者指出，南南合作是國際經濟關係上眾多弱者之間的互濟互助，以共同應對或聯合反抗來自強者或霸者的弱肉強食。作者在論述南南合作的戰略意義中指出：現存的國際經濟體制，是在經濟實力基礎上形成的。要改變它，首先也要靠實力；在經濟上過分依賴發達國家，對發展中國家經濟發展極為不利。加強南南合作，走弱者聯合自強的道路，才是增強自身經濟實力的可靠途徑；南南合作，把各個分散的、在經濟上相對弱小的發展中國家聯合起來，凝聚成一股強大的國際力量，可望提高在南北對話中的地位和能力；南南合作是建立在弱者互助互濟、公平互利的基礎上，是全球合作的新興模式和強大趨勢，本身就是國際經濟新秩序的體現。〔90〕

在專論《南南聯合自強五十年的國際經濟立法反思：從萬隆、多哈、坎昆到香港》中，作者回顧近五十年來南北矛盾與南北合作的史實，總結貫穿全程並將長期存在的發展軌跡，深刻指出，南北矛盾和衝突，南北力量對比上的「南弱北強」，勢必在今後相當長的歷史時期持續存在，鑒此，在南北角力的進程中，南南聯合自強者務必樹立起「持久戰」的戰略思想，逐步更新國際經濟立法、建立起國際經濟新秩序的唯一路徑是南南聯合自強。〔91〕

知識報國、兼濟天下，發出中國和南方學者的時代強音

從作者的治學立場、理念和追求以及對中國特色國際經濟法學的傑出貢獻，我們看到了老一輩知識份子的命運是如何與國家的命運緊密相連，更感受到老一輩知識分子「知識報國、兼濟天下」的歷史責任感、寬廣襟懷、堅定的政治立場和鮮明的價值取向。作者強烈的學術使命感、歷史與現實結合的研究方法及學術成果「國際化」的不懈努力尤其值得我們學習。

（一）強烈的學術使命感

作者指出：「當今發達國家國際經濟法諸多論著的共同基本特點，是重點研究發達國家對外經濟交往中產生的法律問題，作出符合發達國家權益的分析和論證。反觀中國，作為積弱積貧的發展中國家之一員，這樣的研究工作還處在幼弱階段，遠未能適應我國對外交往的迫切需要和對外開放的嶄新格局。」[92] 作者正是懷著強烈的學術使命感，三十多年如一日，身體力行，殫精竭慮，致力於中國特色國際經濟法學的創建。

中國國際經濟法學主要是在引進和借鑑西方國際經濟法學的基礎上產生和發展起來的，國際經濟法學的概念、術語、原則、規則等大多來自西方。汲取和借鑑西方國際經濟法學理論，首先要有「揚棄」精神，「取其精華，去其糟粕」。作者之所以能取得獨樹一幟的國際經濟法研究成果，成就中國和其他發展中國家的「一家之言」，最重要的是堅持「揚棄」精神，獨立思考，勇於創新，具有破舊立新的歷史責任感、決心和勇氣，不迷信權

威，不附和所謂「主流理論」，既能深入鑽研西方國際經濟法理論，又能擺脫西方學者立場、視野所決定的法律觀念或思維定式，特別是擺脫阻礙建立國際經濟新秩序的西方法律觀念的羈絆，為建立國際經濟新秩序而創建和發展新的法律概念、觀念和理論。

（二）歷史與現實結合的研究方法

中國屬於發展中的社會主義國家，中國特色國際經濟法學的研究服務於建立國際經濟新秩序和建立社會主義市場經濟體制的目標，這決定了中國國際經濟法學界在吸收西方國家有關研究成果的同時，應有符合本國國情和目標的研究方法。在種種研究方法中，對創建中國特色國際經濟法學尤為重要的當是歷史和現實結合的方法。

如前所述，作者對南北問題、中國的戰略定位和國際經濟法基本原則的論述，無不採取歷史和現實結合的研究方法。在這方面，中國國際經濟法學界老一輩學者與中青年學者的關注點、敏感度和立場或有不同。老一輩學者曾經歷過「三座大山」壓迫下的舊社會，對西方列強的本質有深刻的認識和高度的警惕。而中青年學者在改革開放的新形勢下，有更多的機會接受西方的法學教育或理論成果，更容易接受西方主導建構的所謂「主流理論」。對中國特色國際經濟法學的一些基本問題，諸如南北矛盾、國家主權等的認識以及對西方理論的「揚棄」精神，中青年學者與老一輩學者尚有一定差距。這從一個側面反映了歷史和現實結合研究方法的重要性，我們需要更深入地了解西方國際經濟

法的緣起、發展及其實質，從中探求中國特色國際經濟法學的歷史使命和發展方向。

（三）學術成果「國際化」的不懈努力

鑒於國際經濟法學的學科特色，中國國際經濟法學者應積極主動地開展國際學術交流和合作，在國際學術論壇上，對國際經濟法學的重要理論和實踐問題提出中國學者的見解，表明中國的立場，為世界性國際經濟法學的發展和繁榮做出應有的貢獻。

作者大學期間專攻法學，外語兼修英語一年，自學俄語、日語，一九八一年以「知天命」之年負笈於美國哈佛大學，即與國際學術同行開展平等交流和對話，受到該校東亞法學研究所所長A. von Mehren教授、副所長F. K. Upham教授的高度評價。[93]作者一直力倡中國國際經濟法學者的學術成果「走出國門」。自一九八一年在美國《國際法與比較法學報》首次發表英文論文以來，作者持續發表和出版英文論著，成果豐碩。[94]特別是，二〇〇六至二〇一〇年在享譽國際經濟法學界的《世界投資與貿易學報》（瑞士日內瓦出版）發表六篇重要論文，創該期刊同期發表論文數的最高紀錄。[95]其英文論著立場堅定，論證嚴謹，特別是具有鮮明的中國特色，因而產生了重要的國際學術影響。發展中國家智庫「南方中心」秘書長Branislav Gosovic先生認為，作者有關南南聯合自強的論述「能給人以清晰鮮明的方針政策性的啟示，會使『南方中心』公報的讀者們很感興趣，特別因為這是您從一個正在崛起的舉足輕重的大國發出的大聲吶喊」[96]。更為難得的是，來自發達國家的多邊投資擔保機構首席法律顧問L.

Weisenfeld先生和ICSID法律顧問A. Parra先生等同樣對作者的學術主張和水準表示由衷讚賞和信服。[97]

中國特色國際經濟法學是世界性國際經濟法學的一個重要組成部分。中國特色國際經濟法學的發展和繁榮在一定程度上有賴於世界性國際經濟法學的發展和繁榮，世界性國際經濟法學的發展和繁榮也不能缺少中國特色國際經濟法學的參與和奉獻。中國特色國際經濟法學的使命是，站在中國和廣大發展中國家立場，緊密聯繫中國和國際實踐，汲取具有普世價值的國際經濟法學精華，維護和發展國際社會普遍認同的國際經濟法原則，積極影響和促進國際經濟法實踐的健康發展。

這是一項長期的、宏大的理論工程，需要幾代人矢志不移、堅持不懈的努力。陳安老師等老一輩國際經濟法學者篳路藍縷，為中國特色國際經濟法學的創建和發展做出了開拓性的貢獻，亦成為後學之師範。近年來，廈門大學國際經濟法學術團隊青年教師積極向國外學術刊物投稿，在國際學術界嶄露頭角，顯示出較強的學術發展潛力。自二〇〇二年以來，廈門大學法學院辯論隊連續參加Willem C. Vis國際商事模擬辯論賽、Jessup國際法模擬法庭辯論賽（英文）和國際人道法模擬法庭辯論賽（英文）等國際性專業大賽，形成優良傳統，屢獲佳績，如榮獲Jessup國際法模擬法庭辯論賽「Hardy C. Dillard」最佳書狀獎第一名」（2006年）和「反方訴狀第一名」（2011年），為中國法學教育贏得了國際聲譽，也給國人莫大的啟示和鼓舞。需要明確的是，上述辯論賽均是在西方主導下進行的西式「遊戲規則」的演練和競爭。鑒此，在研究和掌握這些規則以求「知彼」的同時，更需要獨立思

考，明確「己方」的信念、追求和使命，力求在「知己知彼」的基礎上增強專業能力和創新精神，擔負起建立國際經濟新秩序的歷史重任。相比老一輩國際經濟法學者和我們這一代「老三屆」學者，青年學者和學生後來居上，具有更好的基礎、更高的起點、更好的發展環境和機會，專心致志，自強不息，在創建和發展中國特色國際經濟法學方面當有更大的作為。

六、中國參與經濟全球化管理的戰略思考
——評《陳安論國際經濟法學》的主導學術理念

趙龍躍*

　　國際經濟秩序是指在世界範圍內建立起來的國際經濟關係以及各種國際經濟體系與制度的總和，是使世界經濟作為有內在聯繫和相互依存的整體進行有規律的發展與變化的運行機制；其建立和變遷，取決於國際社會各類成員間的經濟、政治和軍事的實力對比。[98] 現行國際經濟秩序是二十世紀四〇年代以來，在以美國為代表的西方國家的主導和控制下建立起來的，首先體現的是美歐工業國家的利益和要求。隨著經濟全球化的深入發展，國際經濟形勢發生了重大的變化：發展中國家經濟增長迅速，在世界經濟中的比重不斷提升；發達國家經濟不僅增長乏力，而且面臨巨額財政赤字和主權債務等種種危機。然而，國際經濟秩序卻沒有隨著世界經濟格局的變化而進行相應的改革，發達國家繼續掌控著主要的國際經濟組織，竭力維持國際經濟舊秩序，發展中國家被嚴重地邊緣化。

長期以來，陳安教授致力於國際經濟法學的教學與研究工作，高度關注國際經濟秩序的改革與完善，取得了豐碩的成果。陳安教授於二〇〇八年八十大壽之際，出版大型學術專著《陳安論國際經濟法學》，共分五卷；其後在二〇〇九和二〇一〇年又連續發表了《論中國在建立國際經濟新秩序中的戰略定位》等系列論文四篇[99]，從國際經濟法學的角度，分析了現行國際經濟秩序的特點，指出在國際經濟秩序和國際經濟法的發展過程中，始終貫穿著強權國家維護國際經濟舊秩序與貧弱國家爭取建立國際經濟新秩序的矛盾，即南北矛盾。「南北矛盾衝突的焦點和實質，是全球財富的國際再分配。而新、舊國際經濟秩序的根本分野，則在於全球財富國際再分配之公平與否。」[100]呼籲中國應該旗幟鮮明地，積極與發展中國家一起「變法圖強」「通過BRICSM類型的『南南聯合』群體」[101]改變不合理的國際經濟舊秩序。陳安教授一系列獨特的戰略思想和政策建議，喊出了與時俱進、變法圖強的最強音，非常值得我們重視和思考。

現行國際經濟秩序存在嚴重的缺陷

現行國際經濟秩序基本上是以布雷頓森林體系為核心，體現在聯合國、世界銀行、國際貨幣基金組織、關貿總協定以及世界貿易組織等國際機構的有關協定和組織管理中。二戰以來，美國成為這些組織的「所有者」、操控者和經營者，享受著特殊的權利和利益。[102]在過去的六十多年中，國際經濟社會經歷了巨大的變遷，國際經濟管理體系也發生了一些變化，但是西方國家主導現行國際經濟秩序的本質沒有改變，體現為發達國家的「制度

霸權」和「話語優勢」，嚴重地忽略了廣大發展中國家的利益和要求。

發達國家「制度霸權」最明顯也最直觀的體現就是在國際經濟組織中的人事權和決策權，美歐國家不僅始終控制著世界銀行行長、國際貨幣基金組織（IMF）總裁和世界貿易組織總幹事的職位，而且在決策程式上占有絕對的優勢。以IMF為例，IMF實行加權投票表決制，投票權由兩部分組成，每個成員國都有二百五十票的基本投票權和一定份額的加權投票權。因為基本投票權各國都一樣，所以在實際決策中起決定作用的是加權投票權。最近幾年，雖然IMF醞釀改革，希望增加新興國家和發展中國家的投票權，但是美國仍然占有約百分之十七的投票權。按照IMF憲章，重大議題表決需要百分之八十五以上的多數票才能通過，因此美國具有絕對否決權。陳安教授對此等制度設計評價為：「它使寥寥幾個西方發達大國和強國加在一起，就可以操縱全球性重大經濟事務的決策……眾多發展中國家在這種極不合理、極不公平的決策體制下，往往陷入進退維谷的兩難選擇：一是被迫簽字『畫押』，吞下苦果；另一是被迫退出困境，自行孤立。」[103]

除了擁有制度霸權以外，發達國家還擁有強勢的話語體系，通過鼓吹和宣揚利於自身的價值觀念來維持現行國際經濟秩序。二〇〇四年，在美國學界和政界都具有重要影響力的約瑟夫・奈發表了《軟實力與美國外交政策》，他認為「軟實力」的核心為一國文化的吸引力、價值觀念和政策，並指出「當我們〔美國〕的政策在他人看來具有合法性時，我們的軟實力就會得到加強」[104]，其實質即為達到「不戰而勝」的效果。由於其是一種隱形

力量，作用是潛在的，但危害不可小視。陳安教授在其《一論》中，對這種西方主導的話語權進行了精彩的分析。

其實這種價值觀念的輸出在西方早就存在，在美國戰略界，如經濟學家羅伯特・吉爾平提出了「霸權穩定論」，認為國際經濟的穩定與發展取決於一個占絕對優勢的霸權國存在[105]國際問題研究學者羅伯特・基歐漢提出了由美國操控的國際制度能降低合作成本促進合作[106]等等。由於美國占據學術研究的中心，這些思想在中國以及世界影響非常大。而這些思想的潛臺詞就是讓發展中國家「自願」維護現有的國際經濟秩序，借用陳安教授的話就是讓發展中國家自覺「守法」而不去「變法圖強」。國際經濟領域，此類思想更是層出不窮，比較有影響力的有「新自由主義經濟秩序」論、「WTO憲政秩序」論、「經濟民族主義擾亂全球化秩序」論等。「它們雖然在相當程度上激發了新的有益思考，卻也造成了某些新的思想混亂。」[107]以「新自由主義經濟秩序」論為例，它所突出宣揚的是所謂的「華盛頓共識」。諾姆・喬姆斯基曾明確指出華盛頓共識是由美國政府及其控制的國際經濟組織所制定，並由它們通過各種方式進行實施。其奉行的教條是自由化、私有化和政府作用的最小化，「本質是為國際壟斷資本在全球擴張服務的」[108]，對發展中國家造成的傷害是非常嚴重的。「華盛頓共識」曾在拉美國家盛行，以阿根廷為例，在二十世紀九〇年代實行全面的私有化、自由化與市場開放，結果在國際遊資和國內問題的雙重打擊下，金融崩潰，政府垮臺，社會動亂。頗具諷刺意味的是，「面對『華盛頓共識』在拉美國家製造的悲劇，新自由主義的經濟學家緘默了」[109]。

在鼓吹和推行所謂的自由和民主「價值觀」的同時，發達國家還不遺餘力地攻擊發展中國家的自我保護措施，將其貶斥為「經濟民族主義亂序」。「『經濟民族主義亂序』論的實質和效應則在於以莫須有的『罪名』，力圖迫使國際弱勢群體離開原定的建立國際經濟新秩序的奮鬥目標。」〔110〕其實南方發展中國家在面對北方發達國家試圖以各種「迷惑人心的口號」衝破主權限制和掠奪財富時，完全有理由保護自己，這一點是理直氣壯和合情合理的，在西方發達大國的強勢話語影響之下，切不可自先氣短自亂陣腳。陳安教授明確指出：「全球弱勢群體對此類含有精神鴉片或精神枷鎖毒素的理論，亟宜全面深入剖析，不宜貿然全盤接受。」〔111〕

在國際貿易領域的情況完全類似。長期以來，世界貿易組織及其前身關貿總協定，雖然在規範和穩定國際貿易秩序、降低關稅和非關稅壁壘、促進國際貿易發展方面發揮了一定的作用，但是卻嚴重忽略了廣大發展中國家發展的不平衡問題。國際貿易規則主要是在發達國家的操縱下制定的，所以首先體現的必然是這些發達國家的利益。後來在發展中國家的共同努力下，關貿總協定增加了一些給予發展中國家差別待遇或優惠的條款。可是這些條款有些是有名無實，有些是形同虛設，基本沒有得到預期的效果。世界貿易組織成立以來，主要受益者仍然是發達國家，那些看似平等的貿易條款所帶來的利益仍然是不平等的。那麼多哈回合是不是真的要解決這些問題，或者能不能解決這些問題？到目前為止，答案仍然是NO。許多專家學者都懷疑多哈回合究竟是把促進發展中國家的「發展」作為談判的實質內容，還是作為吸

引發展中國家參與談判的誘餌？美國前貿易代表巴爾舍夫斯基就曾經說過：「把多哈回合說成是『發展回合』只是一種喬裝打扮而已。」〔112〕

面對擁有制度霸權和話語優勢的發達國家，面對不平等的國際經濟秩序，弱勢國家應該怎麼辦？我們應該怎麼辦？是「韜光養晦」，去滿足於「搭乘全球化的便車」實現一定程度的發展，還是在力所能及的範圍「有所作為」，團結廣大的發展中國家，爭取推動國際經濟秩序更加公平合理？陳安教授給出了一個肯定的答案：「中國人理應與時俱進，落實科學的發展觀，全面、完整、準確地理解鄧小平提出的『韜光養晦、有所作為』方針」「理應成為建立國際經濟新秩序的積極推手」。〔113〕

現行國際經濟秩序不能適應新的國際經濟形勢

隨著經濟全球化的深入發展，國際經濟形勢發生了重大的變化，現行國際經濟秩序已經不能適應新的國際經濟形勢，構建國際經濟新秩序已經成為當前世界走出危機、重振經濟的當務之急與必然選擇。同時，在當今的國際形勢下，出現了一些有利於推動國際經濟秩序變革的條件，主要表現為新興國家和發展中國家的實力在不斷增強，而發達國家卻面臨新的經濟和社會問題。

當今國際經濟格局最突出的一個變化就是發展中國家經濟增長迅速，在世界經濟中的比重不斷提升，一些新興經濟國家出現在世界經濟舞臺的中心，開始發出不同於西方國家的聲音。從國際貨幣基金組織的統計資料來看，發達國家雖然在經濟總量上仍然占有顯著優勢，但在經濟增長速度上明顯低於發展中國家和新

興經濟國家。高盛公司曾經預測：到二〇一八年『金磚四國』和美國占全球GDP的比例將同為25%；而到二〇五〇年四國將一同躋身全球六大經濟體之列，發展中國家和發達國家在全球經濟總量中的份額將各占50%。」[114]有些學者認為：進入二十一世紀以來，世界經濟的最大特點是，新興經濟體群體性崛起……尤其是中國、印度等新興大國名副其實成為世界經濟的領頭羊，在增強自身經濟實力的同時，改變著世界經濟發展的路徑。」[115]

發達國家不僅經濟增長乏力，而且面臨巨額財政赤字和主權債務等種種危機。西方G7國家的主權債務持續走高，比世界平均水準高出近一倍，比新興國家和發展中國家高出三到四倍。[116]美國二〇一一年財政年度的財政赤字近一點三萬億美元，累計債務高達十四點八萬億美元，幾乎相當於全年的國內生產總值。歐盟國家的主權債務問題更加嚴重，希臘、西班牙、愛爾蘭、葡萄牙和義大利，相繼出現主權債務危機，不僅威脅著歐元區的經濟穩定，而且影響著全球經濟的健康發展。

除此之外，隨著經濟全球化的深入發展，很多全球性問題僅靠西方國家早已不能解決諸如國際能源安全、全球糧食安全、氣候變化和環境問題等等。二〇〇八年金融危機以後，G7首腦峰會轉為G20峰會，就是對這種情況變化的調整，為推動國際經濟秩序的變革提供了新的機會。最近G20坎城峰會所關注的主要議題，如解決經濟失衡、加強金融監管、改革全球貨幣體系、改進全球監管治理等，都涉及對國際經濟秩序的改進。中國國家主席胡錦濤在會上指出：「我們應該充分反映世界經濟格局變化，繼續增加新興市場國家和發展中國家在全球經濟治理中的發言權，

為發展中國家發展創造良好制度環境。」[117]

在推動國際經濟秩序變遷的過程中，既得利益的大國與貧弱的國家之間，圍繞國際經濟制度設計和規則制定的鬥爭是非常複雜的，鬥爭的焦點是全球資源和財富的國際再分配。在發達國家主導的國際經濟秩序中，全球資源和財富的國際再分配必然是不公平的，無論是分工還是交換，發展中國家都處於完全被動的局面，這正是現行國際經濟秩序的最大問題。「從根本上看，世界經濟發展的最大瓶頸在於廣大發展中國家未能實現充分發展，使世界範圍內有效需求增長未能跟上生產力發展步伐。長期以來，發達國家和發展中國家資源占有失衡，財富分配不公，發展機會不均，形成『越不發展越落後，越落後就越難發展』的惡性循環，最終制約了世界經濟持久穩定增長。」[118]

面對不合理的舊秩序及其給世界經濟帶來的問題，思變求新是必然的選擇。但是，在全球化深入發展、經濟依存度越來越高的今天，發達國家占據技術優勢、制度優勢和話語優勢，向它們爭取平等合理的發展機會難度很大。面對當代國際社會「南弱北強」、實力懸殊的戰略態勢，面對國際強權國家集團在國際經濟領域中已經形成的「霸業」格局和「反變法」阻力，國際弱勢群體要求「變法」圖強，當然不可能一蹴而就[119]。權益只有爭取才會獲得，而不是靠施捨。陳安教授通過分析南北關係，總結為螺旋式上升的「6C軌跡」或「6C律」，說明過程雖然是曲折的，但是成果還是顯著的。[120]「6C軌跡」指在南北合作曲折行進的過程中，「國際經濟秩序和國際經濟法律規範的破舊立新、新舊更替，勢必循著螺旋式上升，即Contradiction（矛盾）→ Conflict

（衝突或交鋒）→ Consultation（磋商）→ Compromise（妥協）→ Cooperation（合作）→ Coordination（協調）→ Contradiction New（新的矛盾），逐步實現」[121]。弱勢國家並不是完全無能為力的，而是可以有所作為的。

當然，機會總是與挑戰並存，發展中國家包括新興國家也面臨很多國內外的問題和挑戰。首先，美元主導的國際貨幣體系可以說是根深蒂固，很難撼動，「重建具有穩定的定值基準並為各國所接受的新儲備貨幣可能是個長時期內才能實現的目標」[122]。其次還是主權債務問題，發達國家政府赤字和債務問題在短期內很難解決，必將影響全球金融市場的穩定，這又不可避免地加大了新興市場國家的債權安全與金融風險。美國的債務問題不僅僅是美國的問題，而是全球持有美債的債權人所擔心的問題，必須警惕發達國家轉嫁危機的風險。當然還存在貿易保護主義等其他問題，危機帶來機遇，但帶來的各種不確定因素與風險也須時刻注意。

G20為發展中國家爭取推動國際經濟秩序朝著公平合理方向變革提供了有利的條件，陳安教授通過對二〇〇九年G20匹茲堡峰會和匹茲堡峰會前後的重要國際會議的分析，認為「『匹茲堡發軔之路』之『新』值得重視，就在於它強調和指定歷時整整十年的G20南北對話機制，應當從非正式機制開始轉軌成為正式的、常規的、主要的機制，從而很可能進一步發展成為南南聯合自強、建立國際經濟新秩序的新轉折和新起點」[123]。但是，「從歷史上的經驗教訓看，全球公眾卻同時理應繼續保持清醒頭腦和敏銳目光，預測『匹茲堡發軔之路』今後發展的另一種可能前

景：時過境遷，強權發達國家之『信誓旦旦』迅即轉化為『口惠而實不至』的一紙空頭支票」〔124〕而這個「空頭支票」卻有可能為發達國家換來大量的利益。

中國參與經濟全球化管理的戰略思考

當今世界正處在大發展大變革大調整時期，世界多極化、經濟全球化深入發展。中國經濟社會持續快速發展，融入全球化程度的不斷提高，國際政治、經濟環境對中國的影響越來越大，在國際事務中，中國面臨的問題和挑戰也越來越多。現行國際經濟秩序不僅本身存在嚴重的缺陷，越來越不能適應當前世界經濟發展的新形勢，而且體系中有些條款本身就是用來牽制或限制中國發展的。中國擁有獨特的政治、經濟和社會體制，在世界上扮演著非常獨特的角色。全面準確地把握國際經濟秩序變革的動因和趨勢，積極參與國際規則制定和經濟全球化管理，不僅是維持並進一步開創有利於中國改革開放發展國際環境的需要，而且也是滿足國際社會希望中國在國際事務中發揮更大作用，推動建設和諧世界，促進國際經濟秩序朝著更加公正合理方向發展的需要。

「世界五分之四的人口在發展中國家，發達國家人口只占五分之一。人人都有平等的生存權利。如果廣大發展中國家繼續貧困，說明當今世界是不公平、不和諧的，也注定是不穩定的。」〔125〕物不平則鳴，人亦然。〔126〕面對不平等的國際經濟秩序，「中國既是全球弱勢群體的一員，又是最大的發展中國家之一。中國積極參與和努力推動建立國際經濟新秩序，應屬當仁不讓，責無旁貸」〔127〕。

當然也有不同的看法，其中比較流行也最為荒謬的說法是中國的發展得益於現行的國際經濟秩序，即中國享受了美國霸權提供的穩定的國際經濟體系帶來的發展機遇，享受了美國提供的「公共產品」「搭了美國的便車」[128] 因此，現在中國不是要推動國際經濟體系的變革，而是要主動承擔更多的義務，為現行國際體系提供更多的「公共產品」， 明美國維持現狀。事實上中國不是「搭了現行國際經濟秩序的便車」，而是付出了很高的代價。陳安教授提出，面對建立國際經濟新秩序的大勢所趨，「中國的自我戰略定位理應一如既往，繼續是旗幟鮮明的積極推動者之一，是現存國際經濟秩序的改革者之一，不宜只是現存國際經濟秩序的『改良者』、南北矛盾的『協調者』」[129]。為此，必須處理好「韜光養晦」與「有所作為」的關係，處理好「守法適法」與「變法圖強」的關係。

首先是「韜光養晦」與「有所作為」的關係。陳安教授明確提出應與時俱進，落實科學的發展觀，全面、完整、準確地理解鄧小平提出的「韜光養晦、有所作為」方針，批評了中國只應明哲保身、自顧自己發展，不顧外部是非的傾向。鄧小平在提出「韜光養晦」的同時，一直堅持主張建立國際經濟新秩序，堅持要「有所作為」。陳安教授也批評了建立國際經濟新秩序的鬥爭已經式微，而中國應融入「蓬勃的新自由主義經濟秩序」的錯誤觀點，指出這種觀點源於美國學界，目的是「瓦解南南合作的堅定信心和不懈實踐，從而步步為營，維護少數經濟強權國家在國際經濟舊秩序和國際經濟現有『遊戲規則』下的既得利益」[130]。陳安教授的分析鞭辟入裡，引人深思，事實也正是如此。「韜光

養晦」不是目的，堅持「韜光養晦」是為了「有所作為」，決不能為了「韜光養晦」而「韜光養晦」，不能無原則地「軟弱退讓」，更不能掉進西方的「話語陷阱」，結果被洗腦跟著西方的戰略走。在奉行「強者為王」競爭激烈的國際經濟領域，良好的經濟發展的環境只有爭取才會得到保障，而不是簡單地去追隨強者，靠施捨絕不會自主更不會長久。「在建立國際經濟新秩序的時代總潮流中，中國的自我戰略定位理應一如既往，繼續是旗幟鮮明的積極推動者之一，是現存國際經濟秩序的改革者之一。」[131]

　　其次是「守法適法」與「變法圖強」的關係。陳安教授認為，在國際經濟關係中必須力行法治，但是從法理角度看，當代國際經濟法的「立法」過程中決策權力的國際分配存在著嚴重不公。強者擁有「遊戲規則」的制定權，必然造成全球財富的國際分配嚴重不公，不利於發展中國家。「國際經濟法是鞏固現存國際經濟秩序的重要工具，也是促進變革舊國際經濟秩序、建立新國際經濟秩序的重要手段。」建立國際經濟新秩序，就是要求改變、改革現存的有關「立法」就是要求「變法」。[132]當然，「變法」是一個循序漸進的過程，不可能一蹴而就，要先「適應」和「守法」，在「適應」和「守法」的實踐檢驗中，不斷加深認識。熟悉遊戲規則，使其「為我所用」，同時「又立足於國際弱勢群體的共同權益，進行核對總和判斷，明辨其是非臧否，思考其變革方向」[133]。當然，向強勢國家爭取「變法圖強」，免不了道路曲折反覆，「但勢必與時俱進，前景光明」[134]。

　　隨著中國經濟社會持續快速的增長，國際地位越來越高，國際影響越來越大，國際社會重視來自中國的聲音，希望中國在參

與國際規則制定和經濟全球化管理方面發揮更大的作用，這是中國國際政治、經濟、外交地位不斷提高的必然結果，總體來說是一件好事。同時我們必須意識到，參與全球化管理意味著中國的國際責任和義務愈來愈大，面臨的問題更加複雜，進一步提高中國經濟外交能力和水準的要求更加迫切。參與經濟全球化管理呼喚中國的調整，這裡的調整不僅僅是經濟結構的調整、發展模式的更新，還包括觀念的轉變和角色的轉換。

第一，參與經濟全球化管理，必須按照國際思維方式，研究制定科學的戰略與策略，不斷地提高國際談判藝術和經濟外交能力。特別是在國際談判中，不能過多地受到中國文化的影響和束縛，不宜過早地暴露自己的底線，否則會造出被動局面，甚至付出更大的代價。

第二，參與經濟全球化管理，需要研究制定一個長期的、整體的、系統的和一致的國際行動方案和指導原則，並貫穿於國家有關部門的日常國際事務中。經濟全球化提高了參與國際事務的透明度和關聯度，給中國參與國際合作交流提出了更高的要求。即使在研究制定雙邊的談判和合作方案時，也需要考慮其對多邊合作和區域合作的影響。目前中國的一舉一動，與任何國家的談判口徑或合作行動，都將受到全世界的高度關注。

第三，參與經濟全球化管理，需要大量的國際化的專業人才和對有關專題的深入研究。長期以來，中國政府部門所實行的那種近乎封閉式的用人機制將面臨嚴峻的挑戰，中國需要研究開放式的用人機制，既要加快培養體制內的相關人才，也要充分發揮現有專業人才的作用。根據國際合作的需要，從全國選拔最合適

的專家學者，及時充實有關機構，把握機遇，爭取主動。

同時我們還要重視為國際組織培養輸送管理人才，研究疏通國際組織與國內機構人才互動的機制，把參與國際組織工作作為中國培養國內熟悉國際規則、具有國際領先水準管理人才的平臺之一。在全球化的時代，國內事務與國際事務的界限變得越來越模糊，國內專家和國際專家交互使用，方能相得益彰。

第四，參與經濟全球化管理，中國需要角色的轉換，從過去強調熟悉和接受國際規則，開始轉向修訂、完善現有國際規則，並積極參與制定新的規則。現行規則往往具有發達國家的烙印，不完全是客觀公正的國際規則。中國獨有的經濟體制，在世界上扮演著非常獨特的角色，只能是由自己站出來，爭取建立既適合於中國國情又有利於世界經濟發展、公平公正的國際經濟新秩序。

和而不同，與時俱進：我們學習的楷模

《陳安論國際經濟法學》是一部巨著，全書分五卷共三百一十多萬字，全面彙集了陳安教授從中國改革開放三十多年來潛心國際經濟法學教學和研究的經歷、思想和成果。該書對於我們了解當代國際經濟法學前沿的理論和動態，回顧中國國際經濟法學理論的成長、實踐和發展，展望建立國際經濟新秩序所面臨的機遇和挑戰，都具有重要的學術理論價值和政策實踐意義。拜讀《陳安論國際經濟法學》與《四論》以後，深切地體會到陳安教授數十年磨一劍，在獨樹中華一幟，躋身國際前驅方面的許多獨到之處。特別是在以下三個方面，即對待國外國際經濟法學理論

和流派的態度、理論聯繫實際的學風以及知識報國、兼濟天下的志向，非常值得我們晚輩學習。

第一，對待世界上各種國際經濟法學的理論和流派非常重視，但不迷信。陳安教授非常重視研究世界上有關國際經濟法學的理論和流派，但是從不迷信。陳安教授研究和引進國際經濟法學的現有成果只是一種手段，而博采眾長、消化吸收、開拓創新、創立具有中國特色的國際經濟法學體系才是目的。陳安教授一貫主張：「在國際學術論壇上，中國人既要謙虛謹慎，認真學習和吸收有益的新知，切忌閉目塞聽，妄自尊大；又要敢於對外來的種種『權威』理論，根據國情和世情，深入探討，獨立思考，加以鑒別，乃至質疑，切忌妄自菲薄，盲目附和。」孔子《論語》中宣導的「和而不同」精神，在陳安教授的治學實踐中隨處可見。

第二，堅持理論聯繫實際，學以致用。陳安教授的教學研究工作密切聯繫中國和世界的實際，致力為中國的改革開放提供理論和法律支持。國際經濟法學是規範國際經濟關係中的法律和政策問題的綜合性和邊緣性的學科，過去在很長的一段時間裡，中國參與的不是很多，或者可以說很少。隨著中國改革開放發展程度的不斷提高，中國面臨的國際經濟法律問題越來越複雜，亟須深入研究解決。陳安教授的研究成果，涵蓋了有關國際貿易和投資、雙邊協定和多邊公約以及相關國際組織和管理體制的多個方面，為中國政府有關部門處理國際經濟法律問題，為保護中國有關企業的合法權益，提供了大量的戰略思想和決策建議，具有重要的參考價值。

　　第三，堅持知識報國、兼濟天下的志向。關於中國在建立新的國際經濟秩序、參與國際規則的制定、促進南南合作方面如何發揮作用，陳安教授作出了重要的理論創新，致力為中國和全球弱勢群體在國際經貿大政問題上爭取平等的話語權和參與權。《陳安論國際經濟法學》一書在探索建立國際經濟新秩序的規律和路徑方面旁徵博引，史論結合，提出了螺旋式上升的「6C軌跡」理論，得到了國內外學者的廣泛重視和認可。其中，《南南聯合自強五十年的國際經濟立法反思》一文為促進南南合作、豐富第三世界思想體系做出了重要貢獻；《晚近十年來美國單邊主義對抗WTO多邊主義的三大回合》一文在美國雜誌發表以後，被認為是「當前最受關注的、最引人入勝和最有創見的」文章，專門為發展中國家服務的國際組織「南方中心」將其收輯為中心的專題出版物——《貿易發展與公平》專題議程的系列工作檔之一，以單行本的形式重新出版發行。

　　隨著中國經濟社會持續快速的發展，在國際社會的地位和影響顯著提高，如何才能繼續維持並進一步開創有利於深化改革開放發展的國際環境，全面有效地參與國際規則制定與經濟全球化管理，正成為中國迫切需要解決的問題。研究和借鑑陳安教授提出問題和解決問題的思路，對於中國更深入、更廣泛和更有效地參與國際規則制定和經濟全球化管理，具有更加重要的價值。

注釋

〔1〕　孔子說：「德不孤，必有鄰。」（見《論語·里仁》）。這句話的意思是指凡是有道德、胸懷正氣、追求正義的人，都不會感到孤單無

助、孤掌難鳴、孤立無援。因為，他的四周（鄰）必定有不少志同道合的人，和他價值觀念相同，與他互相呼應，互相幫助，互相配合，共同為正義事業奮鬥。

* 張永彬，復旦大學出版社法學編審、副總編輯，《陳安論國際經濟法學》（五卷本）的責任編輯。本文原載於《中華讀書報》2009年12月9日。

* 張玉卿，中國政法大學國際法學院教授、博士生導師，中國商務部條法司前司長、WTO爭端解決機構專家組指示名單成員、中國國際經濟法學會副會長。本文原載於《國際經濟法學刊》2009年第16卷第3期。

* 張永彬，復旦大學出版社法學編審、副總編輯，《陳安論國際經濟法學》（五卷本）的責任編輯。本文原載於《西南政法大學學報》2012年第2期。

〔2〕 參見《中共中央第十一屆三中全會決議》（1978年12月）、《中共中央關於建國以來黨的若干歷史問題的決議》（1981年6月）。

〔3〕 楊亞男：《為對外開放鋪路 —— 記廈門大學法學教授陳安》，載《人民日報》（海外版）1992年7月7日。

〔4〕 轉引自張永彬：《陳安：知識報國，壯心不已》，載《中華讀書報》2009年12月9日。

〔5〕 參見陳安：《陳安論國際經濟法學》（第五卷），復旦大學出版社2008年版，第2624-2626頁。

〔6〕 參見陳安：《陳安論國際經濟法學》（第五卷），復旦大學出版社2008年版，第2624-2626頁。

〔7〕 同上。

〔8〕 即陳安教授發表的《論中國在建立國際經濟新秩序中的戰略定位》一文，二〇一一年獲得「福建省第九屆社會科學優秀成果獎」一等獎。

〔9〕 參見陳安：《「黃禍」論的本源、本質及其最新霸權「變種」：「中國威脅」論—中國對外經濟交往史的主流及其法理原則的視角》，載《現代法學》2011年 第6期。See also An Chen, On the Source, Essence of "Yellow Peril" Doctrine and Its Latest Hegemony "Variant"—the "China Threat" Doctrine: From the Perspective of Historical Mainstream of Sino-Foreign Economic Interactions and Their Inherent Jurisprudential Principles, *The Journal of World Investment & Trade*, Vol. 13, No. 1, 2012.

〔10〕本系列專著問世後，國內多家主流媒體多次報導，給予密切關注和高度學術評價（參見林鴻禧等：《適應對外開放和發展外向型經濟需要，國際經濟法系列專著問世》，載《光明日報》（海外版）1988年4月26日；長安南等：《人以少勝多，書以優取勝》，載《人民日報》1988年10月26日；余勁松：《評陳安主編：國際經濟法系列專著（1987年版）》，載《中國國際法年刊》，法律出版社1988年版；楊亞男：《為對外開放鋪路──記廈門大學法學教授陳安》，載《人民日報》（海外版）1992年7月7日）。當時主管福建省對外經貿事務的遊德馨副省長特地親筆致函表示讚揚和鼓勵──「陳安教授：感謝你贈送的五本巨作。當前全省上下議外向、想外向、幹外向的形勢下，外向知識何等重要又何等貧乏。這五本書可算及時雨，它大大有助於人們提高外向型知識，推動沿海開放事業發展……」

〔11〕參見陳安：《論國際經濟法學科的邊緣性、綜合性和獨立性》，載陳安：《陳安論國際經濟法學》（第一卷），復旦大學出版社2008年版，第13-16、33-37頁。

〔12〕張永彬：《陳安：知識報國，壯心不已》，載《中華讀書報》2009年12月9日。

〔13〕對本書的學術評價，請參見徐崇利：《新視角：從南北矛盾看國際經濟法──評〈國際經濟法總論〉》，載《廈門大學學報（哲社版）》1992年第3期。

〔14〕對本書的學術評價，請參見車丕照：《「問題與主義」中的「問題」──讀〈國際經濟法學專論〉》，載《政法論壇》2005年第1期。

〔15〕對本書的學術評價，請參見韓德培：《致力知己知彼　出色研究成果──〈美國對海外投資的法律保護及典型案例分析〉序言》，載陳安：《陳安論國際經濟法學》（第五卷），復旦大學出版社2008年版，第2536頁。

〔16〕對本書的學術評價，請參見1965年《華盛頓公約》「解決投資爭端國際中心」（ICSID）在1990年出版的《ICSID訊息》（*ICSID News*）第7卷第1期，宣告：中國正式簽署參加《華盛頓公約》，同時，在「有關ICSID的近期最新論著」專欄中，列出世界各國近期出版的有關ICSID的新著六種，把陳安教授主持撰寫的上述專著列在首位。一九九〇年八月JCSID法律顧問帕拉（A. R. Para）寫信給陳安教授，稱：「您論述『中心』的新書，已在本期的《ICSID訊息》上宣布了有關

的出版消息。根據本書內容目錄的英文譯文來判斷，這肯定是一本極其有益的著作。」當時中國對外經貿部條法司對本書的出版也給予很大的鼓勵和良好的評價，認為：「該書的出版無疑會推動我國學術界對於《華盛頓公約》和『解決投資爭端國際中心』的理論研究，同時亦對我們研究加入該公約的工作具有積極的參考價值和借鑑作用」；「您的大作，對我們的立法工作幫助很大」。參見陳安：《陳安論國際經濟法學》（第五卷），復旦大學出版社2008年版，第八編「來函選輯」之八、九、十、十一、二十；單文華：《深入研究，科學判斷——〈「解決投資爭端國際中心」述評〉簡介》，載《福建日報》1995年3月31日。

〔17〕對本書的學術評價，請參見吳煥寧：《獨樹中華一幟，躋身國際前驅——評陳安主編：〈MIGA與中國〉》，載《文匯讀書週報》1996年3月23日。

〔18〕對本書的學術評價，請參見張乃根：《國際投資爭端仲裁研究的力作——評〈國際投資爭端仲裁機制（ICSID）研究〉》，載《中國圖書評論》2002年第5期。

〔19〕對本書的學術評價，請參見中國商務部條法司來函：《立意新穎務實分析縝密深入理論實踐交融——對陳安主編〈國際投資法的新發展與中國雙邊投資條約的新實踐〉一書的評價》（商法投資函〔2008〕40號）

〔20〕其中發表於外國學術刊物的十八篇英文長篇論文，均收輯於《陳安論國際經濟法學》（第四卷），復旦大學出版社2008年版，第1723-2513頁。

〔21〕李雙元：《中國國際經濟法學研究的現狀和發展趨勢》，載《法學家》1996年第6期，第3-6頁。以上各條注解所列主流媒體、同行學者對陳安教授論著的報導、評論等，均收輯於《陳安論國際經濟法學》（第五卷），復旦大學出版社2008年版，第2515-2626頁。

〔22〕轉引自張永彬：《陳安：知識報國，壯心不已》，載《中華讀書報》2009年12月9日；陳安：《陳安論國際經濟法學》（第一卷），復旦大學出版社2008年版，第104-108頁。

〔23〕參見陳安：《改進我國國際法教育的「他山之石」——歐美之行考察見聞》，載《國際學術動態》1985年第4期。

〔24〕參見劉智中：《從難從嚴訓練，成果人才並出》，載《學位與研究生

教育》1988年第5期。

〔25〕全書從當代國際社會弱勢群體即第三世界的視角，探討和論證國際
　　　經濟法學這一新興的邊緣性、綜合性學科。諸如：闡明獨立的、不
　　　同於發達國家學者的學術理念和學術追求；獨到地探索建立國際經
　　　濟新秩序的規律和路徑；創新地論證當代國際經濟法的基本原則；
　　　鑽研中國古籍，深入探討源遠流長的中國對外經濟交往史及其蘊含
　　　的法理原則；長期重點研究國際投資條約及其相關體制的實際運
　　　行，探討發展中國家如何在這些體制中趨利避害，提供決策諮詢建
　　　議和立法建言；率先剖析評議中國涉外仲裁監督機制立法的優點與
　　　不足，旁徵博引，力排「眾議」，澄清學術訛傳，提出建立嚴格監
　　　督體制、防阻執法腐敗、保證公正仲裁的立法建議；秉持公正公平
　　　原則，具體研析涉外經貿爭端仲裁典案，依法祛邪扶正，並撰文從
　　　理論上伸張正義；致力澄清和批駁外國媒體、政界和學界對中國的
　　　誤解和非難。通過學術論證，努力維護中國的國家尊嚴、國際信譽
　　　和民族自尊，弘揚中華愛國主義。參見陳安：《陳安論國際經濟法
　　　學》（第一卷），復旦大學出版社2008年版，自序。

〔26〕參見朱學山：《一劍淬礪三十年：中國特色國際經濟法學的奠基之
　　　作——推薦〈陳安論國際經濟法學〉》載陳安：《陳安論國際經濟法
　　　學》（第五卷），復旦大學出版社2008年版，第2537-2539頁；李雙
　　　元：《中國國際經濟法學研究的現狀和發展趨勢》，載《法學家》
　　　1996年第6期。

〔27〕詳見陳安近三年來撰寫的四篇系列論文：（1）《論中國在建立國際
　　　經濟新秩序中的戰略定位——兼評「新自由主義經濟秩序」論、
　　　「WTO憲政秩序」論、「經濟民族主義擾亂全球化秩序」論》簡稱
　　　《一論》，收輯於陳安：《陳安論國際經濟法學》（第一卷），復旦大
　　　學出版社2008年版，第109-134頁；其修訂文本發表於《現代法學》
　　　2009年第2期，第3-18頁。（2）《旗幟鮮明地確立中國在構建NIEO中
　　　的戰略定位——兼論與時俱進，完整、準確地理解鄧小平「對外二
　　　十八字方針」》（簡稱《二論》），發表於《國際經濟法學刊》2009
　　　年第16卷第3期。（3）《三論中國在構建NIEO中的戰略定位：「匹茲
　　　堡發軔之路」走向何方——G20南北合作新平臺的待解之謎以及「守
　　　法」與「變法」等理念碰撞》（簡稱《三論》），發表於《國際經濟
　　　法學刊》2009年第16卷第4期。（4）《中國加入WTO十年的法理斷

想：簡論WTO的法治、立法、執法、守法與變法》(簡稱《四論》)，
發表於《現代法學》2010年第6期。

〔28〕參見陳安：《我國涉外經濟立法中可否規定對外資絕不實行國有
化》，載《廈門大學學報（哲學社會科學版）》1986年第1期。See
also An Chen, "Should an Absolute Immunity from Nationalization for
Foreign Investment Be Enacted in China's Economic Law? *Legal Aspect
of Foreign Investment in the People's Republic of China*, China Trade
Translation Co. Ltd., 1988.中英文本分別收輯於陳安：《陳安論國際經
濟法學》(第三、五卷)，復旦大學出版社2008年版，第1197-1209、
2368-2387頁。

〔29〕上述論文中文本發表四年之後，一九九〇年四月全國人大對《中華
人民共和國中外合資經營企業法》加以修訂，在第2條中增補了第3
款：「國家對合營企業不實行國有化和徵收；在特殊情況下，根據
社會公共利益的需要，對合營企業可以依照法律程式實行徵收，並
給予相應的補償。」此項新規定在國有化和徵收問題上區分一般情
況與特殊情況，分別對待。這完全符合當代發展中國家外資立法的
通例，也與一九八六年陳安教授提出的看法和論證即「務必留權在
手，但決不任意濫用」相一致。

〔30〕本長篇論文撰寫並發表於二〇〇一至二〇〇四年，題為《晚近十年
來美國單邊主義與WTO多邊主義交鋒的三大回合：綜合剖析美國
「主權大辯論」(1994)、「301條款」爭端(1998-2000)以及「201
條款」爭端(2002-2003)》，全文約六點五萬字。其部分內容約一
點五萬字最初以《美國1994年的「主權大辯論」及其後續影響》為
題，發表於《中國社會科學》2001年第5期。另一部分內容約二萬
字，題為《美國單邊主義對抗WTO多邊主義的第三回合──「301條
款」爭端之法理探源和展望》，發表於《中國法學》2004年第2期。
此前，本文的英文本 "The Three Big Rounds of U. S. Unilateralism
Versus WTO Multilateralism During the Last Decade: A Combined
Analysis of the Great 1994 Sovereignty Debate, Section 301 Disputes
(1998-2000), and Section 201 Disputes (2002-2003)" 發表於美國*Temple
International and Comparative Law Journal* 2003年第17卷第2期。英文
稿發表後，引起國際人士關注。作者應總部設在日內瓦的六十二個
發展中國家的政府間國際組織「南方中心」(South Centre)約稿，

又結合「301條款」爭端案終審結局，將上述英文全稿再次作了修訂增補，由ICSID作為「T. R. A D. E.專題工作檔第22號」於二〇〇四年七月重新出版單行本，散發給「南方中心」各成員國理事以及WTO各成員常駐日內瓦代表團，供作決策參考：同時，登載於ICSID網站上（http://www. southcentre. org/publications/workingpapers/paper22/wp22. pdf），供讀者自由下載。本文的英文本於二〇〇四年獲得第十二屆「安子介國際貿易研究獎」一等獎；中文本於二〇〇五年獲得「福建省第六屆社會科學優秀成果獎」一等獎。中英兩種文本分別收輯於陳安：《陳安論國際經濟法學》（第一、四卷），復旦大學出版社2008年版，第366-420、1725-1807頁。

〔31〕參見陳安教授的論文《南南聯合自強五十年的國際經濟立法反思：從萬隆、多哈、坎昆到香港》（A Reflections on the South-South Coalition in the Last Half Century from the Perspective of International Economic law-making: From Bandung, Doha and Cancun to Hong Kong）。本長篇專論有中、英兩種文本。隨著「多哈回合」談判形勢的發展，先後數度應邀增訂或改寫，被中國及有關國際組織機關公報等國內外六種權威學刊（含《中國法學》2006年第2期、*The Journal of World Investment & Trade* 2006年第2期等）相繼採用、轉載、轉譯，並被輯入英文學術專著。中英兩種文本已分別收輯於陳安：《陳安論國際經濟法學》（第一、四卷），復旦大學出版社2008年版，第479-506、1808-1852頁。該論文於2007年獲得「福建省第七屆社會科學優秀成果獎」一等獎。

〔32〕參見陳安：《陳安論國際經濟法學》（第一卷），復旦大學出版社2008年版，自序。

〔33〕這些發表於外國學術刊物的十八篇英文長篇論文，均收輯於陳安：《陳安論國際經濟法學》（第四卷），復旦大學出版社2008年版，第1723-2513頁。

〔34〕參見郭壽康：《弘揚中華學術投身國際爭鳴──推薦〈陳安論國際經濟法學〉》載陳安：《陳安論國際經濟法學》（第五卷），復旦大學出版社2008年版，第2539-2540頁。

〔35〕轉引自陳安：《陳安論國際經濟法學》（第五卷），復旦大學出版社2008年版，第2540-2546頁。

〔36〕朱學山：《一劍淬礪三十年：中國特色國際經濟法學的奠基之作──

推薦〈陳安論國際經濟法學〉〉，載陳安：《陳安論國際經濟法學》
（第五卷），復旦大學出版社2008年版，第2537-2539頁。

* 朱欖葉，華東政法大學教授、博士生導師，國際法學院前院長，WTO爭
端解決機構專家組指示性名單成員。本文原載於《西南政法大學學報》
2012年第2期。

〔37〕關於該問題的詳細論述，請參見陳安教授的文章《論國際濟法的產
生和發展》《論中國在建立國際經濟新秩序中的戰略定位》（簡稱《一
論》）、《南南聯合自強五十年的國際經濟立法反思：從萬隆、多
哈、坎昆到香港》，載陳安：《陳安論國際經濟法學》（第一卷），復
旦大學出版社2008年版，第62-64、109-111、479-506頁。

〔38〕參見陳安：《旗幟鮮明地確立中國在構建NIEO中的戰略定位——兼
論與時俱進，完整、準確地理解鄧小平「對外二十八字方針」》，載
陳安：《國際經濟法學刊》2009年第16卷第3期，第55-81頁；陳安：
《三論中國在構建NIEO中的戰略定位：「匹茲堡發軔之路」走向何
方——G20南北合作新平臺的待解之謎以及「守法」與「變法」等
理念碰撞》，載陳安：《國際經濟法學刊》2009年第16卷第4期，第
1-29頁；陳安：《中國加入WTO十年的法理斷想：簡論WTO的法治、
立法、執法、守法與變法》，載《現代法學》2010年第6期，第114-
124頁。

〔39〕關於該問題的詳細論述，請參見陳安教授的文章《論國際經濟法學
科的邊緣性、綜合性和獨立性》《世紀之交在經濟主權上的新爭議與
「攻防戰」：綜合評析十年來美國單邊主義與WTO多邊主義交鋒的三
大回合》，載陳安：《陳安論國際經濟法學》（第一卷），復旦大學出
版社2008年版，第12-16、34-37、370-378頁。

〔40〕關於該問題的詳細論述，請參見陳安：《世紀之交在經濟主權上的
新爭議與「攻防戰」：綜合評析十年來美國單邊主義與WTO多邊主
義交鋒的三大回合》，載陳安：《陳安論國際經濟法學》（第一卷），
復旦大學出版社2008年版，第366-420頁。

〔41〕關於該問題的詳細論述，請參見陳安：《陳安論國際經濟法學》（第
一卷），復旦大學出版社2008年版，第415-420頁。

〔42〕關於該問題的詳細論述，請參見朱學山教授的文章《一劍淬礪三十
年：《中國特色國際經濟法學的奠基之作》、吳煥甯教授的文章《獨
樹中華一幟，躋身國際前驅》，載陳安：《陳安論國際經濟法學》（第

〔43〕關於該問題的詳細論述，請參見陳安教授所撰各篇專論，諸如《論國際經濟關係的歷史發展與南北矛盾》《論源遠流長的中國對外經濟交往及其法理原則》《論中國在建立國際經濟新秩序中的戰略定位》《論馬克思列寧主義對弱小民族國家主權學說的重大貢獻》《論「適用國際慣例」與「有法必依」的統一》《論中國的涉外仲裁監督機制及其與國際慣例的接軌》《再論中國涉外仲裁的監督機制及其與國際慣例的接軌》等等，輯於《陳安論國際經濟法學》一書第一卷、第二卷。

〔44〕朱欖葉編著：《世界貿易組織國際貿易糾紛案例評析》，法律出版社2000年版，第661頁。

〔45〕關於該問題的詳細論述，請參見陳安：《世紀之交在經濟主權上的新爭議與「攻防戰」：綜合評析十年來美國單邊主義與WTO多邊主義交鋒的三大回合》，載陳安：《陳安論國際經濟法學》（第一卷），復旦大學出版社2008年版，第382-385頁。

〔46〕關於該問題的詳細論述，請參見陳安：《論社會帝國主義主權觀的一大思想淵源：民族虛無主義的今昔》，載陳安：《陳安論國際經濟法學》（第一卷），復旦大學出版社2008年版，第421-443頁。

〔47〕關於該問題的詳細論述，請參見陳安：《南南聯合自強五十年的國際經濟立法反思：從萬隆、多哈、坎昆到香港》，載陳安：《陳安論國際經濟法學》（第一卷），復旦大學出版社2008年版，第479-506頁。

〔48〕關於該問題的詳細論述，請參見陳安教授的文章《論中國涉外仲裁程式中當事人的申辯權和對質權》《就中國涉外仲裁體制答英商問》《論涉外仲裁個案中的偏袒偽證和縱容欺詐——CIETAC 1992-1993年個案評析》《論涉外仲裁個案中的越權管轄、越權解釋、草率斷結和有欠透明——CIETAC 2001-2002年個案評析》《論中國法律認定的「違法行為」及其法律後果——就廣東省廣信公司破產清算債務訟案問題答外商摩根公司問》等，載陳安：《陳安論國際經濟法學》（第二卷），復旦大學出版社2008年版，第683-810頁。

〔49〕關於該問題的詳細論述，請參見陳安：《中國「入世」後海峽兩岸經貿問題「政治化」之防治》，載陳安：《陳安論國際經濟法學》（第四卷），復旦大學出版社2008年版，第1650-1677頁。

〔50〕參見陳安：《「黃禍」論的本源、本質及其最新霸權「變種」「中國

五卷），復旦大學出版社2008年版，第2537-2539、2556-2557頁。

威脅」論——中國對外經濟交往史的主流及其法理原則的視角》，載《現代法學》2011年第6期，第10-36頁。See also An Chen, On the Source, Essence of "Yellow Peril" Doctrine and Its Latest Hegemony "Variant"—the "China Threat" Doctrine: From the Perspective of Historical Mainstream of Sino-Foreign Economic Interactions and Their Inherent Jurisprudential Principles, *The Journal of World Investment & Trade*, Vol. 13, No.1, 2012, pp. 1-58.

〔51〕參見一九八七年至二〇〇八年期間中華人民共和國對外經貿部、商務部條法司以及中華人民共和國常駐世界貿易組織代表團團長孫振宇大使先後致陳安教授的函件，載陳安：《陳安論國際經濟法學》（第五卷），復旦大學出版社2008年版，第2546-2547、2585-2591頁。

* 曾華群，時任廈門大學法學院教授、博士生導師。本文原載於《西南政法大學學報》2012年第2期。

〔52〕陳安：《論國際經濟關係的歷史發展與南北矛盾》，載陳安：《陳安論國際經濟法學》（第一卷），復旦大學出版社2008年版，第40頁。

〔53〕同上書，第46-54頁。

〔54〕同上書，第53頁。

〔55〕同上書，第46頁。

〔56〕參見陳安：《列寧對民族殖民地革命學說的重大發展》，生活‧讀書‧新知三聯書店1981年版。該書已輯入《陳安論國際經濟法學》（第一卷），題為「論馬克思列寧主義對弱小民族國家主權學說的重大貢獻」，復旦大學出版社2008年版，第136-342頁。

〔57〕參見陳安：《論社會帝國主義主權觀的一大思想淵源：《民族虛無主義的今昔》，載陳安：《陳安論國際經濟法學》（第一卷），復旦大學出版社2008年版，第421-443頁。

〔58〕參見陳安：《論國際經濟關係的歷史發展與南北矛盾》，載陳安：《陳安論國際經濟法學》（第一卷），復旦大學出版社2008年版，第59頁。

〔59〕同上書，第60-61頁。

〔60〕關於WTO體制的進一步剖析，請參見陳安：《中國加入WTO十年的法理斷想：簡論WTO的法治、立法、執法、守法與變法》，載《現代法學》2010年第6期，第114-124頁。

〔61〕關於該問題的詳細論述，請參見陳安：《論中國在建立國際經濟新

秩序中的戰略定位——兼評「新自由主義經濟秩序」論、「WTO憲政秩序」論、「經濟民族主義擾亂全球化秩序」論》，載陳安：《陳安論國際經濟法學》（第一卷），復旦大學出版社2008年版，第120-134頁。

〔62〕近年來，西方學者除上述國際經濟秩序論外，還提出了所謂全球治理論。如在國際投資法領域，提出了所謂「外國直接投資的全球治理體系」（the global governance system for FDI）的概念，並指出這一體系主要是由BITs構成的。See Axel Berger, China's New Bilateral Investment Treaty Programme: Substance, Rational and Implications for Investment Law Making, paper for the American Society of International Law International Economic Law Group (ASIL IELIG) 2008 Biennial Conference "The Politics of International Economic Law: The Next Four Years", Washington, D. C., November 14-15, 2008.

〔63〕陳安：《論國際經濟法的產生和發展》，載陳安：《陳安論國際經濟法學》（第一卷），復旦大學出版社2008年版，第64頁。

〔64〕參見陳安：《南南聯合自強五十年的國際經濟立法反思：從萬隆、多哈、坎昆到香港》，載陳安：《陳安論國際經濟法學》（第一卷），復旦大學出版社2008年版，第500-502頁；陳安主編：《國際經濟法學專論（第二版）》，高等教育出版社2007年版，第246、324-326頁。

〔65〕關於南南合作問題的系統論述，參見An Chen, Weak Versus Strong at the WTO, the South-South Coalition from Bandung to Hong Kong, *The Geneva Post Quarterly: The Jounal of World Affairs*, 2006, pp. 55- 107。

〔66〕關於「中國威脅」論的歷史考察，參見陳安：《「黃禍」論的本源、本質及其最新霸權「變種」：「中國威脅」論——中國對外經濟交往史的主流及其法理原則的視角》，載《現代法學》2011年第6期。See also An Chen, On the Source , Essence of "Yellow Peril" Doctrine and Its Latest Hegemony "Variant"—the "China Threat" Doctrine: From the Perspective of Historical Mainstream of Sino-Foreign Economic Interactions and Their Inherent Jurisprudential Principles, *The Journal of World Investment & Trade*, Vol. 13, No. 1, 2012.

〔67〕陳安：《我國涉外經濟立法中可否規定對外資絕不實行國有化》，載陳安：《陳安論國際經濟法學》（第三卷），復旦大學出版社2008年版，第1209頁。

〔68〕更詳細的論述，請參見陳安：《論源遠流長的中國對外經濟交往及其法理原則》，載陳安：《陳安論國際經濟法學》（第一卷），復旦大學出版社2008年版，第98頁。

〔69〕更詳細的論述，請參見陳安教授的論文《論中國在建立國際經濟新秩序中的戰略定位──兼評「新自由主義經濟秩序」論、「WTO憲政秩序」論、「經濟民族主義擾亂全球化秩序」論》，載陳安：《陳安論國際經濟法學》（第一卷），復旦大學出版社2008年版，第109-120頁。在該文發表之後，作者相繼發表有關中國在建立國際經濟新秩序中戰略定位的專論，包括：陳安：《再論旗幟鮮明地確立中國在構建NIEO中的戰略定位──兼論與時俱進，完整、准確地理解鄧小平「對外二十八字方針」》，載陳安：《國際經濟法學刊》2009年第16卷第3期；陳安：《三論中國在構建NIEO中的戰略定位：「匹茲堡發軔之路」走向何方──G20南北合作新平臺的待解之謎以及「守法」與「變法」等理念碰撞》，載陳安：《國際經濟法學刊》2009年第16卷第4期；陳安：《中國加入WTO十年的法理斷想：簡論WTO的法治、立法、執法、守法與變法》，載《現代法學》2010年第6期；An Chen, What Should Be China's Strategic Position in the Establishment of New International Economic Order? With Comments on Neoliberalistic Economic Order, Constitutional Order of the WTO and Economic Nationalism's Disturbance of Globalization, *The Journal of Word Investment & Trade*, Vol. 10, No. 3, 2009; An Chen, Some Jurisprudential Thoughts upon WTO's Law-Governing, Law-Making, Law-Enforcing, Law-Abiding and L.aw-Reformiing, *The Journal of Wold Investment & Trade*, Vol. 11, No. 2, 2010。

〔70〕陳安：《論經濟主權原則是當代國際經濟法首要的基本規範》，載陳安：《陳安論國際經濟法學》（第一卷）復旦大學出版社2008年版，第344頁。

〔71〕同上書，第346頁。

〔72〕See John H. Jackson, *Sovereignty, the WTO, and Changing Fundaments of International Law*, Cambridge University Press, 2006.

〔73〕See B. Boutros-Ghali, B. Gosovic, *Global Leadership and Global Systemic Issues: South, North and the United Nations in 21st Century World*, Transcend University Press, 2011.

〔74〕參見陳安：《論經濟主權原則是當代國際經濟法首要的基本規範》，載陳安：《陳安論國際經濟法學》（第一卷），復旦大學出版社2008年版，第347-348頁。

〔75〕同上書，第351-359頁。

〔76〕參見陳安：《世紀之交在經濟主權上的新爭議與「攻防戰」綜合評析十年來美國單邊主義與WTO多邊主義交鋒的三大回合》，載陳安：《陳安論國際經濟法學》（第一卷），復旦大學出版社2008年版，第366-420頁。

〔77〕同上書，第420頁。

〔78〕陳安：《我國涉外經濟立法中可否規定對外資絕不實行國有化》，載陳安：《陳安論國際經濟法學》第三卷），復旦大學出版社2008年版，第1197-1209頁。

〔79〕陳安：《論中國在「入世」談判中應當堅持經濟主權原則》，載陳安：《陳安論國際經濟法學》（第一卷），復旦大學出版社2008年版，第360頁。

〔80〕參見陳安：《中外雙邊投資協定中的四大「安全閥」不宜貿然拆除──美、加型BITs談判範本關鍵性「爭端解決」條款剖析》，載陳安：《陳安論國際經濟法學》（第三卷），復旦大學出版社2008年版，第1079-1108頁。

〔81〕參見陳安：《區分兩類國家，實行差別互惠：再論ICSID體制賦予中國的四大「安全閥」不宜貿然全面拆除》，載陳安：《陳安論國際經濟法學》（第三卷），復旦大學出版社2008年版，第1109-1146頁。

〔82〕參見陳安：《論國際經濟法中的公平互利原則是平等互利原則的重大發展》，載陳安：《陳安論國際經濟法學》（第一卷），復旦大學出版社2008年版，第446-447頁。

〔83〕參見周鯁生：《國際法》（上冊），商務印書館1981年版，第213頁。

〔84〕參見陳安：《論國際經濟法中的公平互利原則是平等互利原則的重大發展》，載陳安：《陳安論國際經濟法學》（第一卷），復旦大學出版社2008年版，第444頁。

〔85〕參見陳安：《論國際經濟法中的公平互利原則是平等互利原則的重大發展》載陳安：《陳安論國際經濟法學》（第一卷），復旦大學出版社2008年版，第449頁。

〔86〕同上書，第449-450頁。

〔87〕 同上書，第448-449頁。

〔88〕 參見陳安：《全球合作的新興模式和強大趨勢：南南合作與「77國集團」》，載陳安：《陳安論國際經濟法學》（第一卷），復旦大學出版社2008年版，第463-466頁。

〔89〕 參見陳安：《南北合作是解決南北矛盾的最佳選擇》，載陳安：《陳安論國際經濟法學》（第一卷），復旦大學出版社2008年版，第455-459頁。

〔90〕 參見陳安：《全球合作的新興模式和強大趨勢：南南合作與「77國集團」》，載陳安：《陳安論國際經濟法學》（第一卷），復旦大學出版社2008年版，第463頁。

〔91〕 參見陳安：《南南聯合自強五十年的國際經濟立法反思：從萬隆、多哈、坎昆到香港》，載陳安：《陳安論國際經濟法學》（第一卷），復旦大學出版社2008年版，第479頁。

〔92〕 陳安：《〈陳安論國際經濟法學〉自序》，載陳安：《陳安論國際經濟法學》（第一卷），復旦大學出版社2008年版，第3頁。

〔93〕 參見《（美國）哈佛大學法學院斯托利講座教授、東亞法學研究所所長A. von Mehren教授致陳安教授函（1982年10月25日）》《（美國）波士頓大學法學院教授、哈佛大學東亞法學研究所前所長F. K. Upham教授致陳安教授函（1982年11月29日）》，載陳安：《陳安論國際經濟法學》（第五卷），復旦大學出版社2008年版，第2613-2614頁。

〔94〕 陳安教授的主要英文著述，載於《陳安論國際經濟法學》（第四、五卷），復旦大學出版社2008年版，第1725-2513頁。

〔95〕 參見康安峰、蔣圍：《致力「走出去」：廈門大學國際經濟法研究團隊科研「國際化」的初步實踐》，載陳安：《國際經濟法學刊》2011年第18卷第2期，第264-282頁。

〔96〕 《南方中心秘書長Branislav Gosovic致陳安教授函（2006年2月1日）》載陳安：《陳安論國際經濟法學》（第五卷），復旦大學出版社2008年版，第2591-2592頁。

〔97〕 參見《「多邊投資擔保機構」MIGA）首席法律顧問L. Weisefeld致陳安教授函（2004年5月12日）》《「解決投資爭端國際中心」ICSID）法律顧問A. Para致陳安教授函（1990年3月22日，1990年8月22日）》，載陳安：《陳安論國際經濟法學》（第五卷），復旦大學出版

社2008年版，第2599-2602頁。

* 趙龍躍，時任南開大學周恩來政府管理學院教授、博士生導師，世界銀行兼職研究員，美國喬治城大學特聘教授。本文原載於《西南政法大學學報》2012年第2期。

〔98〕參見陳安：《論中國在建立國際經濟新秩序中的戰略定位——兼評「新自由主義經濟秩序」論、「WTO憲政秩序」論、「經濟民族主義擾亂全球化秩序」論》，載陳安：《陳安論國際經濟法學》（第一卷），復旦大學出版社2008年版，第109-134頁。其修訂文本發表於《現代法學》2009年第2期，第3-18頁。

〔99〕陳安教授的四篇系列論文包括：《論中國在建立國際經濟新秩序中的戰略定位——兼評「新自由主義經濟秩序」論、「WTO憲政秩序」論、「經濟民族主義擾亂全球化秩序」論》（簡稱《一論》），載《現代法學》2009年第2期；《旗幟鮮明地確立中國在構建NIEO中的戰略定位——兼論與時俱進，完整、準確地理解鄧小平「對外二十八字方針」》（簡稱《二論》），載《國際經濟法學刊》2009年第16卷第3期；《三論中國在構建NIEO中的戰略定位：「匹茲堡發軔之路」走向何方——G20南北合作新平臺的待解之謎以及「守法」與「變法」等理念碰撞》（簡稱《三論》），載《國際經濟法學刊》2009年第16卷第4期；《中國加入WTO十年的法理斷想：簡論WTO的法治、立法、執法、守法與變法》（簡稱《四論》），載《現代法學》2010年第6期。

〔100〕陳安：《論中國在建立國際經濟新秩序中的戰略定位——兼評「新自由主義經濟秩序」論、「WTO憲政秩序」論、「經濟民族主義擾亂全球化秩序」論》，載陳安：《陳安論國際經濟法學》（第一卷），復旦大學出版社2008年版，第110頁。

〔101〕參見陳安：《旗幟鮮明地確立中國在構建NIEO中的戰略定位——兼論與時俱進，完整、準確地理解鄧小平「對外二十八字方針」》，載陳安：《國際經濟法學刊》2009年第16卷第3期，第80頁。

〔102〕See G. John Ikenberry, *Liberal Leviathan: The Origins, Crisis, and Transformaion of the American World Order*, Princeton University Press 2011.

〔103〕陳安：《中國加入WTO十年的法理斷想：簡論WTO的法治、立法、執法、守法與變法》，載《現代法學》2010年第6期，第115頁。

〔104〕Joseph S. Nye, Jr., Soft Power and American Foreign Policy, *Political*

Science Quarterly, Vol. 119, No. 2, 2004, pp. 255-270.

〔105〕See Robert Gilpin, *War and Change in World Politics*, Cambridge University Press, 1981.

〔106〕See Robert O. Keohane, *After Hegemony*: *Cooperation and Discord in the World Political Economy*, Princeton University Press, 1984.

〔107〕陳安：《陳安論國際經濟法學》（第一卷），復旦大學出版社2008年版，第120頁。

〔108〕同上書，第121頁。

〔109〕房寧：《迷夢的遠逝：「華盛頓共識」與拉美困境》，載《社會觀察》2005年第3期，第11-12頁。

〔110〕房寧：《迷夢的遠逝：「華盛頓共識」與拉美困境》，載《社會觀察》2005年第3期，第130頁。

〔111〕陳安：《旗幟鮮明地確立中國在構建NIEO中的戰略定位——兼論與時俱進，完整、準確地理解鄧小平「對外二十八字方針」》，載陳安：《國際經濟法學刊》2009年第16卷第3期，第79-80頁。

〔112〕Cf. Daniel Atman, Charlene Bashefsky on Doha (2007) Managing Globalization Weblog—The International Herald Tribune, http: // blogs. iht. com/tribtalk/business/globalization/ ? p=342.

〔113〕陳安：《旗幟鮮明地確立中國在構建NIEO中的戰略定位——兼論與時俱進，完整、準確地理解鄧小平「對外二十八字方針」》，載陳安：《國際經濟法學刊》2009年第16卷第3期，第80頁。

〔114〕佚名：《調整全球經濟格局面臨三大挑戰》，載《上海金融報》2010年4月20日第A02版。

〔115〕陳鳳英：《新興經濟體與21世紀國際經濟秩序變遷》，載《外交評論》2011年第3期，第1頁。

〔116〕See IMF, World Economic Outlook, April, 2011.

〔117〕《胡錦濤在二十國集團領導人第六次峰會上的講話》，http:// finance. jrj. com. cn/2011/11/04054211487860. shtml。

〔118〕同上。

〔119〕參見陳安：《旗幟鮮明地確立中國在構建NIEO中的戰略定位——兼論與時俱進，完整、準確地理解鄧小平「對外二十八字方針」》，載陳安：《國際經濟法學刊》2009年第16卷第3期，第66-67頁。

〔120〕陳安教授對南北經濟談判過程與效果進行系統分析，可參見《南南

聯合自強五十年的國際經濟立法反思》，載陳安：《陳安論國際經濟法學》（第一卷），復旦大學出版社2008年版，第479-506頁。

〔121〕陳安：《論中國在建立國際經濟新秩序中的戰略定位——兼評「新自由主義經濟秩序」論、「WTO憲政秩序」論、「經濟民族主義擾亂全球化秩序」論》，載《現代法學》2009年第2期，第4頁。

〔122〕周小川：《關於改革國際貨幣體系的思考》，http://www. gov. cn/gzdt/2009-03/23/content_1266412. htm。

〔123〕陳安：《三論中國在構建NIEO中的戰略定位：「匹茲堡發軔之路」走向何方——G20南北合作新平臺的待解之謎以及「守法」與「變法」等理念碰撞》，載陳安：《國際經濟法學刊》2009年第16卷第4期，第1-29頁。

〔124〕同上。

〔125〕《溫家寶在聯合國千年發展目標高級別會議上的講話》。http://www. fmiprc. gov. cn/ce/cgstp/chn/zt_1/ zgwj/t764048. htm。

〔126〕韓愈在《送孟東野序》中说：「大凡物不得其平則鳴……人之於言也亦然。有不得已者而後言，其歌也有思，其哭也有懷。凡出乎口而為聲者，其皆有弗平者乎！」

〔127〕陳安：《旗幟鮮明地確立中國在構建NIEO中的戰略定位——兼論與時俱進，完整、準確地理解鄧小平「對外二十八字方針」》，載陳安《國際經濟法學刊》2009年第16卷第3期，第80頁。

〔128〕參見〔美〕羅伯特·吉爾平：《國際關係政治經濟學》，楊宇光等譯，上海人民出版社2006年版。

〔129〕陳安：《旗幟鮮明地確立中國在構建NIEO中的戰略定位——兼論與時俱進，完整、準確地理解鄧小平「對外二十八字方針」》，載陳安：《國際經濟法學刊》2009年第16卷第3期，第80頁。

〔130〕同上書，第67頁。

〔131〕陳安：《旗幟鮮明地確立中國在構建NIEO中的戰略定位——兼論與時俱進，完整、準確地理解鄧小平「對外二十八字方針」》，載陳安：《國際經濟法學刊》2009年第16卷第3期，第80頁。

〔132〕參見陳安：《中國加入WTO十年的法理斷想：簡論WTO的法治、立法、執法、守法與變法》，載《現代法學》2010年第6期，第116頁。

〔133〕同上書，第119頁。

〔134〕同上書，第120頁。

《中國的吶喊》書評薈萃

編者按：

陳安教授所撰《中國的吶喊》一書，自德國Springer出版社向全球推出以來，已引起國內外學界同行的廣泛關注，學者們紛紛撰文評論與回應，迄今已經收到書評二十四篇，並已匯輯在一起，由北京大學出版社出版的《國際經濟法學刊》第十九卷第二期至二十三卷第二期特闢《中國的吶喊》書評專欄，以中英雙語集中發表[135]薈萃聚合，形成對外弘揚中華學術正氣、追求國際公平正義的共鳴強音，藉以進一步擴大其國內外的學術影響。

編者：陳欣、楊帆[136]

二〇一七年六月十日

Editorial Note:

After the publication of Prof. An Chen's monograph——*The Voice from China: An CHEN on International Economic Law* through world renowned Springer, it has atracted extensive attention and provoked intensive interest in the academic circles, both from domestic and abroad. Scholars have in succession responded with comments and reviews. As of today we have received 24 such book reviews, the bilingual (Chinese and English) versions of which are all ready to compile together and publish in a special book-review column for *The Voice from China* in the *Journal of International Economic Law* (China) through the Peking University Press. It is our wish that these leading comments will help to forge and converge a stream of strong resonances to advance and enrich the righteous viewpoints of Chinese scholars, and to pursue equity and justice at the international level.

June 10，2017

一、中國吶喊　發聲振聵

　　耄耋高齡的廈門大學法學院國際經濟法學教授、中國國際經濟法學會榮譽會長陳安教授所撰英文專著《中國的吶喊：陳安論國際經濟法》(*The Voice from China: An CHEN on International Economcc Law*)，新近由享有國際學術盛譽的德國權威出版社Springer向全球推出，在國際經濟法學界引起廣泛關注。

　　本書匯集作者自一九八〇年以來三十多年不同時期撰寫的二十四篇英文專論。全書八百五十二頁，分為六部分，分別探討和論證當代國際經濟法基本理論和重要實踐的學術前沿重大問題。這些英文專論原稿絕大部分發表於中外知名學刊，立足於中國國情，以馬克思主義為指導，從當代國際社會弱勢群體即第三世界的視角，有的放矢，針對當代國際經濟法學科領域的基本理論以

及熱點難點實踐問題，發出與西方強權國家主流觀點截然不同的呼聲和吶喊。在積極參與國際學術爭鳴當中，大力宣揚眾多發展中國家共同的正義主張和基本立場，有理有據地揭示某些西方主流理論誤導之不當和危害，從而避免在實踐上損害包括中國在內的國際弱勢群體的公平權益。這也正是本書命名為《中國的吶喊：陳安論國際經濟法》之由來。

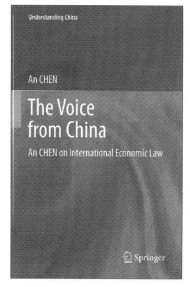

這部英文專著文稿於二〇一三年十一月獲得「國家社會科學基金中華學術外譯專案」正式立項，據悉，這是中國國際經濟法學界獲得此立項的第一例。按照全國社科規劃辦公室檔解釋，「中華學術外譯專案」是二〇一〇年由全國社會科學規劃領導小組批准設立的國家社科基金新的重大項目，旨在促進中外學術交流，推動中國社會科學優秀成果和優秀人才走向世界。它主要資助中國社會科學研究的優秀成果以外文形式在國外權威出版機構出版，進入國外主流發行傳播管道，增進國外對當代中國、中國社會科學以及中國傳統文化的了解，提高中國社會科學的國際影響力。

誠如專家評審意見所指出的那樣，這部英文專著「**對海外讀**

者全面了解中國國際經濟法學者較有代表性的學術觀點和主流思想具有重要意義。全書結構自成一體，觀點新穎，具有中國風格和中國氣派，闡釋了不同於西方發達國家學者的創新學術理念和創新學術追求，致力於初步創立起以馬克思主義為指導的具有中國特色的國際經濟法理論體系，為國際社會弱勢群體爭取公平權益鍛造了法學理論武器」。

陳安教授《中國的吶喊》一書，在展現作者中國特色學術思想和創新成果的同時，也為中國國際經濟法學界向世界發聲搭建了國際傳播平臺。本專著出版之後，反響強烈，國內外高端學者紛紛撰文評論與回應，迄今已經收到書評十四篇，即將由北京大學出版社出版的《國際經濟法學刊》第二十一卷第四期特闢專欄，以中英雙語集中發表，薈萃聚合，形成弘揚中華學術正氣、追求國際公平正義的共鳴強音。另外，鑒於此書出版後國際學術效應良好，德國Springer出版社又主動提出進一步開展學術合作的建議，要求陳安教授主持組織另外一套系列英文學術專著，總題定名為「當代中國與國際經濟法」（Modern China and International Economic Law），遴選和邀請一批中外知名學者圍繞這個主題，撰寫創新著作，提交該出版社出版，每年至少推出兩部。經認真磋商，雙方現已達成協議，正式簽署合同，並已啟動執行。相信此舉將會為進一步提升中華法學學術在世界學術界的知名度和影響力做出新的貢獻。

中國國家主席習近平曾經指出，「文明因交流而多彩，文明因互鑒而豐富」；「文明是平等的，人類文明因平等才有交流互鑒的前提」〔137〕近來他又強調中國在國際事務中應當積極「提出

中國方案、貢獻中國智慧」〔138〕。可以說，陳安教授上述力作向全球發行及其良好效應和後續舉措，對於促進**中外不同特色**的文明在**平等前提**下交流互鑒，對於在國際事務中提出中國方案，提升中國的話語權，都將起到應有的積極作用。

（林伍／報導）

The Enlightening and Thought-provoking Voice from China

The English monograph of Prof. An Chen, an octogenarian prominent professor at School of Law, Xiamen University and the Honorary Chairman of Chinese Society of International Economic Law (CSIEL for short, a nation-wide academic society), was recently published by Springer, a Grermany-located yet world-renowned Publisher, under a broad title *The Voice from China*: *An CHEN on International Economic Law*". It has now entered the main disseminating channel of academic works, arousing extensive atention in the circles of international economic law.

This monograph, with a total six parts and a colossal volume of 852 pages, has compiled within it 24 of Prof. Chen's articles written in English since early 1980s. These English articles were mostly published by well-known academic journals in and out of China. Guided by Marxism, they are all based on a common stand of China's national conditions and a consistent perspective of world weak groups, endeavoring to speak up a completely different voice from those of mainstream Western powers as regards the fundamental theoretical problems and hot or controversial issues in practice in the field of contemporary international economic law. During his active participation in world academic debates, Prof. Chen persistently advocates for the just proposals of the many developing countries, and tries his best to reveal the improperness and potential hazard of those misguiding mainstream theories from the West, so as to protect the equitable rights and interests of world weak groups including China. This is why the monographis entitled *"The Voice from China"*.

This English monograph has successfuly won the support of the Chinese Academic Foreign Translation Project (CAFTP), making itself the first of such kind within the academic circles of International Economic Law in China. According to the official specifications from the National Social Science Fund of China (NSSFC), CAFTP is one of the major categories of projects set by the NSSFC and approved by the National Philosophy and Social Science Planning Leading Group of China in 2010. This Project aims to promote Sino-foreign academic exchanges, and to facilitate the outstanding works as well as prominent scholars in the field of philosophy and social science towards the world's academic stage. For this purpose, a major part of such funding is allocated to sponsor the aforesaid achievements to be published in foreign language through authoritative publishers abroad. It is expected that, by such way of accessing and participating in foreign mainstream distribution channels, foreigners could have a better understanding of contemporary China, its philosophy and social sciences and its traditional culture. It is also expected that Sino-foreign academic exchange and dialogue would hence be more active, and the overseas influence of Chinese philosophy and social science would be enhanced.

In the Expert Review Report, some of the most professional peers opine that Prof. Chen's book "contributes vastly in the sense of introducing onto the world arena a series of typical academic views and mainstream ideas of Chinese International Economic Law scholars. The whole book is well and uniquely structured, and loaded with creative points of views. With its obvious Chinese character and style, this book has illustrated various innovational academic ideals and pursuits that are different from those voices & views preached by some authoritative scholars from Western developed powers. The author has endeavored to create a specific Chinese theoretical system of International Economic Law under the guidance of Marxism, to further serve as a theoretical weapon for the weak groups of international society to fight for their equitable rights and interests."

Apart from spreading the China-specific academic thoughts and creative achievements, Prof. Chen's monograph has also set up an international platform for Chinese scholars in international economic law to disseminate their viewpoints to the world. With the publishing of Prof. Chen's monograph, scholars as well as practitioners from domestic and abroad have one after another responded with book reviews and relating comments, which have now converged into a strong resonating voice of advancing and enriching China's academic justice and righteous proposals on international issues. As till now, 14 such reviews have been received and are to be published by Peking University Press as a special bilingual column in the forthcoming Chinese *Journal of International Economic Law* (Vol. 21, No.4). In light of this favorable and positive outcome, Springer offered to build a further cooperative relation, by asking Prof. Chen to preside and organize a whole series of English monographs entitled "Modern China and International Economic Law". This band new series will select and invite a batch of well-known scholars from China and abroad to contribute their innovative works around the theme of this series, at least two volumes of which will be published by Springer per year. After conscientious consultation, the two sides have reached and executed the final agreement. It is believed that such cooperation will make new contributions to promote the popularity and influence of China's legal academic research.

China's President Xi Jinping once pointed out in his speech in the UNESCO (United Nations Educational, Scientific, and Cultural Organization), that "[I]t is through communication that civilizations can show their multicolor, and it is through learning from each other that civilizations can be abundantly enriched ... All civilizations are equal, which forms the very premise for the communication and mutual learning." [139] He further emphasized that we should actively "raise

Chinese proposals and contribute Chinese wisdom" in international affairs.[140] It could be predictedthat, the above-referred book of Prof. An Chen, together with its consequent influences and follow-up measures, will prove its positive utility in boosting the equal communication and mutual learning among civilizations of different characteristics, as well as in enhancing China's voice of contributing its own prescriptions as to world affairs.

（翻譯：林　伍）

二、晨起臨窗坐　書香伴芳菲
—— 喜覽《中國的吶喊：陳安論國際經濟法》

郭壽康*

　　昨天傍晚收到了一批書報雜誌的郵件，今晨逐件拆封、翻閱時，忽然發現一本裝幀精美的全英文書。書名很別緻，*The Voice from China*（《中國的吶喊》或《來自中國的聲音》）。初想，平日與新聞、文藝各界接觸很少，剛要放在一邊，忽然發現，本書作者的署名，是大名鼎鼎的陳安教授，翻閱內容，主要是一九八〇年以來陳老在國外著名刊物上發表的二十四篇關於中國國際經濟法學的論文集合，這又是陳老的一大創舉。

　　陳安老先生是中國國際經濟法學界馳名中外的泰斗和大師，而且是中國特色國際經濟法學科的創始人之一，發表了一系列有分量的扛鼎之作。陳老也在國外著名刊物上發表了許多影響很大

的學術論文。但是，用時卻很難找到。這一次集二十四篇在國內外發表的中國國際經濟法學方面的論文成卷出版，給國內外業界專家提供了很大方便，使人們更便於聽到來自中國國際經濟法學界的聲音，功德無量。

陳老這個頭帶得很好。據我所知，國內專家也有在國外報、刊發表學術作品，但往往難於尋找。在中國出版的五卷本《陳安論國際經濟法》以及筆者的《郭壽康法學文選》中，都包括一部分在國外發表的論文作品，但全書用英文出版的，尚屬罕見。希望有更多的學者，用外語在國外權威出版社出版學術專著，從而進入國外學術著作主流發行傳播管道，以滿足世界上迫切需要聽到「來自中國的聲音」的日益強烈的要求。

（編輯：龔　宇）

By the Casementat Dawn, in the Fragrance of New Book

—A Joyful Browse of *The Voice from China:*
An CHEN on International Economic Law

Guo Shoukang*

This morning when I was sealing off and leafing through a pile of newly received books, journals and magazines, a rather weldesigned English book suddenly caught my eyes. With its unconventional title: *The Voice from China*, it first occurred to me that I seldom had contacts with media and literature circles. When I was just about to put it aside, I suddenly saw that the author of this book is Prof. An Chen, a widely renowned scholar. After I skipped through the contents, I found it a compilation of 24 articles successively published by Prof. Chen since 1980 in foreign journals, all with a focus on the topic of Chinese school of International Economic Law (IEL). This should be deemed as another pioneering work of Chen.

Mr. An Chen, an elderly gentleman, is a master of the discipline of IEL, and has a worldly recognized reputation in this academic circle. He is also one of the founding members of the Chinese School of IEL, or IEL with Chinese characteristics, for he has published a series of heavy-weight masterpieces, as well as a number of research papers in well-known journals. These journal articles are, however, not that handy when people feel the need to refer to. Now that Prof. Chen's 24 articles on Chinese IEL are compiled into one volume, it will be bound to foster a more convenient way for peers, both from domestic and abroad, to hear a Voice from Chinese academic circle of IEL. The benefits that go along with this publication are definitely beyond measure.

Mr. Chen has set a very instructive leading example. As far as I know, there are other scholars of China who have also published their research results in foreign journals. But these articles share a common deficit of being inconvenient to find and collect. In the domestically published works such as *An CHEN on International Economic Law* (Five Volumes), and my *Guo Shoukng's Selected Works on Law*, there are some thesis writen in English, too. But it is rather rare, at least for now, that a published book of Chinese scholar is all in English. It is my sincere hope, that more scholars of China can publish their works through authoritative foreign press, and enter the worldwide mainstream transmission channel of academic works, so as to fulfill the increasingly strengthened demands of world people to hear the "Voice from China".

（翻譯：楊　帆）

三、弘中華正氣　為群弱發聲

曹建明*

中華人民共和國最高人民檢察院

弘中華正氣　為群弱發聲

尊敬的陳安教授：

當我收到您的英文專著《中國的吶喊：陳安論國際經濟法》，欣喜之外，更是一種感動和震撼。多年來，您一直希望我們以文會友、以書會友。這些年我先後收到了您的《陳安論國際經濟法》五卷本、《國際經濟法學芻言》上下卷等鴻篇巨著。我的書架上，整整齊齊排列著您主編的《國際經濟法學刊》，至今已是第二十一卷！打開您《中國的吶喊》，更是讓我感到份量很重、很重……

這是您的又一部力作。這部專著不僅深刻闡述了當代國際經

濟法的基本理論問題，而且緊密結合國際經濟法理論與實踐，深入探討了構建國際經濟新秩序的熱點難點問題，自成體系，相容並包，翔集事理。我知道，字裡行間，凝聚的都是您幾十年潛心學術研究之成果，是您又一部研精覃思的著作。這本專著作為國家社科基金中華學術外譯項目以英文正式出版，對於促進世界更加了解和理解當代中國必將產生重要影響，無疑是中國國際經濟法學界的一件大事。

讓我感動的是，您在國際經濟法學方面的造詣很深，學術成就斐然。但是，耄耋之年，您至今仍在孜孜不倦，辛勤耕耘，不斷深入思考國際經濟法學特別是中國國際經濟法學的發展，並為之奉獻了自己的全部心血和智慧。先生的精神實乃難能可貴，足以讓那些心浮氣躁、急功近利的後輩晚生汗顏。我們年輕一代，無論是法學研究工作者還是司法工作者，都應當學習和弘揚您這種嚴謹治學、學為人師的學術品格和行為風範。

世界多極化、經濟全球化和社會資訊化的趨勢深入發展，科技進步日新月異，各種文化碰撞交融，使當今世界正經歷著前所未有的歷史性變革。中國已經歷了三十多年的改革開放歷程，中國比以往任何時候更加重視國際法的研究，更加重視國際規則的制定和運用。全面推進依法治國，離不開法學理論的繁榮發展。構建開放型新經濟新體制，離不開國際經濟法的研究。可以說，擺在我們面前的一系列國際法問題包括國際經濟法問題，既是理論研究，更是應用研究，我們必須理論聯繫實際。我們需要學習借鑑外國法學先進理論，更需要立足於複雜多變的國際形勢和國際關係，立足於國際經濟法理論與我國對外開放實踐的緊密結

合，積極推動建立公正合理的國際政治經濟新秩序，有自己的思考和建議，並且敢於發出中國聲音。

在這本英文專著第一編裡，我看到其中一篇熟悉的文章，即《「黃禍」論的本源、本質及其最新霸權「變種」:「中國威脅施」》。這篇專論我有幸在二〇一二年就拜讀過，它以史實為據，史論結合，深入剖析和批判「中國威脅論」的本質和危害，讀了之後令人蕩氣回腸、拍案叫好，這些年來，您始終立足中國國情和廣大發展中國家的共同立場，始絳秉持國家經濟主權原則，強調維護發展中國家利益，宣導公平互利、南北合作、南南合作，探索建立國際經濟新秩序的規律和路徑，實事求是，與時俱進，不斷探索，追求真理，特別是敢於提出與西方國家傳統觀點乃至主流觀點截然不同的觀點，真正響亮地發出了中國的聲音，不斷推動著中國國際經濟法學的理論創新與實踐創新。從您的身上，我更是深深感受到了我們每一個國際法學者和法律工作者義不容辭的責任和使命。

真誠感謝您為國際經濟法學界奉獻了又一部力作！衷心祝願您健康長壽！

曾建明

二〇一四年九月十六日

Spreading China's Justice, Voicing for the Global Weak

Cao Jianming*

Dear Esteemed Prof. An Chen

Upon receiving your recent published English writing monograph
—*The Voice from China: An CHEN on International Economic Law*, I
felt more touched and shocked than delighted. For decades, you have
been encouraging us to meet friends through sharing our articles and
books. I alone have successively received a number of big treatises of
yours, such as *An CHEN on International Economic Law* (Five Volumes),
and *CHENS Papers on International Economic Law (Two Volumes)*. On
my bookshelf arrays neatly a complete serie of Chinese *Journal of
International Economic Law* (from Vol. 1 to the present Vol. 21!). I can
literally feel the heavy weight of your new book when I hold it in hand
and turn over the cover...

Undoubtedly this is your another masterpiece. It has not only
elaborated in depth the many fundamental theoretical problems of
contemporary international economic law (IEL), but also deeply discussed
some hot and controversial issues regarding the establishment of a new
international economic order (NIEO), with a close integration of relating
IEL theory and practice. By adopting an all-inclusive approach to
synthesize facts and reasonings, this new monograph has created a
unique system similar to no other. As I see, this new monograph, which
is pervaded among the words and lines with all your hard work,

condenses your meticulous research and thorough thinking, and embodies your decades' devotion to and fruits of this subject. Supported by the Chinese Academic Foreign Translation Project of the China National Social Sciences Fund, the publishing of this English monograph must bring significant influence on promoting the global understanding of contemporary China, and is with no doubt a major event in the Chinese academic circle of international economic law.

What moves me most is that, apart from your many academic accomplishments in the field of IEL, and despite of your **eighties-odd age, you have not yet ceased in thinkng and writing on this subject, and still are tirelessly and entrely devoted your heart and wisdom to promoting the development of Chinese school of IEL. Such spirit of yours is quite rare and commendable**, and can shame all the youngsters who are impatient and eager for quick success. We younger generations of legal researchers and practitioners shall earn and carry forward such academic personality and behavioral demeanor of yours, to carry out meticulous research and to disseminate righteous knowledge orideals.

With the continuous deepening of world multipolarization, economic globalization and society informatization, as well as the fast innovation of science and technology, the collision and fusion of various cultures, contemporary world is now experiencing an unprecedented historical change. After over three decades of opening-up and reformation, China is now attaching importance more than ever before to there search of international law, and the making and application of international rules. The comprehensive promotion of managing state affairs according to law is indispensable to the prosperity of legal theoretical research. The establishment of a novel economic system that opens up to the world is indispensable to there search of IEL. A series of problems that we encounter,no matter regarding International law or IEL, are of theoretical research as well as of practical one. We must thus link theory to practice. Also, we need to learn and benefit from the Foreign advanced theories; especially need to base on the complicated and changeable International situations and international relations, as well as a close combination of international economic legal theory with our past open-up practices. Furthermore, we also need to actively promote the establishment of a fair and reasonable new international economic and political order, to form our own thoughts and suggestions, and dare to express our own Voice from China.

I have found a familiar article in Part I of your English monograph, namely "On the Source, Essence of 'Yellow Peril' Doctrine and Its Latest Hegemony 'Variant' —The 'China Threat' Doctrine", which I had the fortune to read when it first came out in 2012. This article has carried out a very thorough dissection of and pointed critique against the"China Threat" Doctrine. Based on historical facts and with a well-organized integration of history and theory, this article is soul-stirring, making readers can't help striking the table and shouting bravo. For he past decades, you have been consistently standing on China's situations and the common ground ofthe vast developing countries, adhering to the principle of national economic sovereignty, emphasizing the preservation of national interests of the weak groups, advocating equity and mutual benefit, South-North C ooperation and South- South Cooperation, and exploring the rules and approaches to establishing a new international economic order. You have been persistently advancing with the times, keep exploring and pursuing the truth from facts, and especialy daring to express thought-provoking viewpoints that are diferent from or even contrary to traditional or mainstream views fromthe West. Such resounding Voices from China of yours have been keeping pushing forward the innovation of international economic legal theory and practice with Chinese characteristics. You have set up a model, from whom I have deeply felt the responsibility and mission that every international law scholar and practitioner is bound to and shall under take.

I sincerely thank you for contributing another new masterpiece to the academic circle of IEL, and cordially wish you good health and along life!

CAO Jianming

September 16, 2014

（翻譯：楊　帆）

四、老艄公的鏗鏘號子 [*]　發出時代的最強音

—— 《中國的吶喊：陳安論國際經濟法》讀後的點滴感悟

曾令良^{**}

金秋收穫時節，欣悉《中國的吶喊：陳安論國際經濟法》
（ *The Voice from China: An CHENon International Economic Law* ，以
下簡稱《中國的吶喊》）面世。這部新著集中了中國國際經濟法
學奠基人之一陳安先生三十多年學術研究之精華，由舉世聞名的
國際權威出版社同時向全球推出紙質版精裝本和電子版。晚輩獲
陳老前輩惠贈其巨著，受寵若驚，感激之餘，不禁感歎如下數
語，以饗讀者。

創新遠征　教材開路

陳先生不愧為學界泰斗，學術常青常新。他數十年如一日，
研究不息，筆耕不止，出版和發表的著述字數以數百萬計。根據
晚輩初步觀察，中國改革開放後的頭二十年，陳先生研究的重心
主要是通過主編不同版本的《國際經濟法》教材、創辦和主編
《國際經濟法論叢》及其改版的《國際經濟法學刊》，創立和不
斷完善中國的國際經濟法學體系。此外，他還在國際商事仲裁和
國際投資爭端解決等領域著書立說。與此同時，陳先生在國
（境）內外一系列重要學術刊物上就國際經濟法基本理論和實踐
中的重大和熱點問題分別用中文和英文發表了數十篇具有重要影
響的論文。

「三步進行曲」與「陳氏國際經濟法」

進入二十一世紀，陳先生的學術成就集中體現在其先後出版的三部巨著之中。這三部代表作可謂是陳先生近十幾年來學術創新的「三步進行曲」，節節攀升，直至巔峰。首先，由北京大學出版社於二〇〇五年推出《國際經濟法學芻言》上、下兩卷本，共計二百一十餘萬字。三年後的二〇〇八年，在原有著述的基礎上由復旦大學出版社推出了《陳安論國際經濟法學》五卷本，共計三百餘萬字。誠如先生自言：這部新著「並不是《芻言》的簡單再版或擴容」，而是作者「針對本學科領域新問題進行探索的心得體會的全面增訂和創新匯輯」。更令人震撼的是，如今，雖然先生已八十五歲高齡，但是追求學術之壯心不已，再次由國際權威出版機構向全球推出其英文巨著《中國的吶喊》。至此，「陳氏國際經濟法」不僅深深紮根和流行於華語世界，而且將在全球各種不同文化的國家和地區廣泛傳播和推廣，必將產生深遠的國際影響。

「三性」理論與「6C律」

《中國的吶喊》重申和再現了「陳氏國際經濟法」。[141]二十世紀九〇年代初，陳先生率先提出了國際經濟法學的「三性」基本特徵，即「邊緣性」「綜合性」和「獨立性」，並將這一新的理論貫穿於此後他主編的教材、出版的著作和發表的論文之中。「三性」理論科學地揭示了國際經濟法學作為一門新興學科的內涵和外延，闡明了國際經濟法與其他相鄰學科之間的區別與聯繫，論證了這一新興學科體系上的綜合性和相對獨立性。如今，

「三性」理論早已被國際經濟法學界所普遍接受，廣泛應用於中國的國際經濟法教學與研究之中，結束了曾長期困擾學界的關於國際經濟法學的定性之爭。

《中國的吶喊》創造性地揭示了國際經濟關係、國際經濟秩序和國際經濟法發展與更新「6C律」。「6C律」是陳先生通過洞察和總結數十年來圍繞建立國際經濟新秩序的南北鬥爭的歷程而得出的規律性認識，並預言這一規律在全球化快速發展的當下和明天將持續下去。所謂「6C律」（依筆者看來，似乎是「7C律」），就是描述國際經濟秩序和法律規範破舊立新的螺旋式上升軌跡，即「矛盾」（Contadition）→「衝突或交鋒」（Conflict）→「磋商」（Consultation）→「妥協」（Compromise）→「合作」（Cooperation）→ 協調「Coordination」→「新的矛盾」（Contradiction New）。[142] 陳先生巧妙地運用七個英文單詞的首字母予以概括和表述，既貼切，又便於記憶，其學術智慧可見一斑。

捍衛弱者主權　抨擊國際霸權

《中國的吶喊》向國際社會闡釋中國對外經濟交往的法理內涵和原則，揭露當今美國等國宣揚的「中國威脅」論是近代西方列強「黃禍」論的翻版，二者的DNA 一脈相承，其本質是「政治騙術」，其目的是蠱惑人心，誤導國際輿論，貶損中國。[143] 陳先生鋒利的言辭依據的是歷史和事實，秉持的是正義和公理，捍衛的是中國的正面形象和正當合法的利益。

《中國的吶喊》先後三論中國在建立國際經濟新秩序中的戰略定位。陳先生主張中國應成為「建立國際經濟新秩序的積極推

手」「南南聯合自強的中流砥柱之一」；中國應「既堅持戰略原則的堅定性」，「又審時度勢，堅持策略戰術的靈活性」。[144] 依陳先生之見，正在和平崛起的中國「不宜只是現存國際經濟秩序的『改良者』、南北矛盾的『協調者』而應是『改革者』之一」[145]。我堅信，這一觀點道出了中國和其他發展中國家及其國際經濟法學界共同的心聲，並且已經得到一些歐美學者的贊許。

旗幟鮮明、直抒己見，是陳先生為人、做事、治學的原則和特點，這同樣貫穿於《中國的吶喊》之中。這裡僅舉一例。近年來，在改革現有國際經濟法及國際經濟秩序的問題上，西方國際法學界一度流行「新自由主義經濟秩序」論、「WTO憲政秩序」論、「經濟民族主義擾亂全球化秩序」論。對此，陳先生告誡中國和廣大發展中國家及其學人，不可盲從或附和，應實行有鑒別的取捨，尤其要警惕西方「淡化」「弱化」主權和鼓吹主權「過時」的「理論陷阱」。[146]

《中國的吶喊》將廣大發展中國家描述為「全球弱勢群體」，強調這些弱勢群體國家應「珍惜和善用經濟主權」，呼籲「南南聯合自強」，反對美國的單邊主義和西方強勢群體國家在國際經濟和貿易關係中實行「雙重標準」，堅持多邊主義，以爭取和維護全球弱勢群體在國際經濟秩序中的平等地位和公平權益。[147]

旗幟鮮明　中國風格　中國氣派　時代強音

總之，《中國的吶喊》具有鮮明的中國風格和中國氣派，代表著中國國際經濟法學先進的理論，發出的是全球弱勢群體國家強烈呼籲建立公平、公正的國際經濟新秩序的共同心聲。《中國

的吶喊》的出版，再次體現了一代宗師非凡的學術氣度和追求學術卓越的精神。陳先生不愧為中國國際經濟法學的舵手和國際經濟秩序「破舊立新」的旗手。更重要的是，陳先生學術成就的重大意義和影響已經超越了國際經濟法學本身，正如有關國際機構的高級人士所評價的，「(《中國的吶喊》) 是對當代世界政治研究和認識的重要貢獻」；同時，「應成為了解和研究中西關係人士的必讀物，尤其是應作為發展中國家的領導人、高級經貿談判官員培訓的指導用書」，甚至作為這些國家高等院校的教材。[148]

總之，《中國的吶喊》無疑是中國國際經濟法學界具有代表性的學術權威之音，是向世界發出的強音和高音。我堅信，這部巨著的出版將對國際經濟法學的發展產生深遠的影響！

（編輯：龔　宇）

The Sonorous Work Song of an Old Helmsman of International Economic Law

—Some Reflections and Thoughts After Reading *The Voice from China: An CHEN on International Economic Law*

Zeng Lingliang*

In this golden harvest season, it is delighted to know that *The Voice from* China: An CHEN on International Economic Law (hereafter referred as *The Voice from China)* was published by Springer, the world-wide well-known publisher, both in paper and electronic versions. This new monograph colects the very essence of academic research achievements of Professor An Chen for the past 30-odd years, who is one of the founders of Chinese international economic law. I, as a younger generation of the discipline and receiver of this great book, thank him for his kindness. In addition to gratefulness to him, I would like to make a few words of my superficial understanding of this book as follows:

Professor Chen has proved himself to be a leading scholar of the discipline of Chinese international economic law. His academic research is evergreen and often up-dated. He has never stopped studying and writing for several decades, producing numerous publications both at home and abroad. According to my preliminary observation, his studies in the first twenty years after China engaged itself in "reform-and-open policy", focused on creation and completion of the Chinese discipline of international economic law by means of compiling international economic law textbooks in various editions and founding Journal of International Economic Lawin Chinese as editor-in-chief. In addition, some parts of his writings relate to theory creation in the areas of international commercial arbitration and international investment dispute resolution. At the same time, he published quite a number of articles on key and hot issues both concerning basic theories and practices of international economic law in some important academic journals in Chineseor English.

Since the 21th century, Professor Chen's academic achievements have been reflected intensively and respectively in his three masterpieces.

These three magnificent masterpieces might be well-caledas "trilogy" of his academic creation in the most recent twenty years, which steadily climbs up to the peak. He firstly published the monograph entitled *CHENS Papers on International Economic Law* (two volumes) in Peking University Press in 2005. Three years later in 2008, he published the new expanded edition (five volumes altogether) entitled *An CHEN on International Economic Law* in Fudan University Press. This new edition, as its author described, "is not simply a re-edition or expansion in volume, but a collection of comprehensive revision and enlargement as well as creation made by the author after his continuous exploration of new issues arising in the discipline". Today, in spite of his age of 85, he continues pursuing his academic excellence by publishing hisgreatwork *The Voice from China* in English version in Springer who enjoys high international reputation. Hence, Chen's doctrines of international economic law not only has been deeply rooted and popular in the Chinese society, but also will spread and extend globally, thus resulting in far-reaching international influence.

The Voice from China reaffirms and reproduces the theory of "three basic features" [149] persistently advocated by Professor Chen for decades. This theory was first put forward by him in early 1990s, namely the marginality, comprehensiveness and independence of international economic law discipline. Since then on, he has penetrated and integrated the theory into his subsequent textbooks, monographs and published articles as well as various lectures on international economic law. This new theory scientifically brings to light the connotation and extension of international economic law as a newly-born discipline, and identifies the differences from and links to other neighboring disciplines. Nowadays, the theory of "three basic features" has been widely recognized by international economic law scholars and extensively applied in teaching and studying of international economic law courses in China's universities and colleges, thus ending the debates on definition of international economic law which had persecuted scholars ever before.

The Voice from China creates the "6C Track" or "6C Rule" format embedded in the law-making process of international economic relations since the end of the Second World War. The "6C" means Contradiction → Conflict → Consultation → Compromise → Cooperation → Coordination → Contradiction New. [150] It seems to be a "7C" process instead. This format description demonstrates via the author's critical eyes the track of struggles between the North and the South in establishing international economic order for the past several decades and expects that this track of development in spirals will be continuing in today's and future world of globalization. Professor Chen skillfully uses the seven key English words which all share the first letter "C" to summarize this circle development tendency, which is both precise and easy for memory. We could appreciate the wisdom of an academic master underlying it.

The Voice from China explains to the international society the Chinese jurisprudence and legal principles in international intercourses, exposes that "China Threat" Doctrine advocated by the U.S. and a few other countries today is in essence the refurbished version of "Yellow Peril" Doctrine advocated by the western powers in the past. He sharply observes that the DNA of the two theories is the same and their essence is a "political trickery".[151] His sharp words are based on history and facts, uphold the justice and generally acknowledged truth and maintain the positive image of China and its legitimate rights and interest.

The Voice from China contributes a special Part (part III) to analyze China's strategic position on contemporary international economic order issues. It proclaims that China, as the biggest developing country, should "play an active part in promoting the establishing of the NEIO", "become one of the driving forces and mainstays of the South-South Coalition".[152] In the course of establishment the NEIO, China should adhere to the firmness its strategic principles on the one hand and tactical flexibility on the other hand. In the view of Professor Chen, the peacefully rising China should not only be an "ameliorator" of the current international economic order and "intermediary" of the South-North contradiction, but also one of the "reformers" of the order,[153] which I believe expresses the common voice and wishes of the vast developing countries and their scholars and deserves the blessing of some European and American academics.

Up-holding clear-cut stand and speaking his mind is the principle and feature of Professor Chen in his behavior, research and dealing with matters, which is also reflected in *The Voice from China*. For instance, in recent years, theories of "neoliberalistic economic order", "constitutional order of WTO" and "economic nationalism's disturbance of globalization" have been popular in western academics of international law. However, Professor Chen warns China and vast developing countries and their international economic law scholars not to follow these theories blindly, but make choices identifiably, with special guard against "theories trap" which fades out and weakens sovereignty or claims sovereignty old-fashioned. [154]

The Voice from China describes the vast developing countries as the "global weak group" and stresses that these weak countries should "cherish and take a proper use of sovereignty". The author calls for the "South-South coalition and self-improvement" to oppose unilateralism of the U.S and "double standards" by the strong group of western countries and persist in multilateralism so as to strive for and maintain the equal rights and fair interests in the international economic order. [155]

In short, *The Voice from China* bears a distinctive Chinese-style ballet. The book represents the advanced theory of the discipline of Chinese international economic law and delivers the common voice of the weak group countries calling for the establishment of a new international economic order with fairness and justice. It reproduces a master's spirit of extraordinary academic tolerance and pursuing academic excellence. Professor Chen deserves the title of "helmsman" of Chinese international economic law and "the flag bearer" of the international economic order who promotes to "destroy the old and establish the new". What is more important is that the significance of his academic achievements surpasses the discipline of international economic law itself. Just as a retired official of the UNATAD observed, Professor Chen's work is "an important contribution to the study and understanding of contemporary world politics", and "should be made subject for required reading and study by leaders and policy makers in all developing countries" and "should also be part of the curriculum in developing countries ministries, universities, and institutes of higher learning that prepare new cadres and officials for participating and work in the multilateral sphere". [156]

In conclusion, *The Voice from China*, just like the sonorous work song of an old helmsman, is undoubtedly a representative academic voice of the Chinese academics of international economic law as well as its high and strong voice to the whole world. I am confident that the publication of this master work will produce a far-reaching significance for the development of international economic law studies.

（翻譯：曾令良）

五、天下視野　家國情懷　公平秉守
——讀《中國的吶喊：陳安論國際經濟法》

車丕照*

　　由國際著名出版社Springer出版發行的陳安先生的英文著作《中國的吶喊：陳安論國際經擠法》（*The Voice from China: An CHEN on International Economic Law*）已經問世。該書彙集了陳安先生數

十年來在國際經濟法研究方面的重要學術成果，集中向世界展示了一位資深的中國國際經濟法學者的立場、觀點和方法。如果我們要對該書所反映出的陳安先生的學術思想與學術風格作一個簡單概括，或許可以歸結為這樣三句話：天下視野、家國情懷和公平秉守。

天下視野

國際經濟法學者原本就應具有觀察問題的天下視野。但事實上，許多學者的學術視野局限於西方發達國家的國際經濟法理論與實踐，甚至完全唯西方標準馬首是瞻，以至於「法律全球化」成了「美國法的全球化」。[157]

陳安先生的研究雖然仍關注美國等西方發達國家的理論與實踐，但卻具有更為廣闊的視角，即國際經濟秩序的視角。法律的首要價值是其秩序價值。「秩序構成了人類理想的要素和社會活動的基本目標。」[158]同樣的道理，國際經濟法的首要價值應該是其在確立國際經濟秩序方面的功能。事實上，當今的國際經濟秩序是在各種國際經濟法律規範的共同作用下得以維繫的。在這些法律規範中，既有國際法規範，又有國內法規範；既有私法規範，又有公法規範。陳安先生在二十多年前即已為我們清晰地描繪出這樣一個支撐國際經濟秩序的國際經濟法體系。[159]由於國際社會並不存在代表社會利益的「世界政府」，因此，國際經濟秩序的形成，即國際經濟法律制度的形成是各國及其他各類實體長期行為積累的結果。由此形成的秩序，儘管優於無秩序，但卻可能並非公平。正因為如此，從二十世紀六〇年代起，世界上形

成了以「公平」為價值追求的「建立國際經濟新秩序」的思潮和運動。這場運動雖然尚未達到預期的效果，但仍舊取得了一些現實的成果。國際貿易領域中的「普惠制」和國際環境領域中的「共同卻有區別的責任」就是其中的代表。中國國際經濟法學者雖然也關注過國際經濟新秩序的研究，但少有像陳安先生那樣持續、深入地對國際經濟新秩序加以探索和研究的。在中國老一輩國際經濟法學者當中，陳安先生關於國際經濟新秩序的研究應該是最具代表性的。儘管「建立國際經濟新秩序」的運動在二十多年前即已開始陷入低潮，但陳安先生的相關研究依舊勢頭不減，並鼓勵大家繼續深化該領域的研究。在《中國的吶喊》中，陳安先生高瞻遠矚地指出：「建立國際經濟新秩序乃是數十億人爭取國際經濟平等地位的共同目標和行動綱領。自通過南南合作而建立國際經濟新秩序的方針形成以來，弱勢國家爭取平等國際經濟地位的努力，雖歷經潮起潮落，但不斷衝破明灘暗礁，持續向前。因此，應從長遠的戰略視角對這場運動予以分析和評估，而不宜從短期戰術角度考慮其得失。」〔160〕中國優秀知識份子歷來就有「先天下之憂而憂，後天下之樂而樂」的價值取向，而這樣一種以天下為己任的胸懷，對於當代知識份子來說，首先就應表現為學術研究的「天下視野」。

家國情懷

在以天下為視野的同時，陳安先生的學術研究也明顯地表露出家國情懷。這種家國情懷主要體現為兩個方面：一是對中國國家利益的深切關注，二是以國家為中心的研究進路。

　　陳安先生的學術研究始終表現出對中國國家立場和國家利益的關切。在《論中國在建立國際經濟新秩序中的戰略定位》（What Should Be China's Strategic Position in the Establishment of New International Economic Order?）一文中，陳安先生指出：「在建立國際經濟新秩序的時代大潮流中，中國的自我戰略定位理應一如既往，繼續是旗幟鮮明的積極推動者之一，是現存國際經濟秩序的改革者之一。不宜只是現存國際經濟秩序的『改良者』南北矛盾的『協調者』」[161] 在《中外雙邊投資協定中的四大「安全閥」是否應貿然拆除？》（Should the Four "Great Safeguards" in Sino-foreign BITs Be Hastily Dismantled?）一文中，陳安先生語重心長地建議：在中外雙邊投資協定談判中，中國應堅持有關國際法授權的規定，善於掌握四大「安全閥」[162]，以有效保護中國的國家利益，並在確立合理的外國投資法律規範及建立國際經濟新秩序的過程中發揮示範作用。[163] 陳安先生的學術研究始終跟蹤中國政府的相關實踐。他所帶領的學術團隊與國家商務部等政府部門一直保持很好的互動關系。他的許多研究成果都得到中國相關政府部門的重視和採納。陳安先生的學術研究中所包含的這份家國情懷令人感動、值得稱讚。

　　陳安先生的學術研究中還表現出另外一種「家國情懷」，即以國家為中心的研究進路。如前所述，陳安先生很早就界定了國際經濟法的範圍，指出：「由於國際經濟法是用來調整各種公、私主體之間跨國經濟關係的法律規範。所以，它並非專屬於單一的國際公法，不單純是國際公法的分支，不僅僅是適用於經濟領域的國際公法。恰恰相反，它的內涵和外延早已大大突破了傳統

的國際公法的局限，與國際私法和國際商法交叉，並及於國內經濟法、民法和商法，從而構成了一個多門類、跨學科的邊緣性綜合體。」[164] 儘管如此，陳安先生的國際經濟法研究基本上是以國家為中心展開的，而幾乎不涉足私人之間交易的法律問題。於是，在《中國的吶喊》一書中，我們看到陳安先生關於美國單邊主義與WTO多邊體制衝突的研究（The Three Big Rounds of US Unilateralism Versus WTO Multilateralism Duringthe Last Decade）、對中國在建立國際經擠新秩序中的戰略立場的研究（What Should Be China's Strategic Position in the Establishment of New International Economic Order?）、對建立國際經擠新秩序過程中南南合作的研究（A Reflection of the South-South Coalitioninthe Last Half Century from the Perspective of International Economic Lawmaking: From Bandung, Doha, and Cancun to Hong Kong）以及關於中國夕蔔資政策與法律的研究（To Open Wider or to Close Again: China's Foreign Investment Policies and Laws）等。即使是就具體案例所進行的研究，陳安先生也是圍繞著國家與私人的關係而展開的。陳安先生的這種研究進路反映出他對國家這一國際社會的基本主體的重視。儘管私人之間的國際經濟交往是國際經濟法現實的和邏輯的起點：沒有私人之間的國際經濟交往，就沒有國家對國際經濟交往的管理；沒有國家對國際經濟交往的管理，也就沒有國家之間的衝突、協調和合作。但與私人相比，國家是更為重要的國際經濟法主體。在調整私人之間交易關係的民商法性質的規範逐漸趨同的情況下，國際經濟法體系中更為活躍的部分是國際經濟活動的國家管理制度及國家間的協調和合作制度。陳安先生歸納

出的「6C律」Contradiction（矛盾）→ Conflict（衝突或交鋒）→ Consultation（磋商）→ Compromise（妥協）→ Cooperation（合作）→ Coordination（協調）→ Contradiction New（新的矛盾）[165] 系統而準確地闡明了國家行為與國際經濟法的關係及演變規律。

公平秉守

　　陳安先生學術研究的另外一個特色就是對公平的執著秉守。

　　如果我們從國家層面觀察國際經濟法，如果我們將國際經濟法的形式限定為制定法和習慣，那麼，當今的國際經濟法從整體上看只能達到「互惠」（reciprocity），而無法達到「公平」（equity）。「互惠」是相互對等的讓與，而「公平」則要求考慮特定情形下的利益分配，這種分配並不要求是互惠和對等的。由於當今的國際經濟法是歷史上各類規則的積累，平等地適用這些規則，以致創設新的「互惠」規則，都無法在國際社會成員間實現真正的公平，因此，「建立新的國際經濟秩序」也就是要「建立公平合理的國際經濟秩序」。如前所述，陳安先生的研究所貫穿的一個基本思想，就是追求國際經濟秩序的公平合理。「公平」是比「秩序」更高一級別的價值。人類社會中的「秩序」僅僅表明穩定的社會關係的存在，而「公平」則深入到對「秩序」內容的評判或「秩序」模式的選擇。在《關於WTO的法治、立法、執法、守法與變法的法理思考》（Some Jurisprudential Thoughts upon WTO's Law-Governing, Law-Making, L.aw- Ef forcing, Law-Abiding, and Law-Reforming）一文中，陳安先生指出：「面對當今現存的各種國際經濟立法，包括形形色色的國際經貿『遊戲規則』，國際弱勢群

體固然不能予以全盤否定，也無力加以徹底改造，但更不能全盤接受，服服帖帖，心甘情願地忍受其中蘊含的各種不公與不平。」[166] 關於建立公平合理的國際經濟秩序的途徑，陳安先生認為其根本途徑在於弱小國家的團結合作。他認為：「在今後一系列全球性問題的國際論壇和多邊談判中，南方各發展中國家比以往任何時候都更加需要采取集體行動，才能贏得公平、公正和合理的結果。為了維護發展中國家共同的根本利益，必須適應形勢的變化，通過精心研究和科學設計，調整和更新77國集團的綱領，協調不同的利益，以增強共識和內部的凝聚力。」[167]

陳安先生對國際經濟秩序的公平與合理的不懈和熱切的追求——無論建立國際經濟新秩序的運動是處於高潮或低谷，除其他原因外，與其自身經歷有關。他在《中國的吶喊》一書的前言中寫道：「我年輕的時候，在學習中華燦爛文明的同時，也從教育中知曉並親身感受到中華民族的悲慘危機。複雜的情緒逐漸培養起我強烈的民族自豪感和愛國主義的思想，我的反對國際霸權主義的決心，以及我的努力實現社會公正和支持世界上所有弱小國家的志向。」[168]

陳安先生與姚梅鎮先生等一起在中國開創了國際經濟法學這門學科，並繼姚梅鎮先生之後成為中國國際經濟法學界的旗手。他在九〇年代初就系統地論述了國際經濟法學的邊緣性、綜合性和獨立性，[169] 並對質疑國際經濟法學的「不科學」或「不規範」論、「大胃」論或「長臂」論、「浮躁」論或「炒熱」論以及「翻版」論或「舶來」論作出了系統的批駁，[170] 為國際經濟法學的發展奠定了堅實的基礎。如今，陳安先生的英文著作又結集出版，

在國際學界發出了中國國際經濟法學者的聲音。我們期待隨著陳安先生的引領，中國學者將在國際社會發出更為響亮的和聲。

（編輯：龔　宇）

Global Perspective, State Position and Equity Pursuance

—Introducing *The Voice from China: An CHEN on International Economic Law*

Che Pizhao

Professor An Chen's book, *The Voice from China*: An CHEN on International Economic Law, newly published by internationally leading academic publisher Springer, contains representative articles written by the author over the past three decades, showing specific ideas of a senior and eminent Chinese scholar of international economic law. We may sum up the author's wisdom and style reflected in this book with several words, namely: the global perspective, the state position, and the equity pursuance.

1. Global Perspective

A scholar of international economic law is expected to observe issues with a global perspective. However, the views of many scholars are limited to the theories and practices of Western developed countries, and globalization of laws, for them, is the globalization of the laws of the United States. [171]

Although Professor Chen has been paying close attention to the theories and practice of the United States and other developed countries, he insists on studying from a broader perspective—the international economic order. The primary value of law is order. "Order constitutes the ideal element of mankind as well as the basic target of social activities." [172] Similarly, the most essential value of international economic law is its function on establishing international economic order. In fact, the current international economic order is maintained by the co-function of various rules of international economic laws, which include both international law and domestic law, private law and public law. Such a system of international economic law maintaining the international economic order was first demonstrated to us by Professor Chen as early as more than 20 years ago. [173] Due to the absence of a world government to represent the interests of the international society, the formation of international economic order, as well as the international economic legal system is a result of historically accumulated practices of states and other actors. Such an order, though better than disorder, may be far from equity. This is why a trend of thought and movement of the new international economic order aiming at achieving equity was radically developed since 1960s. There have been some fruits from this movement, such as GSP arrangements in international trade law and the principle of common but differentiated responsibilities in international environment law, although there is still a long road to achieve its expected objectives. There are Chinese scholars paying attention to the study of the new international economic order (NIEO), but few like Professor Chen who keeps continuous and in-depth studies on the new international economic order. Among the senior generation of Chinese scholars in the area of international economic law, Professor Chen's study on the new international economic order may be the most representative one. Although the movement of establishing the new international economic order began to hit its bottom about 20 years ago, Professor Chen has never been disappointed; rather, he has consistently encouraged others to further study in this field. In *The Voice from China*, Professor Chen shows great foresight that "the establishment of NIEO is the common goal and program of action of billions of people who are striving for equal international economic status. Since the formation of the policy of establishing the NIEO by way of South-South Coalition, the movement of striving for equal international status of the weak states has undergone ebb and flow, and kept on progressing in a spiral course in spite of layers of barriers. Therefore, the analyses and evaluation of the movement should be carried out from a long-term strategic perspective, not from a perspective of gains or loss in the short run." [174] "Feeling anxious before all the others and enjoying happiness after all the others" is the creed of outstanding Chinese scholars in history. For today's scholars, to have the world in mind, should firstly keep a global perspective in academic studies.

2. State Position

While taking a global perspective, Professor Chen's book is an embodiment of the standpoint of the state. The state position is clearly expressed by his profound concern for China's interests and his state-centered research approach.

Professor Chen's academic study always shows his profound concern for China's interests. In "What Should Be China's Strategic Position in the Establishment of New International Economic Order", Professor Chen points out that "in the course of establishing the NIEO, China should adhere to her self-positioning, i.e., an active promoter who takes a clear-cut stand and a reformer of the existing international economic order, but not just an ameliorator of the existing order or an intermediary of the South-North Contradiction." [175] In "Should the Four 'Great Safeguards' in Sino-foreign BITs Be Hastily Dismantled?", Professor Chen advises earnestly that China, in the course of negotiating BITs, should insist on stipulating in related BITs such rights authorized by the relevant international law, to well control the four "Great Safeguards", [176] so as to effectively protect China's national interest as well as to play a model role in the course of establishing reasonable legal norms toward foreign investment and the new international economic order. [177] Professor Chen always combines his academic study with the practice of Chinese government, and his team has been working with the Ministry of Commerce of China and other governmental departments smoothly. Many of his suggestions in his studies have been adopted by relevant governmental agencies. Professor Chen's patriotic ideas and feelings are really precious and deserve high praise.

Another embodiment of state position is Professor Chen's state-centered research approach. As mentioned earlier, professor Chen defined the scope of international economic law very early, saying that "as international economic law refers to legal norms that are used to adjust the cross-border economic relations of various public and private subjects, it can thus not be categorized solely to public international law and cannot be merely deemed as a branch of public international law that applies to economic issues. On the very contrary, its connotation and denotation have largely broken the constrains of public international law in its traditional sense and have crossed partially with private international law, international business law and relating domestic economic law, civil law, and commercial law. Thus, it formed an interdisciplinary marginal synthesis of multi-branches." [178] However, Professor Chen's study seems always focusing on state, and seldom concerned with transnational business transactions among individuals. Thus, in *The Voice from China*, we can find Professor Chen's analysis on the conflicts between US unilateralism and WTO multilateralism ("The Three Big Rounds of US Unilateralism Versus WTO Multilateralism During the Last Decade"), his insight on China's strategic position in the establishment of the new international economic order ("What Should Be China's Strategic Position in the Establishment of New International Economic Order?"), the study on South-South coalition in the process of establishing the new international economic order ("A Reflection of the South'South Coalition in the Last Half Century from the Perspective of International Economic Lawmaking: From Bandung, Doha, and Cancún to Hong

Kong") and his study on China's policy and law on foreign investment ("To Open Wider or to Close Again: China's Foreign Investment Policies and Laws"). Even in the articles mainly adopting case-study, Professor Chen's analysis is also developed around the relations between the state and individuals. This approach reflects Professor Chen's attention on states, the basic actor of the international society. Admittedly, transnational business transaction between individuals is in fact the logical starting point, as without individuals business transactions there would be no governmental administration on them, and no conflicts and coordination among states concerning international economic transactions. However, compared with individuals, the state is a more important actor. While civil law and commercial law regulating business transaction tend to converge, the law regulating governmental administration becomes a more essential part of international economic law. The "6C rules" concluded by Professor Chen, namely Contradiction→Conflict→Cons ultation→Compromise→Cooperation→Coordination→Contradiction New [179], systematically and accurately expounds the relationship between state behavior and international law and their road of evolution.

3. Equity Pursuance

Another character of Professor Chen's study is his pursuance to equity.

If we observe international economic law from a perspective of international relations, and confine the law to international convention and custom, we may find today's international economic law in general is a system in the nature of reciprocity, but not equity. Reciprocity means mutual and equal concession between countries, while equity requires specific allocation of interests under particular situations, which does not necessarily require reciprocity. Since current international economic law is a legal system containing historically accumulated rules, it is difficult to achieve equity among members of the international society by applying those rules equally or establishing new reciprocal rule. Therefore, to establish a new international economic order is to establish an equitable and reasonable international economic order. As mentioned earlier, an idea permeated through Professor Chen's studies is pursuing the equity and reasonableness of international economic order. Equity is a value of law superior than order. Order only means stable social relations, while equity requires the judgment on the content of order or the choosing of the pattern of order. In"Some Jurisprudential Thoughts upon WTO's Law-Governing, Law-Making, Law-Enforcing, Law-Abiding, and Law Reforming", Professor Chen explains that"facing the existing IEL, including varieties of'rules of game'for international economic and trade affairs, the international weak groups certainly cannot deny them all, nor are they capable of remaking the rules entirely. However, the weak groups cannot either accept all the therein embedded unfairness and injustice willingly, docilely, and obediently." 〔180〕 With respect to the road to establish an equitable and reasonable international economic order, Professor Chen believes the fundamental way lies in the cooperation among the small and weak countries. He holds that "in the later international fora and multilateral negotiations on a series of global issues, it is more necessary than ever for the developing countries of the South to take actions to win an equitable, justified and reasonable outcome. To defend the fundamental common interests of developing countries, it is imperative for the South to adapt itself to the change of circumstances, through delicate research and scientific design, and to reorient and renew the guidelines of the Group of 77, harmonizing various interests and reinforcing common understanding and internal cohesion." [181]

Professor Chen's unremitting pursuance to equity and reasonableness of the international economic order, no matter whether the movement for establishing the new international economic order is rising or falling, in addition to other factors, relates to his personal experiences. He recalls in the preface of *The Voice from China* that "when I was young, I was told of the glorious civilization of China, but I was also educated by and personally experienced the sad national crisis of China. Such complex emotions gradually nurtured my strong sense of national pride and patriotism, my determination to fight against international hegemonism, and my ambition to strive for social justice and to support all other weak countries in the world." [182]

Together with other pioneers, such as professor Yao Meizhen, Professor Chen created the discipline of international economic law in China, and succeeded professor Yao as the standard-bearer of China's international economic law academia. He expounded and proved systematically that international economic law "formed an interdisciplinary marginal synthesis of multi-branches" as early as in the 90s of last century. [183] He also argued convincingly against queries towards the discipline of international economic law including the queries of "nonscientific or nonnormative", "polyphagian or avaricious", "fickle fashion or stirring eat" and "duplication version or importing goods", [184] and laid firm foundation for the discipline of international economic law in China. The publication of Professor Chen's works in English makes it more convenient for foreign readers to hear the voice from Chinese international economic law scholarships. We expect that following the voice from Professor Chen, there shall be a loud and clear cantata by much more Chinese scholars in international stage.

（翻譯：車丕照）

六、「提出中國方案、貢獻中國智慧」[185]的先行者
——評《中國的吶喊：陳安論國際經濟法》
趙龍躍*

　　廈門大學陳安教授的英文專著《中國的吶喊：陳安論國際經濟法》（*Tlie Voice from China: An CHEN on Internationil Economcc Laiw*，以下簡稱《中國的吶喊》），近期由在國際學術界享有盛譽的德國出版社Springer在全球出版發行，令人非常欽佩。作為中國國際經濟法學界的學術泰斗，陳安教授耄耋之年，筆耕不輟，知識報國，堪稱楷模。《中國的吶喊》順應中國和平發展的要求，從積極參與國際規則制定和全球治理的角度，就國際經濟

法的基本理論、當代國家經濟主權的論爭以及中國在構建國際經濟新秩序中的戰略定位等重大問題進行了獨特的戰略思考，提出了許多切實可行的政策建議。陳安教授立足中國國情和維護廣大發展中國家合法權益的需要，學貫中西，獨樹一幟，從完善國際經濟法的角度，為中國參與國際規則制定，建立國際經濟新秩序發揮了重要作用，是中國為國際社會「提出中國方案、貢獻中國智慧」的先行者。

　　隨著經濟全球化的深入發展，國際政治經濟格局正在發生著深刻的變化，中國和廣大發展中國家在國際舞臺上的地位和作用日益重要。積極參與國際規則制定、參與全球經濟治理，不僅是實現中華民族偉大復興之中國夢的重要戰略選擇，而且也是滿足國際社會希望中國在重塑國際經濟新秩序過程中發揮更大作用的需要。

　　中國新一屆黨和國家領導人高度重視這項工作。習近平總書記在出任國家主席後的第一次對非訪問中，就明確提出要推動建設全球發展夥伴關係、加強宏觀經濟政策協調、共同參與國際發展議程制定、推動國際秩序朝著更加公正合理的方向發展等倡議。[186] 之後他在各種場合多次強調中國要全面參與國際規則制定、參與全球經濟治理。

　　二〇一四年七月，在出席金磚國家領導人第六次會晤，對巴西、阿根廷、委內瑞拉、古巴進行國事訪問並出席中國—拉美和加勒比國家領導人會晤的前夕，習近平主席接受了巴西《經濟價值報》、阿根廷《國民報》、委內瑞拉國家通訊社和古巴拉丁美洲通訊社的聯合採訪，就中國的國際作用回答記者的提問時，進

一步承諾中國「將更加積極有為地參與國際事務，致力於推動完善國際治理體系，積極推動擴大發展中國家在國際事務中的代表性和發言權」，「將更多提出中國方案、貢獻中國智慧，為國際社會提供更多公共產品」〔187〕

二〇一四年十二月，習近平總書記在中共中央政治局第十九次集體學習中指出，中國「是經濟全球化的積極參與者和堅定支持者，也是重要建設者和主要受益者」。對於參與國際經貿規則制定、爭取全球經濟治理的制度性權力，中國「不能當旁觀者、跟隨者，而是要做參與者、引領者」，「在國際規則制定中發出更多中國聲音、注入更多中國元素」〔188〕

從加入世界貿易組織以來，中國無論在學術研究方面，還是在政策實踐方面，對參與國際經貿規則制定的認識和重視都還很不夠，甚至還存在不同的看法，歸納起來可以分為「階段參與論」「能力不足論」和「避免麻煩論」等觀點。〔189〕陳安教授對於現行的世界貿易組織體制和規則，以及中國參與國際經貿規則制定的問題一直有他自己的獨立思考和鮮明觀點，早在二〇一〇年便在他紀念中國加入世界貿易組織十週年的論文中作了全面的闡述，提出了立法、執法、守法和變法的辯證關係。〔190〕陳安教授在堅持國際經濟關係必須力行法治的基礎上，深入地剖析了國際經濟立法中決策權力分配不公的事實，指出由此而形成全球財富分配嚴重不公的後果，即發達國家主導國際經貿規則的制定權，發展中國家權益嚴重受損。所以，中國和廣大發展中國家弱勢群體既要在現行的多邊貿易機制中「守法」和「適法」，熟悉運行規則，爭取為我所用，最大限度地趨利避害；又要在實踐中

明辨是非，系統排查現行體制中對國際弱勢群體明顯不利和顯失公正公平的條款、規則，研究探索變革方向，通過「南南聯合」，推行「變法圖強」，促使多邊貿易體制和規則與時俱進，造福全球。

事實上，現行國際經貿體系主要是在二十世紀四〇年代以後，在美歐等西方發達國家的主導下建立起來的，首先體現和維護的是西方國家的利益和價值。這些國際規則不僅沒有考慮中國和其他發展中國家的實際情況，而且有些規則還是專門針對中國和一些發展中國家的，最為典型的例子就是所謂的「特殊保障條款」，以及在貿易補救條款下的「非市場經濟」地位。隨著經濟全球化的深入發展，現行國際經貿體系已經不能很好地適應新的國際經濟格局。中國與世界的關係在發生變化，中國同國際社會的聯動更加密切，中國和平發展追求的不僅是中國人民的福祉，也是世界人民共同的福祉，所以必須統籌考慮和綜合運用國際國內兩個市場、國際國內兩種資源、國際國內兩類規則。

陳安教授心懷報國之志，以強烈的學術使命感，長期奮戰在國際經濟法教學和研究的道路上，獨立思考，積極探索，先後在國內外發表了一系列重要的學術論文和論著，包括「國際經濟法學系列專著」、《國際經濟法總論》和《陳安論國際經濟法學》等鴻篇力作，為發展完善具有中國特色的國際經濟法學做出了巨大的貢獻。英文專著《中國的吶喊》的出版，不僅讓國際社會聽到了中國的聲音，而且也正式揭開了中國學者全面系統地參與國際經濟法學研究交流的序幕。

在參與國際規則制定、構建新的國際經濟秩序的過程中，發

展中國家與發達國家必然會發生一些利益上的摩擦和碰撞。西方國家極力維護現存的體現其利益的經濟秩序，發展中國家希望建立新的更加公平合理的國際經濟秩序，改變全球資源和財富分配不合理的現狀。圍繞新制度的設計和相關規則的制定，南北方國家之間的鬥爭是非常激烈和複雜的，在國際經濟法學界也出現了「新自由主義經濟秩序」論、「WTO憲政秩序」論和「經濟民族主義擾亂全球化秩序」論等理論誤區。陳安教授在《中國的吶喊》一書中，對這些西方理論界的誤區逐一地進行了分析批判，並呼籲中國在構建國際經濟新秩序中要發揮領導作用，堅持和平發展、合作共贏的原則，推動國際經濟新秩序和國際經濟法體制的新老交替，實現世界共同繁榮。[191]

隨著經濟全球化的不斷深化，國家主權原則是否過時，成為當代國際法學界另一重大的理論和實踐問題。二十世紀九〇年代前後，西方國家憑藉自身經濟實力的優勢，出現了種種否定和淡化國家主權的思潮，美國國際公法專家、曾任美國國際法學會會長的路易士・漢金教授就曾提出「主權過時論」和「主權有害論」世界貿易組織成立以後，美國國會擔心加入世界貿易組織可能影響美國的國家主權，從而引發了美國法學界關於國家主權的大辯論。美國另一位國際經濟法學專家、被譽為「世界貿易組織之父」的約翰・傑克遜教授則提出所謂的「現代主權論」和「主權有效論」，他認為傳統主權的核心沒有過時，仍然有效，現代主權的核心是權力的分配問題。[192]陳安教授對於美國的這場「主權大辯論」進行了深入的研究和分析，發現漢金教授的「主權過時論」和傑克遜教授的「主權有效論」貌似相反，實則相成：都是為了限制其他國家的主權，而維護美國的霸權地位。[193]

當我看到《中國的吶喊》第四章的時候，就不由地想起陳安教授與約翰・傑克遜教授就國家主權問題的一次面對面的精彩辯論，那是二〇〇五年在美國首都華盛頓，美國國際法學會舉辦的「國際貿易與和平、自由、安全」國際研討會上。陳安教授是受邀出席該研討會的第一位演講嘉賓，他提交的論文就是《綜合評析美國單邊主義與WTO多邊主義交鋒的三大回合》。[194]陳教授從美國隨意使用「201條款」和「301條款」等國內貿易法規出發，揭示了美國實行單邊貿易保護主義不僅是WTO多邊貿易機制所面臨的挑戰，而且直接影響世界的和平、自由與安全。美國一九九四年主權大辯論的實質就是維護美國的霸權主義，限制其他國家的主權，從而將美國的主權和利益凌駕於其他國家和國際組織之上。陳教授的精彩演講給當時在美國喬治城大學任職的我以及與會的各國專家學者留下了深刻的印象，也使我有幸與陳安教授結下了忘年之交的深厚友誼。

　　實現中華民族偉大復興的中國夢，積極參與國際規則制定和全球經濟治理，推動完善國際機制，建立公正合理的國際經濟新秩序，需要中國社會各界的努力合作。陳安教授耄耋之年，筆耕不輟，博覽中外，厚積薄發，向世界國際經濟法學界發出了代表中國的吶喊，不僅為國際社會了解中國國際經濟法學的主流思想和價值取向提供了途徑；為傳播中華文化的先進思想和理念、建立完善中國國際經濟法學派做出了傑出貢獻；而且也為促進中外學術交流、豐富完善國際經濟法理論做出了傑出貢獻，堪為我們晚輩努力學習的楷模。

（編輯：龔　宇）

A Pioneer in "Providing China's Proposal and Contributing China's Wisdom"*

—Review on *The Voice from China: An CHEN*

on International Economic Law

Zhao Longyue**

Professor An Chen of Xiamen University has recently published an English book *The Voice from China: An CHEN on International Economic Law*, which is distributed globally by Springer, a Germany press with high reputation in the international academic circle. That should be greatly admired. As a leading magnate in China's international economic law and jurisprudential circle, the octogenarian, Professor An Chen has never stopped writing and been insisting on making contributions to our country with knowledge, who is an excellent model. The book complies with the requirements of peaceful development in China, particularly ponders such significant problems as the basic theory of international economic law, the debate on modern economic sovereignty and the strategic position of China in building a new international economic order, etc. and presents numerous feasible policy suggestions from the perspective of active participation in making international rules and global governance. Basing on the China's national conditions and the requirements of maintaining legal interests of developing countries, Professor An Chen is well versed in both Chinese and western learning, develops a school of his own and plays an important role in assisting China in participating in making international rules and building a new international economic order from the perspective of perfecting international economic law, who will be a Chinese pioneer in "Providing China's Proposal and Contributing China's Wisdom" for the international society.

In the wake of the in-depth development of economic globalization, international political and economic pattern is undergoing profound changes, China and other developing countries play an increasingly important position and role on international stage. The proactive participation in making international rules and global economic governance is not only an important strategic choice achieving Chinese dream of bringing about a great rejuvenation of the Chinese nation, but also a desire satisfying the international society that hopes China to play a greater role in rebuilding a new international economic order.

The new Chinese Party and State leaders have attached great importance to the work. The Party General Secretary Xi Jinping explicitly put forward suggestions in the aspects of promoting and constructing global development partnership, strengthening macroeconomic policy coordination, jointly participating in making international development agenda and driving international order toward a more just and rational direction during his first visit to Africa after he was elected as the president. [195] Afterwards, he has stressed that China should comprehensively participate in making international rules and global economic governance for several times in different occasions. Afterwards, he has stressed that

China should comprehensively participate in making international rules and global economic governance for several times in different occasions.

Chinese President Xi Jinping received the joint interview of Brazil *Valor Economico*, Argentina *National Newspaper*, Venezuela news agency and Cuba Latin America news agency on the previous day of attending the 6th summit of BRICS leaders for official visit to Brazil, Argentina, Venezuela and Cuba and attending the leaders' summit between China-Latin America and Caribbean countries in July, 2014. When answering the question of journalist about China's international role, he made a further commitment that China would further proactively participate in international affairs and perfecting international governance system, promote and enlarge the representative right and speaking right of developing countries in international affairs, present more Chinese schemes and contribute more Chinese wisdom and provide more public products for the international society. [196]

The Party General Secretary Xi Jinping indicated in the 19th collective learning of CPC Central Committee Political Bureau in December, 2014 that China is the active participant and firmed supporter and also the main constructer and beneficiary of economic globalization. China may act as a participator and leader rather than an onlooker and follower with regard to the institutional power participating in making international economic and trade rules and seeking for global economic governance. China may present more suggestions and implant more Chinese elements in making international rules. [197]

Since accessing to the WTO, China has not paid enough attention to the participation in making international trade and economic rules either in the aspect of academic research or policy practice. There were even various different views such as "theory of participation by stages", "theory of scarce capacity" and "theory of avoiding trouble", etc. [198] As for the existing WTO systems and rules and the problem regarding China's participating in making international economic and trade rules, Professor An Chen has his own independent thoughts and distinct viewpoints. He has comprehensively expounded the dialectical relationship between legislation, enforcement, law-abiding and law-reforming in the paper in memory of 10th anniversary of China's accessing to the WTO as early as in 2010. [199] On the basis of performing laws in international economic relationship, Professor Chen deeply dissected the fact of maldistribution in decision-making power in international economic legislation and pointed out the consequence of serious maldistribution in global wealth, namely the developed countries dominate the right of making international trade and economic rules and the rights and interests of developing countries are seriously damaged. China and the vulnerable groups in developing countries shall "abide by laws" and "make laws" in existing multilateral trading system and use the operation rules for ourselves and draw on advantages and avoid disadvantages to the maximum extent. They shall also distinguish right from wrong, systematically survey the articles and rules obviously disadvantageous to international weak groups and losing just and fair in existing system, explore and study the reform directions and promote the multilateral trade systems and rules to keep pace with the times and benefit the world through "South-South" Coalition and "law-reforming".

In fact, the existing international economic and trade system was built after 1940s under the leading of western developed countries inclusive of America and European countries, giving priority to safeguarding of benefits and value of western countries. These international rules do not take the actual conditions of China and developing countries into account, and also some rules especially direct at China and some developing countries. The most typical example is the so-called "special safeguards measures" and "non-market economy" position under trade remedy terms. Along with the in-depth development of economic globalization, the existing international economic and trade system can'not well adapt to the new international economic pattern. The relationship between China and the world has been changing, and the linkage between China and international society is more frequent. What the peaceful development China pursues is not only the well-being of Chinese, but also the well-being of the world's people. Therefore, it shall overall consider and comprehensively utilize international and national markets, resources and rules.

With the will of serving the country and strong academic sense of mission, Professor An Chen has fought in the teaching and research road of international economic law for a long time. Upon independent thinking and proactive exploration, he has published a series of important academic papers and works successively at home and abroad, including

Monographs of International Economic Law Series, Pandect of International Economic Law and An CHEN on International Economic Law, etc. He has made great contributions to developing and perfecting international economic law with Chinese characteristics. The English book of *The Voice from China* not only makes the international society hear Chinese voice, but also officially ushers the Chinese scholars comprehensively and schematically in participating the research and communication of international economic law.

Some interest frictions and collisions will certainly occur between the developing countries and developed countries during the process of participating in making international rules and constructing a new international economic order. The western countries make an utmost effort to maintain the existing economic order representing their benefits, while the developing countries are willing to build a fair and rational new international economic order to change the unreasonable distribution of global resources and wealth. The Southern and Northern countries fight intensively and complexly centering about the design of new systems and the making of relevant rules. The theoretical misunderstandings of "Neoliberalistic Economic Order", "Constitutional Order of the WTO" and "Economic Nationalism's Disturbance of Globalization" also exist in international economic jurisprudential circle. Professor An Chen seriatim analyzes and criticizes the misunderstandings in western theory field in this book, and appeals to China playing a leading role in building a new international economic order, insisting on the principle of peaceful development and win-win cooperation, driving the alternation of new international economic order and international economic law system and achieving coprosperity in the world. [200]

Along with the deepening of economic globalization, whether the principle of state sovereignty is behind the times has become another important theory and practice problem in modern international jurisprudential circle. Before or after 1990s, the ideological trend of negating and fading state sovereignty appeared in western countries by virtue of their own economic strength. Professor Louis Henkin, an expert in American public international law and the former president of American Society of International Law has ever presented "a theory of outmoded sovereignty" and "a theory of harmful sovereignty". After setting up the WTO, United States Congress worried about influencing state sovereignty after accessing to the WTO, hereby giving rise to a mass debate about state sovereignty in American jurisprudential circle. Another American expert in international economic law, John Jackson with the reputation of "Father of the WTO" presented the so-called "modern theory of sovereignty" and "theory of effective sovereignty". In his opinion, the core of traditional state sovereignty is not outmoded and the core of modern state sovereignty is the power distribution. [201] Professor An Chen deeply researched and analyzed the "mass debate about sovereignty", discovering that Henkin's "theory of outmoded sovereignty" and Jackson's "theory of effective sovereignty" are opposite in appearance, while complementary in reality: both theories are presented to limit the sovereignty of other countries and safeguard the hegemony position of America. [202]

While reading Chapter IV of *The Voice from China*, I can't help thinking of the face-to-face and wonderful debate between Professor An Chen and Professor John Jackson about state sovereignty in the international conference on International Trade and Peace, Freedom and Security held by American Society of International Law in Washington D.C. in 2005. Professor Chen is the first speaker to give a presentation in the conference. The paper he submitted is "The Three Big Rounds of US Unilateralism Versus the WTO Multilateralism During the Last Decade". [203] Professor Chen revealed that the unilateral trade protectionism of the United States not only threatened WTO multilateralism trade mechanism, but also directly influenced the peace, freedom and security of the world by taking the random use of "Article 201", "Article 301" and other domestic trade laws. The essence of sovereignty debate in 1994 is safeguarding the American hegemonism, limiting the sovereignty of other countries and outmatching American sovereignty and benefits above other countries and international organizations. The splendid speech of Professor Chen made a profound impression on me and the experts and scholars from different countries attending the conference. Since then, I have the honor to be a close friend of Professor Chen in spite of the big difference of age.

All sectors of society in China shall cooperate to achieve the Chinese dream of bringing about a great rejuvenation of the Chinese nation, proactively participate in making international rules and global economic governance, driving the perfection of international mechanism and building a fair and reasonable new international economic order. The octogenarian, Professor An Chen has never stopped writing whilst has been accumulating knowledge in China and foreign countries and uttering a voice to the circle of international economic law on behalf of China, not only providing channels for international society to understand the mainstream ideology and value orientation in China's international economic law and making great contributions to spreading advanced ideology and ideas in Chinese culture and to build China's own school of international economic law, but also making great contributions to promoting academic communication between China and foreign countries and enriching and perfecting the theories in international economic law. He is an excellent model from whom the young generations should learn.

（翻譯：趙龍躍）

七、追求全球正義　抵制國際霸權

〔韓〕李庸中**

小　引

　　陳安教授經過長期刻苦鑽研，完成了鴻篇巨著，邀請我撰寫書評。對我而言，為這樣一位令人敬仰的學者撰寫書評，是喜出

望外的殊榮。第一次見到陳安教授，可以回溯到二〇一一年。當時，經蔡從燕教授推薦，我代表韓國《東亞與國際法學刊》（*Journal of East Asia and Internationa Law*），專程前往廈門米訪陳安教授。米訪在廈門大學法學院的大樓進行。我還記得，廈門大學法學院靠近景色優美的海濱，整個廈門大學法學院的氣氛非常專業化，穩重溫文，具有合作精神。陳安教授和廈門大學法學院的其他教師如陳輝萍教授，以及陳安教授親切和善的女兒陳仲洵的熱情接待，給我留下深刻的印象，令我有賓至如歸之感。我走進寬敞的會面房間，就看到陳安教授已經帶著溫暖的笑容在等我。我立刻意識到他是一位名副其實的學者，是一位具有深厚美德的「士」善於以其無比頑強的力量對抗任何壓制真理（verias）的行為。在我誠摯問候之後，他謙遜且友好地說：「李博士！我們之間有兩個共同之處。首先，中國和韓國都曾經遭受日本軍國主義的侵略。其次，我和你都推崇孔儒之道，因為你的名字『庸中』與一部儒家經典著作《中庸》密切相關。」確實如此，我們之間的會面訪談也正是在這些共識的基礎上積極地展開的。

陳安教授在米訪過程中提到的許多有趣故事，深深地吸引了我（整個米訪的問答記錄刊登在英文版《東亞與國際法學刊》第四卷第二期，並被輯入《中國的吶喊：陳安論國際經濟法》（以下簡稱《中國的吶喊》）這本書的導言部分 [204]。作為中國國際經濟法的旗手學者，他具有卓越的才華和堅守的原則，思維清晰，博聞廣識，嚴謹縝密，充滿智慧。他對國際法的重要性具有深刻厚實的理解。

在我回到韓國之後，我們之間一直保持頻繁的聯繫。二〇一

四年，陳安教授邀請我為《中國的吶喊》一書撰寫書評。一開始我有所猶豫，因為我覺得自己不夠資格為這樣一位我從心底深深敬佩的傑出學者的著作撰寫書評，這將會是我要承擔的最艱難的任務之一。然而，最後我還是接受了陳安教授的提議，因為我覺得我有責任祝賀他把自己的學術主張傳播到國際社會。我的評論本身也許並非對這一著作的確切評價，但我的粗淺評說卻表達了一位年輕外國學者對作者的仰慕和敬意。

作者簡介

陳安教授在一九二九年五月出生於福建省東北部的一個小山村，在其成長過程中，很大程度上受到父親的影響和教育。他的父親是位儒家學者和詩人，一九四五年辭世。一九四六年，十七歲的陳安教授考進廈門大學開始學習法律。此後，由於歷史的原因，自一九五三年起他的法學學習和研究令人遺憾地中斷了二十七年，直到一九八〇年廈門大學法學院重新建立。那時，陳安教授已經五十來歲。他敏銳地意識到中國不僅需要建立國內法律體系，而且，由於中國開始實施對外開放的戰略，還需要有自己的國際經濟法體系。陳安教授決定專注從事國際經濟法的研究。然而，在那個時代，中國缺乏現代的法律教科書，更遑論有關國際經濟法的各種文獻。一九八一年，一個偶然的機會，陳安教授遇到美國的Jerome Cohen教授並與之就學術觀點展開爭論，最後，陳安教授被邀請到哈佛大學繼續從事法學研究。從此之後，他利用所有到國外訪問和參加學術會議的機會，帶回大量相關的英文書籍和資料。輯入《中國的吶喊》一書的一系列專論就是其研究

的主要成果。它們反映了陳安教授嚴謹的學術素養、愛國主義情懷和歷史責任感。陳安教授是「新中國國際經濟法學的奠基人之一」，他的學術生涯和中國改革開放的國策息息相關。在法學實踐中，他又是一名國際商事領域的律師，多家跨國企業的法律顧問，同時還是ICSID、ICCC、IAI和RIA的仲裁員。

除了國際經濟法，陳安教授還愛好詩歌、文學和書法藝術。在東亞，一名完美的學者通常都有這些方面的修養。他性格溫和、熱心，有勇往直前的信念。他經歷了中國被外國占領、內戰和社會革命的歷程。所有這些，都不能阻止他對人類社會真理、公平的追求。甚至可以說，這些磨難幫助他在中國學術乃至國際學術上達到難以超越的高峰。陳安教授經常論證對人類社會和平以及共同繁榮的崇高追求，不失為我們這個時代的一位傑出的良師益友。

著作內容

《中國的吶喊》這部專著，匯輯了陳安教授在過去三十多年所撰寫的二十四篇英文論文，是陳安教授從一九八〇年開始多年從事國際經濟法學術研究的代表作。這本書涵蓋了中國所面臨的有關國際經濟法的許多疑難問題。在該書中，這二十四篇文章被分為六部分：當代國際經濟法的法理；當代經濟主權論；中國在當代國際經濟秩序中的戰略定位；當代雙邊投資條約；中國的涉外經濟立法；當代中國在國際經濟爭端解決中的實踐。各部分的內容相互聯結並保持良好平衡。陳安教授的法理觀念和學術見解在許多方面不苟同於美國和歐洲國際法研究的主流觀點。《中國

的吶喊》這本著作的出版具有相當重大的意義，因為它打造了中國在國際經濟法領域話語權的堅實基礎。通過陳安教授周全深入的研究，中國開始在世界上發出自己的聲音，表達自己的理念。從這個意義上說，《中國的吶喊》這一標題有相當深刻的喻義。除了學術內容精彩獨到之外，這本書由久負盛名的斯普林格出版社負責出版，編輯加工十分專業，裝幀精美，封面設計也很典雅大方，值得稱道。

「黃禍」論（Yellow Peril）

中國對於西方來說一直是個神秘的國度。其主要原因在於中國具有廣闊的疆土，大量的人口，漫長的歷史和古老的文明，現代的共產主義理念，而且在一九七八年之前一直堅持閉關鎖國的政策。但是，更關鍵的是，在西方人思想的深處，曾經不知不覺地根植了所謂「黃禍」論的傳言。最近，這種思想又從他們的潛意識中悄悄爬出來，進入真實的世界，變成為一個惡毒的說法，即「中國威脅」論。在《中國的吶喊》第三章，陳安教授分析了「黃禍」論以及其現代變種「中國威脅」論的起源、演變和在國際社會的法律意義。一些中國學者似乎也同樣意識到這兩個概念之間的歷史聯繫。例如，中山大學陳東教授指出：「『中國威脅』論並非是在過去二十年才出現的新的概念。它可以回溯到十九世紀，例如，在沙俄時代米哈伊爾‧巴枯寧撰寫的《國家制度與無政府狀態》一書中，就談到了『來自東方（中國）的巨大和可怕的威脅』。德皇威廉二世製作的形象漫畫《歐洲人啊，保衛你們的信仰和家園》，就描述了十九世紀末歐洲人對中國的普遍看

法。」[205]陳東教授還指出：「『黃禍』論的根源在於一些歐洲人將黃色面孔的中國人視為『不文明的』和愚蠢的破壞者，他們對西方的『文明社會』可能造成巨大的威脅。」[206]

　　然而，單憑這種歷史回溯的方法，往往還不是認識現今「中國威脅」論的關鍵所在。當代美國霸權版的「中國威脅」論最早出現在二十世紀九〇年代中葉，其主要鼓吹者是布希政府下的美國政客和學者。到了二十一世紀的最初幾年，這一讕言開始變得相當尖銳刺耳。看來當時布希政府是刻意地杜撰出「中國威脅」論這個口號，意在阻止經濟和政治影響力迅速增長的中國進一步擴展，影響到亞洲——太平洋地區，以便於美國全盤統治東亞。對當時唯一的「超級大國」美國而言，中國可能是美國在這一地區軍事和經濟霸權主義的潛在威脅。「中國威脅」論正是在此種權力交替的國際環境中產生。「中國威脅」論可能不是「黃禍」論在當代的簡單轉型，因為「黃禍」論主要是歐洲人在特定環境下的看法，「黃禍」論的產生實際上起源於十三世紀蒙古人入侵歐洲後，歐洲人面對黃色臉孔的中國人和中國文明產生的根深蒂固的自卑情緒。因此，「黃色」一詞可能不是指亞洲人皮膚的顏色，它指的是蒙古騎兵在入侵過程中掀起的黃色沙暴。對當時的歐洲人而言，他們是魔鬼，只有全能的上帝能戰勝他們。

　　這一假設在陳東教授的《誰在威脅誰？「中國威脅」論和布希政策》一文中得到很好的論證。陳東教授認為，布希政府抱有「單極世界的夢想」可以解釋「中國威脅」論的來由。[207]陳東教授引用伊肯貝利撰寫的論文《美國的帝國野心》，指出，美國人將布希的政策視為「美國能保持單極世界從而沒有任何競爭者

的宏偉的戰略」，但這有可能造成「世界更加危險和分裂，因此也會威脅到美國的安全」[208] 陳東教授還特別援引福音教派的理論作為論證布希政策的基礎。他認為，「中國威脅」論是布希構建以美國為中心的單極世界的實用工具。[209]

陳安教授在《中國的吶喊》一書中對前述布希政策下的種種「中國威脅」論作了概括總結。陳安教授認為：

它們是美國出現的層次最高、頻率最繁、影響最大的美國官方版的「黃禍」論──「中國威脅」論。它們是美國國會、美國國防部、美國高層智囊「三結合」產物。美國國防部門的部門利益昭然若揭……（蘇聯解體）和冷戰結束後，對於始終保持著「古怪癖好」的慣性思維的美國人而言……他們需要找到（蘇聯以外）另一個明確的、強大的新「威脅」，而中國正好就是美國人一向極力虛構的危及美國安全的新的「嚴重威脅」[210]

我十分贊同陳安教授對「中國威脅」論的看法，即「中國威脅」論就是「21世紀美國霸權最新修訂版的「黃禍」論，它體現為美國「鷹派」反華議員每年一度集中渲染「中國威脅」的《中國軍力報告》，美中經濟與安全審議委員會的《審議報告》，以及各種媒體的呼應鼓噪。[211]

經濟主權

在《中國的吶喊》一書的第四章和第五章，陳安教授探討了更為根本性的經濟主權問題。隨著經濟全球化和各國間互相依存

性的增強，單個國家的經濟主權成為論戰的焦點之一。陳安教授對WTO的多邊主義和美國的單邊主義作了對比分析。他非常精彩地比較分析了美國漢金教授和傑克遜教授關於美國單邊主義和WTO多邊主義的不同觀點。他引用許多相關案例批判美國單邊主義凌駕於其他國家主權之上。他的分析和評論有意識地涵蓋《美國貿易法》中的201條款和301條款，WTO體系形成過程中的各種主權衝突，美國國內的一九九四年主權大辯論，美國的主權和其他國家的主權之間的關係，美國與歐盟之間經濟主權的爭奪，美國與日本之間的汽車爭端，美國與歐盟之間的香蕉爭端，WTO爭端解決機構針對美國301條款的專家組報告等。

陳安教授探討了多邊體制時代各主權國家合作協調的問題。他的觀點諒必建立在中國過往歷史經驗的基礎上，包括被列強侵佔的災難和國內戰爭的痛楚，這些災難和痛楚陳安教授都曾經親身經歷過。我完全贊同陳安教授的觀點。絕大多數亞洲國家都曾經一度淪為殖民地，對亞洲人說來，「主權」不應該是個虛構的神話，它是民族自決的現實。

結論

陳安教授《中國的吶喊》一書，無論對中國、整個亞洲，還是對國際社會，都是一項重大的成就和貢獻。此書追求和論證的目標是，國家間應當在公平和均衡的基礎上開展經濟合作。這本著作的核心和焦點可以概括為：為世界群弱吶喊，追求全球正義，抵制國際霸權。

這也是「了解中國」系列專著的出發點，即從建立國際經濟

新秩序的角度來理解和看待中國。對於今後願意追隨陳安教授的學術界人士和實務工作者而言，《中國的吶喊》將會成為傑出的範本。就我而言，我正處在陳安教授開始從事國際法研究的年齡。他不渝不懈的努力和學術熱情會一直激勵著亞洲乃至全球的國際法工作者。陳安教授的精神也一直鼓舞我保持永無止境的求知欲。無論何時，我都熱切地期待未來新的一卷《中國的吶喊》問世。由於陳安教授老當益壯，依然矍鑠健朗，我希望新書的出版不會等待太久。在這裡，我再次對《中國的吶喊》一書出版，表達發自內心的深深的祝賀之忱。

（翻譯、編輯：陳　欣）

Pursuing Global Justice Resisting International Hegemony

Eric Yong Joong Lee*

Introduction

It is an incredible honor for me to have this opportunity to review the product of a long and painstaking research conducted by an honorable scholar like Professor An Chen. My first encounter with Professor Chen traces back to 2011 when I visited Xiamen in order to interview him for the Journal of East Asia and International Law with the recommendation of Professor Congyan Cai. The interview was held in the building of School of Law, Xiamen University which is close to the coast of the beautiful ocean. The atmosphere of the School of Law was very professional, gentle and cooperative. I was fully impressed by the warmhearted hospitality of Professor Chen and other staff members of including Professor Huiping Chen and Professor Chen's lovely daughter Carol. It made me feel at home. When I entered the wide room for the interview, Professor Chen was waiting with his gentle smile. I could instantly recognize he is a true scholar and a man of immense virtue （士） with the invincible power against anything suppressing "veritas" （真理）. After my deeply felt greetings, he modestly and friendly said: "Dr. Lee, We are sharing two common things. First, both of us (China and Korea) have suffered severely from Japanese militarism. Second, we (Professor Chen and Lee) in common respect Confucius, considering that your name Yong Joong （庸中） is related to one of the holy books of Confucius. The relating specific holy book is named with '中庸' (Chinese pronounced as Zhong Yong)." Indeed，our interview started on a positive note based on these commonalities. Professor Chen spoke about many interesting stories during the interview sufficient to enthrall me (The transcript of the whole interview has been published in volume 4, number 2 of the Journal of East Asia and International Law as well as in the introduction section of *The Voice from China* [212]). As a flag-holder Chinese scholar of international economic law, he is a man of exceptional brilliance and principles with clear, broad, rigorous thinking and wisdom. He has a profound understanding of the importance of international law.

Since my return home, we have maintained frequent contact with each other. In 2014, Professor Chen requested me to review *The Voice from China*. I was hesitant at first because I thought I was not entitled to comment on something by an outstanding scholar whom I respect from the bottom of my heart. It would thus be one of the most difficult tasks I have endured. However, I finally decided to accept his proposal because it would be my duty to celebrate his voice toward the global community. My review may not contain an evaluation per se, but my humble comments as a young foreign scholar admiring the author.

The Author

Professor Chen was born in May, 1929 in a small mountainous town in northeast Fujian Province, China and grew up there profoundly influenced and educated by his father who was a Confucian scholar and poet, dying in 1945. He began studying law at Xiamen University in 1946 when he was 17 years old. Due to historical reasons, his legal studies were unfortunately interrupted for 27 years until 1980 when the Law School of Xiamen University was reestablished. By that time, he was already in his fifties. He had the keen insight to recognize that China would need to establish not only its domestic legal regime, but also international (economic) law, especially when China opened up to the world. Professor Chen decided to focus on international economic law (IEL). At that time, however, there were few modern legal reference texts in China, not to mention IEL literature. In 1981, he occasionally met and argued with Professor Jerome Cohen and was finally invited to

Harvard Law School to continue his legal studies. Afterwards, he took all opportunities of travelling abroad for conferences and visits to bring back relevant books and articles in English. The series works of The Voice from China are the main products of his research. They reflects his academic rigor, patriotism and historical responsibility. Professor Chen is "one of the founders of international economic law in new China" and his academic life is closely connected with reform and opening up. In his legal practice, he is also a concurrent lawyer of international business, legal adviser of several transnational corporations, as well as an arbitrator of the ICSID,ICC, IAI and RIA.

In addition to the IEL, Professor Chen likes poetry, literature and calligraphy, which are grounds to be an ideal scholar in East Asia. He is a true man of gentle, warmhearted and courageous personality. In his lifetime, China has experienced foreign occupation, civil war and the socialist revolution. All these, however, could not stop his longing for the truth and justice in human society. Rather, those trials have made him an insurmountable peak of Chinese as well as world academia. Professor Chen always tells his lofty messages and ideas for peace and co-prosperity of human society as a great mentor of our time.

Book

The monograph entitled *The Voice from China: An CHEN on International Economic Law*, is a collection of 24 English articles written by Professor An Chen over the past 30 years. *The Voice from China* is a representation of his academic life of IEL, starting from 1980. The book covers areas of IEL questions that China has been asking. These 24 articles are divided into six parts in his book, namely: Jurisprudence of Contemporary International Economic Law; Contemporary Economic Sovereignty; China's Strategic Position on Contemporary International Economic Order; Contemporary Bilateral Investment Treaties; China's Legislation on Sino-Foreign Economic Issues; and Contemporary Chinese Practices on International Economic Disputes; which are all very well balanced. His jurisprudential idea and academic opinions show different aspects of international law from those of the United States and Europe that were mainstream. This publication has great significance considering that it is the firm ground of Chinese discourse on IEL. With his thorough research, China began expressing her ideas in her own voice. In that sense, the title, *The Voice from China* has deep implications. In addition to academic contents, the book is professionally edited and beautifully bound by a highly renowned publisher, Springer. The cover design is also appreciable.

"Yellow Peril" Doctrine

China is a mysterious country to the western people. It is mainly due to her vast national territory, large population, long history and civilization, modern communism and her closed-door policy up until 1978. One more critical point is, however, the so-called "Yellow Peril" Doctrine, which is unconsciously rooted in the western mind. Recently, this "Yellow Peril" Doctrine began creeping out of their sub-consciousness into the real world as a poisonous concept of the so-called "China Threat" Doctrine. In Chapter 3 of *The Voice from China*, Professor Chen has analyzed the origin, evolution and international legal significance of the "Yellow Peril" Doctrine and the "China Threat" Doctrine, which is its modern style transformation. Some Chinese scholars seem to perceive these two concepts to be historically connected. For example, Professor Chen Dong at Sun Yat-sen University stated:

> The term "Chinese Threat" has not been a novel wording for the past twenty years. Its references date as far back to the nineteenth century, e.g., in Mikhail Bakunin's work entitled *On Statism and Anarchism*, which implies the "tremendous and dreadful threat from the East". Wilhelm II von Deutschland's vivid cartoon "The Yellow Peril" (Vôlker Europas, wahrt eure heiligsten Güter) depicted a common European perception of China at the turn of the nineteenth century. [213]

He also added:

> The core of the "Yellow Peril" theory lay in the fact that some Europeans regarded yellow-faced Chinese as "uncivilized" and stupid locusts causing great, albeit potential, threats to the "civilized (western)" world. [214]

Such a historical approach is, however, not always the key to understanding the current recognition of the contemporary US hegemonic version of "China Threat" Doctrine, which was firstly referred to in the mid-1990s, mainly by US politicians and scholars under the Bush administration. It became shrill in the early 2000s. The then Bush administration seemed to intentionally fabricate the political slogan, "China Threat" Doctrine in order to dominate East Asia by preventing China whose economy and political influence were fast growing from expanding to the Asia-Pacific region. For the US, who was "the only superpower" at that time, China might be a potential threat to the American military and economic hegemony in the region. The concept, "China Threat" Doctrine seemed to be initiated under this global environment of power shift. The so-called "China Threat" Doctrine thus might not simply be a modern transformation of the "Yellow Peril" Doctrine, which was largely European oriented. The "Yellow Peril" Doctrine was actually coined because of the Mongol invasion of Europe in the thirteenth century which led to the deep-rooted inferiority complex of the Europeans toward Chinese (Yellow-faced Asian) people and civilization. Herewith, the word, "yellow" might not mean the skin color of Asian, but the color of sand storms that the Mongol cavalry made while aggressing. For the then Europeans, they were evils that could be surmounted only by the omnipotent God.

This hypothesis is well evidenced by Professor Dong Chen's article, "Who Threatens Whom? The 'Chinese Treat' and the Bush Doctrine". In his article, Dong Chen states "Bush's dream for the unipolar world" to explain the "China Threat". [215] Citing Ikenberry's article, America's Imperial Ambitions, he argues that Americans regard the Bush strategy as "a 'grand strategy' that begins with fundamental commitment to maintaining a unipolar world in which the US has no peer competitor," and that threatens to "leave the world more dangerous and divided-and the US less secure." [216] Furthermore, Professor Dong Chen specially refers to evangelical Christianity as the basis of the Bush doctrine. [217] According to him, China Threat is an implementative tool of the Bush doctrine to build the unipolar world with the US in the center.

An abovementioned statement to that effect on "China Threat" under the Bush doctrine may be wrapped up in *The Voice from China*. Professor An Chen said:

> They could be fairly deemed as the official American versions of "Yellow Peril" and "China Threat" on the highest level, at the highest frequency... They are the outcome of the following triple sources: American Congress, the US Department of Defense, and various high-ranked think tanks... The departmental interests of American Department of Defense could be easily discerned in this regard... After the Cold War was over, it was always the inertial thinking of "curious" Americans... to find a definite and powerful new "threat". And China is the new "serious threat" on security that Americans have been endeavoring to establish. [218]

I would fully agree with the position of Professor An Chen that the China Threat is "the twenty-first century version of 'Yellow Peril' which has been repeatedly advocated by American hawkish anti-China congressmen, as evidenced in the annual Report of China's Military

Power and in the annual Report of US-China Economic and Security, and the echoing of media along with them." [219]

Economic Sovereignty

In Chapters 4 and 5 of *The Voice from China*, Professor Chen discusses a more fundamental question of economic sovereignty. As the economic globalization and interdependency between nations are deepening, sovereignty of each nation State is getting to a point of controversy. Professor Chen refers to the comparison between the WTO multilateralism and the US unilateralism. He compares the ideas of Professor L. Henkin to those of Professor J. Jackson with regard to unilateralism (US) and multilateralism (WTO) very well. Professor Chen has cited pertinent cases in order to critically discuss the US unilateralism over the sovereignty of other states. His analytic statement purposefully covers Sections 201 and 301 of the US Trade Act, conflicts of sovereignties in the formation of the WTO system, the Great 1994 Sovereignty Debate, sovereignty of the US and other States, the US EU economic sovereignty disputes, the US-Japan auto disputes, the US EC banana disputes, the WTO / DSB Panel Report on the Section 301 case, etc.

Professor Chen discusses the coordination of national sovereignty in the time of multilateralism. His idea might be set up based on the China's historical experience including horrible foreign occupation and the civil war that Professor Chen himself got through in his lifetime. I fully second his opinions. For Asians, most of whom were once colonized, "sovereignty" is not myth; it is the reality to self-determination.

Conclusion

The *Voice from China* is a great achievement and contribution by Professor An Chen to China, to the whole of Asia, as well as to the global community, which is searching for a new discourse in the promotion of economic cooperation in a fair and balanced manner between states. The core and focus of this monograph could be summarized as Voicing for Worldwide Weaks, Pursuing Global Justice, Resisting International Hegemony.

It should be a triggering point for the series of "Understanding China" with a viewpoint of establishing a new international economic order. This publication will be an outstanding model of other academics and practitioners who are willing to follow him. Personally, I am now of the age in which Professor Chen began studying international law. His constant efforts and enthusiasm is a consistent stimulant for the passion of international lawyers in Asia as well as the whole world. My eternally curious mind is also deeply inspired by Professor Chen. I am eagerly awaiting a future volume of *The Voice from China*, whenever it is manifest. Since Professor Chen is enjoying green old age, I hope it would not entail much waiting. Once again I extend the deepest and heartfelt celebration to the publication of *The Voice from China*.

八、國家主權等國際經濟法宏觀問題的深刻反思

—— 評《中國的吶喊：陳安論國際經濟法》

〔加拿大〕派特麗莎・沃特絲*

《中國的吶喊：陳安論國際經濟法》一書的作者是中國國際經濟法學界泰斗、廈門大學法學院陳安教授，該書彙集了作者自一九八〇年以來三十多年不同時期撰寫的二十四篇專論。該書的學術專論和案例分析論及國際法諸多議題，卻又服務於一個共同的主題，即發出作者對國際經濟法的獨特的「中國聲音」。

全書分為六個部分：當代國際經濟法的基本理論；當代國家經濟主權的「攻防戰」；中國在構建當代國際經濟新秩序中的戰略定位；當代國際投資法的論爭；當代中國涉外經濟立法的爭議；若干涉華、涉外經貿爭端典型案例剖析。該巨著共七八九頁，含正文二十四章及參考文獻和附錄（包括對陳教授論著的各種書刊評論）。

讀者開篇即可看出作者的主要意圖——闡述自己對國際（經濟）法的中國特色和獨有路徑的看法。「序言」開宗明義：

……中國學者不應盲目附和和全盤接受某些西方觀點。正確的態度理應是獨立思考，明辨是非，批判地吸收。秉持這一態度，我和我的中國同仁在晚近三十年的研究和著述中，一直立足於中國國情和其他弱小國家的基本立場，努力剖析、辨別、探討西方各種法學理論的真偽，從而決定取捨。除了對西方法律理論「取其精華，去其糟粕」外，我們還努力推陳出新，開拓創新，

針對若干重大法律問題提出一系列自己的觀點，積極參與國際學術爭鳴，形成了自己的理論體系……我們的理論與現有的某些西方觀點截然不同（第vi頁）

我的研究領域是國際水資源和國家主權理論，故急切想看看陳安教授在《中國的吶喊》一書中如何看待主權這一問題。本書索引列舉了大量與主權有關的討論，為探討這一複雜問題提供了多種方便路徑。例如，對**國家主權至上**這一問題，作者主張：「在當代國際法的規範體系和理論體系中，國家主權原則乃是第一性的、居於最高位階的基本原則。」（第326頁）為此，作者認為：「從這個意義說，MFN待遇原則乃是國家主權原則的衍生物，它應當附屬於、服從於國家主權原則。」（第326-327頁）然而，「即使是居於最高位階的國家主權原則，也可以依締約主權國家的自由意志，通過平等磋商，作出適當的真正平等互惠的自我限制」（第327頁）。雖然這一主張貌似誇大了國際法的基本原則，但作者以中國為例解釋了為什麼要對這些原則如此強調和全面闡釋。在中國，「歷史上喪權辱國的慘痛，人們記憶猶新」（第327頁）。雖然作者在這裡討論的是國際經濟法，其寓意卻是深遠的，特別有助於人們充分理解和領會中國對國家主權的立場。「如今，已經站起來了的中國人民，已經恢復和強化了完全獨立自主的主權國家身份……」（第317頁）

本書其他部分亦從不同角度探討國家主權理論。由於本書主要論及國際經濟法，大量論述的是「經濟主權」（有20次之多），「單個國家的主權」討論過一次，「永久主權」兩次，「聯合主權」

兩次，「國家主權」八次。「主權」一詞貫穿全書，通過剖析西方特別是美國的相關理論與實踐，全面闡述中國對主權的立場。舉例來說，陳教授質疑「跨國法」學說，認為這是一種否定弱國主權，鼓吹美國霸權的學說，是一種有毒的「舶來品」（第38頁）。他認為：「傑塞普鼓吹的『跨國法』，打著『世界政府』『聯合主權』『國際法』優先的旗號，為覬覦、削弱、否定眾多弱小民族的國家主權提供『法理依據』，其宗旨在於促使弱國撤除民族與國家藩籬，擯棄主權屏障，從而使美國的國際擴張主義和世界霸權主義得以通行無阻。」（第38-39頁）

本書附錄收錄了Branislav Gosovic的一篇論文，總結陳教授對國家主權的看法。他認為，國家主權理論是中國外交戰略的基石（該戰略在1982年《憲法》中確立，即「和平共處五項原則」：相互尊重主權和領土完整、互不侵犯、互不干涉內政、平等互利、和平共處）。Gosovic認為：「今後若干年，學者們可以用實踐來檢驗陳教授的論點和論據，如果證明他是對的，則可對抗西方凡夫俗子思想模式下廣泛流傳的觀點。」（第773頁）「西方」觀點認定，中國的和平崛起會……演變為霸權主義、擴張主義和侵略主義，會仿效並追隨過往的侵略者和殖民者，繼而將全球瓜分為各自的勢力範圍。」（第773頁）陳教授《中國的吶喊》一書則從中國的國際法觀出發，作出了完全不同的論斷。

換個角度說，陳教授的國家主權觀是從中國實際出發，為我們理解中國的跨界水實踐提供了新的洞見。跨界水問題是當今中國和亞洲地區迫在眉睫、亟待解決的問題。中國與二十個主權國家和地區有四十多條跨界河流，多數情況下中國處於上游，中國對這些河流的淡水使用和開發頗受質疑。爭議的焦點是國家主權

以及外交政策如何落實國家主權。具體而言，就是中國在管理跨界水資源時，如何根據國際法，既滿足自身經濟發展的需要，又考慮鄰國的需求。雖然有不少外國研究者批評中國的跨界水實踐有「霸權性質」，說中國是（無情的？）地區「超級大國」，只片面考慮自身利益，但是，如果仔細加以研究，會發現這些研究者大都有同樣的重大疏忽，即沒有探究中國的國際法觀對跨界水問題的內在影響。用跨界水涉及的國際法規則來評估和分析中國的相關條約和國家實踐，我們發現中國一貫採取相當一致的立場（雖然該立場尚未得到充分研究），這一立場符合中國的國家主權觀，反映的是領土主權有限論（Wouters and Chen, 2013; Xue, 1992; Saul, 2013）。陳教授在《中國的吶喊》中提出的強有力的法律論據，有助於人們更好地理解將來中國在跨界水實踐方面的可能走向。的確，對於中國涉水行業的外國投資政策這一重要問題，現有研究極少（H. Chen, 2015），今後需要更多細緻研究。《中國的吶喊》一書充分展現出來的跨學科新思維，為更多的創新思路提供了基礎。中國需要新的法律思維來管理跨界水資源，從而平衡經濟發展與環境保護問題，環境問題現在已成為國內的重要議題。當今全球自然資源過度開發，缺乏保護。中國在該領域的國家實踐，不僅對其自身的國家資源，而且對地區和全球經濟和環境資源，都有重大意義。如何以支援經濟發展的方式來解決全球水／能源／食品／環境等問題，是一個熱點問題，也是世界經濟論壇熱議的話題。世界經濟論壇是全球思想家和政策制定者的重要年度會議。在最近一次世界經濟論壇會議上（二〇一五年一月在達沃斯召開），中國總理李克強說：「文化多樣性與生物多樣性一樣，是我們這個星球最值得珍視的天然寶藏。人類社

會是各種文明都能盛開的百花園，不同文化之間、不同宗教之間，都應相互尊重、和睦共處。同可相親，異宜相敬。國際社會應以海納百川的胸懷，求同存異、包容互鑑、合作共贏。」（二〇一五年一月二十三日，達沃斯）「中國提出『一帶一路』建設，願與相關國家需求相結合，合作推進。」中國如何在實踐中，尤其是在面臨諸多複雜挑戰時，根據中國的國家主權觀和國際法，實施這一雄心勃勃的外交政策，人們拭目以待。也許陳教授的洞見能夠指點迷津？

對於解決這些相當複雜又頗有爭議的問題，本書極富啟迪意義。本書詳加探討的是國際經濟法理論與實踐，作者卻常將之歸依為國際公法的普遍問題。因此，《中國的吶喊》具有更宏大的魅力。本書還討論了許多相互關聯而又高度相關的國際法問題。諸如：南南合作發展戰略（「發展中國家對自己的自然資源應該享有和行使永久主權；對發展中國家的經濟援助應該嚴格尊重受援國家的主權，不附帶任何條件，施援國不得要求任何特權」第176頁）論鄧小平對國際經濟新秩序理論的貢獻）；以理論聯繫實際的方法來研究國際經濟法諸議題（包括外國投資），等等。作者反覆呼籲並詳細論證，國際（經濟）法領域需要更加獨立的研究和批判性思考。

對於那些對國際法感興趣的人而言，《中國的吶喊》提供了廣闊的天地，尤其是從中國的視角來看。以下前瞻性的論斷，非常振奮人心，將激勵學者們接受挑戰：

學術上原無什麼絕對的「專屬區」，更不該有什麼「獨家禁

地」，不許他人涉足。因此，中國法學界的志士仁人，不論其擅長或專攻何門類、何學科，似均宜摒除、捐棄任何門戶之見，從各自不同的角度，各盡所能，齊心協力，盡力地開拓和盡多地產出具有中國特色的法學碩果和上佳精品，共同為振興中國法學，躋身國際前列，並進而為世界法苑的百花爭妍和絢麗多彩，做出應有的貢獻！（第42-43頁）

總之，我希望本書廣傳於世，激發更多人從更廣闊的國際法維度研究國際經濟法。此外，我們也需要更多人從事自然資源和涉水資源的研究，既考慮中國的見解，又參考國際最佳實踐，綜合評估各方意見。

來自中國的吶喊必須認真傾聽。陳教授的專著及時問世，必將引發更多創新性的研究。

參考文獻

（詳見本書評英文版）

（翻譯：陳輝萍，校對、編輯：陳　欣）

Reflections on State Sovereignty and Other Grand Themes of International Law

Patricia Wouters*

The monograph, *The Voice from China: An CHEN on International*

Economic Law is a collection of some 24 papers written over 3 decades (from the 1980s) by China's eminent professor in this field—Professor An Chen (School of Law, Xiamen University). It includes scholarly writings and case analyses, which together aim at consolidating the author's views on the distinctive "Voice of China" in the area of international economic law, touching also on a range of related themes in international law.

Presented in six parts—Jurisprudence of Contemporary International Economic Law; Great Debates on Contemporary Economic Sovereignty; China's Strategic Position on Contemporary International Economic Order Issues; Divergences on Contemporary Bilateral Investment Treaty; Contemporary China's Legislation on Sino-Foreign Economic Issues; Contemporary Chinese Practices on International Economic Disputes (Cases Analyses)—the work comprises 24 chapters, with references and an Annex that includes comments about Chen's writings. It is a large volume, covering 789 pages.

The reader quickly discerns the primary objective of the author—to present his personal views on the Chinese characteristics of, and approach to, international (economic) law. The preface provides:

> ...we Chinese law scholars, should not blindly follow and completely accept these Western opinions. Rather, a correct attitude is to contemplate independently and critically in order for us to be able to distinguish right from wrong. By holding such kind of attitude, in my later three decades of research and writing, I,

together, with my Chinese colleague, have always bene trying to analyse, distinguish, ascertain, absorb, or reject Western legal theories while steadily taking into account the national situation of China and the common position of the weak countries. In addition to "keeping the essence while discarding the dross" of the Western legal theories, we have raised a series of our own innovative ideas and actively participated in international academic debates, which have helped us to shape our systematic theories on various legal subjects... Our theories are significantly and substantially different and independent from some of the existing Western ones. (p.vi)

As my own research looks at the notion of state sovereignty (in the context of international freshwater resources), I was keen to explore how Professor An Chen addresses this topic in The Voice from China. The index offers a list of sovereignty-related discourse, each providing diverse inroads on this complex notion. As just one example, on the particular issue of the supremacy of state sovereignty, the author asserts, "State sovereignty is still the primary rule and occupies the highest hierarchical position within the norm-system and theory-system of international law" (p.326). In accordance with this view, the author holds that MFN treatment is "merely a derivative of state sovereignty", "which should be subordinated to and serve the supreme principle of state sovereignty" (pp.326-327). He continues by observing, "However, even if the principle of state sovereignty occupies the supreme place, it can still be appropriately constrained by the states themselves on the basis of real equality, reciprocity, willingness, and equal negotiation" (p.327). While such an assertion might seem to over-state these bedrock principles of international law, the author explains why, in China's case, these need to be reiterated and fully understood. "The serious consequences of humiliation of nation [sic] and forfeiture of sovereignty are unfaded bitter lessons in history" (p.327). Although this passage deals ostensibly with international economic law issues, its relevance is more broad-based, especially when one tries to fully discern and appreciate China's approach to state sovereignty. "Nowadays Chinese people have stood up and recovered and have also intensified the sovereignty status of complete independence..." (p.317)

Other parts of the book also explore the notion of state sovereignty, albeit in different contexts. Understandably, considerable reference is made to "economic sovereignty" (with some 20 citations); "individual sovereignty" is discussed once; "permanent sovereignty", twice; "united sovereignty", also with two entries. "State sovereignty" garners some 8 mentions. A summary of these entries sprinkled throughout the book reveals a rather comprehensive elaboration of China's approach to sovereignty, discussed primarily vis-à-vis western thought and practice, especially US doctrine. As just one example, Professor Chen challenges the "Transnational Law Doctrine" (TLD) as "a doctrine that negates the sovereignty of weak nations, while preaches the hegemony of the United States and is thus a poisonous imported product" (p.38). He continues, "Jessup's TLD, by flaunting the banners of 'world government', 'united sovereignty' and 'priority of IL' [international law], intends to provide the jurisprudential basis of coveting, weakening, and negating the state sovereignty of the vast nations. It purports to force the weak nations to discard the fence of nation and state sovereignty, so that the US expansionism and world hegemonism could go through without hindrance" (pp.38-39).

Interestingly, Professor Chen's treatment of the theme of state sovereignty is summarised in a paper by Branislav Gosovic included in the Annex, where the notion is cast as the anchor for China's foreign policy strategy (defined in the 1982 Constitution—the so-called Five Principles of Peaceful Co-existence—"the mutual respect to each other's sovereignty and territorial integrity, mutual nonaggression, mutual non-interference in each other's domestic affairs, equality and reciprocity, and peaceful coexistence"). Gosovic argues that "In the years and decades to come, scholars will be able to test empirically Professor Chen's thesis and arguments and, if he is proven right, counter the widespread view in the realist mode of thinking, especially in the West" (p.773). The "western" view is described as positing that China's declared peaceful rise will "...morph into a hegemonic, expansionist, aggressive mode of reasoning and planetary behaviour, imitating and following the former oppressors and colonizers with whom it will proceed to carve the planet into respective spheres of influence" (p.773). The Voice from China suggests an entirely different outcome, based fundamentally on China's approach to international law.

In another vein, Professor Chen's treatment of the notion of state sovereignty (unabashedly from a Chinese perspective) provides new insights for China's transboundary water practice—a contemporary pressing issue for the country and the region. China, upstream on most of its 40+ major transboundary waters, shared with more than 20 other sovereign nations and autonomous regions, is often challenged with regard to its international freshwater use and development. At the heart of this debate is state sovereignty and how it is implemented in foreign policy, generally, and more specifically, as regards China's management of these transboundary resources in ways that, not only meet its own national economic imperatives, but also take into account the needs of its riparian neighbours, in accordance with international law. While there is a significant body of research that refers to China's transboundary state practice as "hegemonic", casting China as the regional (and ruthless?) "super-power" that acts unilaterally in its own self-interests, upon closer scrutiny, most of these studies suffer the same glaring oversight—they fail to interrogate the integral role that China's approach to international law plays in this domain. A critical analysis of China's treaty and state practice, evaluated in the light of rules of international law in this field, reveals a rather coherent, albeit not yet fully developed approach, aligned with China's approach to state sovereignty, and reflected in the theory of limited territorial sovereignty (Wouters and Chen, 2013; Xue, 1992; Saul, 2013). Professor Chen's "Voice of China" provides substantive legal arguments that contribute to a better understanding of how China might go forward with its transboundary water practice. Indeed, China's foreign direct investment policy on water-related matters needs more rigorous study, with few writings on this important topic (Chen, H. 2015). Such cross-over connected thinking, richly demonstrated in *The Voice from China*, provides a foundation for innovative approaches.

New legal approaches will be required in order to manage China's transboundary water resources in ways that balance economic growth with environmental issues is now high on the domestic agenda. As the world's natural resources continue to be over-exploited and under-protected, China's practice in this field will have a bearing, not only its national resources, but with respect to regional and global economic and environmental resources. Addressing global water / energy / food / environmental issues in ways that support economic growth is now a key topic debated at the World Economic Forum, the leading annual meeting of the globe's thinkers and policy-makers in this area. At the most recent meeting of the World Economic Forum (Davos, January 2015), Chinese Premier Li Keqiang stated that "Cultural diversity, like biodiversity, is a most precious treasure endowed to us on this planet... Like the vast ocean admitting all rivers that run into it, members of the international community need to work together to expand common ground while accepting differences, and seek win-win progress through inclusive cooperation and mutual learning." (Davos, 23 January 2015) "China has put forward the initiatives to build the Silk Road Economic

Belt and the 21st Century Maritime Silk Road. China hopes to work with other countries to advance these initiatives and ensure that they are brought forward in ways that meet the actual needs of countries concerned." How China implements this ambitious foreign policy in practice, especially in the context of complex contemporary challenges, and in light of China's approach to state sovereignty and international law, will be watched closely. Will Professor Chen's insights offer guidance for the future?

The collected work sheds light on these highly complex and controversial topics through its elaborate discussion of international economic legal theory and practice, which the author often locates within more general themes of public international law. Thus, The Voice from China has broad appeal. A number of inter-connected (and highly relevant) international legal topics are touched upon—as just some examples: South-South development policies ("developing countries possess the right to exercise permanent sovereignty over their natural resources; economic aid to the developing countries should be strictly based on respect towards the aided countries sovereignty, attaching with it no conditions or privileges for aiding countries extra benefit", p176—reviewing Deng Xiaoping's contribution to the notion of a New International Economic Order); theoretical and practice based approaches to international economic law topics (including foreign investment); and other areas, always with repeated calls and detailed justification for more independent and critical thinking in the field of international (economic) law.

The Voice from China provides a fascinating backdrop for all those interested in international law, especially from the Chinese perspective. It is compelling reading for scholars, who are wholeheartedly urged on by this forward looking visionary to take up the research challenge:

> There is and shall be no "exclusive zone" or "prohibited area" for academic research, into which outsiders are forbidden to enter. As a result, all those Chinese scholars with far vision and lofty ideal [sic] shall discard any parochial prejudices, no matter which fields they are specialized in; shall do their best and make concerted efforts respectively from different fields; and coordinatingly endeavour to take exploration and produce as many china-specific research results as possible. In this way, we can make our significant contributions for the revival and prosperity of legal study in both China and the world. (p.43)

In closing, it is the reviewer's hope that this collected work will be read by a wide audience and lead to more academic research in this area, considered within the broader canvas of international law. In particular, more scholarship in the field of natural and water-related resources is needed, infused with Chinese approaches, building on international best practice, rigorously evaluated.

China's voice must be heard—Professor Chen's book is a timely contribution that invites more innovative study in this field.

References:

H. Chen, The Human Right to Water and Foreign Investment: Friends or Foes? Water International, Vol.40, Iss.2, 2015; Manuscript on File with the Author.

Chinese Premier Li Keqiang's Speech at Davos 2015 (23 January, 2015), https://agenda.weforum.org/2015/01/chinese premier li keqiangs speech at davos 2015/.

B. Saul, China, Natural Resources, Sovereignty and International Law, Asian Studies Review, Vol.37, Iss.2, 2013, pp196-214.

Y. Su, Contemporary Legal Analysis of China's Transboundary Water Regimes: International Law in Practice, *Water International*, Vol.39, Iss.5, 2014, pp705-724.

S. Vinogradov & P. Wouters, Sino-Russian Transboundary Waters: A Legal Perspective on Cooperation, Stockholm Paper, Retrieved 12 02, 2014, http://www.chinainternationalwaterlaw.org/pdf/resources/20131216_001.pdf.

P. Wouters & H. Chen, China's "Soft-Path" to Transboundary Water Cooperation Examined in the Light of Two UN Global Water Conventions: Exploring the "Chinese Way", *Journal of Water Law*, Vol.22, 2013, pp229-247.

P. Wouters & H. Chen, Editors' Introduction to the "China Water Papers", *Water International*, Vol.40, Iss.2, 2015, pp1-20.

P. Wouters, The Yin and Yang of International Water Law:

China's Transboundary Water Practice and the Changing Contours of State Sovereignty, *RECIEL*, Vol.23, Iss.1, 2014.

Hanqin Xue, Relativity in International Water Law, *Colorado Journal of International Environmental Law and Policy*, Vol.3, No.1, 1992.

九、精當透徹的論證　盡顯大師的風采
——簡評《中國的吶喊：陳安論國際經濟法》
黃雁明*

捧讀陳安教授的皇皇巨著《中國的吶喊：陳安論國際經濟法》，以下簡稱《中國的吶喊》（ *The Voice from China: An CHEN on International Economic Law* ），不禁為他的學術碩果與駕馭英文的能力所折服。

陳教授是中國國際經濟法學界的大師、旗手，筆者曾是其麾下的普通成員。作為從事國際商事仲裁的工匠，筆者希圖從此視角對《中國的吶喊》中的兩宗案件的法律意見書（第20、21、22、23章〔220〕）略作評述。

案一，英國X公司v.英國Y保險公司。X公司與中國B公司成為一九九六年十二月成立的中國C電力公司的中外合作雙方。Y公司作為X公司的擔保人，承保的風險中包括政府徵用險。因中國國務院〔1998〕第31號通知與國務院辦公廳〔2002〕第43號通知（以下簡稱「兩通知」，依Y公司對X公司的保單，後者要求前者賠償在保險期內因中國政府（可能）的徵收而發生的損失，Y

公司拒絕，在仲裁案中列為被申請人。

陳教授應對的關鍵問題是「兩通知」是否構成（中國政府）對C公司與對X公司在C公司的投資權益的徵收；是否據此X公司可以向承保人Y請求賠償，之後Y公司是否可以獲得X公司的代位求償權。或許還可以用另一種方式表述，即在C公司的合作合同符合當時的《中外合作企業法》規定而獲得批准的前提下，被國際普遍接受的「當事人意思自治」與「法無溯及力」原則是否在作為法治國家的中國存在。

案二，廈門買方Zhonghe v.新加坡賣方Bunge於二〇〇四年二月二十五日簽訂銷售合同，標的物是五點五萬公噸巴西大豆，準據法是英國法。合同規定Zhonghe要在Bunge所接受的中國一流銀行開立以後者為受益人的信用證。

陳教授的法律意見書涉及的核心問題是中國國家品質監督檢驗檢疫總局（以下簡稱「檢驗總局」）的禁令對中國進口公司、中國的銀行及其海外分行是否具有強制性約束力；係爭合同開立信用證義務的履行地是否在中國；係爭合同的準據法是英國法，中國強制性規則對中國法人是否有約束力，上述禁令能否導致係爭合同落空。

在法律意見中，陳教授對於以中國法為準據法的案件，關注從中國憲法的有關法條到與案件及爭議問題密切相關的法律、法規、規章與行政命令等；對以英國法為準據法的合同，他根據《國際合同義務法律適用公約》（即《羅馬公約》）、英國《1990年合同法》、英國法院在長期的司法實踐中所確立的判例、英國權威學者提煉與歸納的為國際社會所普遍接受的法律衝突規範，

對它們的相互關係與不同效力層層分析，透澈論證自己的見解與觀點。

他的結論是否定徵收的構成與存在，確認法無溯及力等兩項原則在中國同樣有效；中國的強制性命令對中國法人有約束力，中國是合同開立信用證義務的履行地，前述強制性命令導致系爭合同落空。

拜讀之，筆者不禁想起一九八五至一九八六年中國改革開放與法制建設初期，曾經協助某前輩出具法律意見書的經歷。其中一份意見書是給中國香港地區的銀團出具的，涉及銀團向國內某公司的貸款，貸款合同的準據法是美國紐約州的法律。銀團律師聘請中國內地律師以查明與確認借款人與擔保人的身份、營業範圍、財政狀況、關於借款與擔保的償還能力與各自董事會的決定、借款與擔保獲得國家外匯管理局批准的情況、各自委派的簽約人等等。兩家擔保人中的一家是非金融企業，其主營業地在香港，並在香港擁有很高的商譽。但是，我們獲悉其註冊地是北京，因而要求其向國家外匯管理局申請批准對外債的擔保，提供批准檔。當時中國的法規有限，要適用內部文件所涉及的有關政策。可見，在貸款合同的準據法為美國紐約州法律的情況下，中國法律涉及中國當事人的權利能力和行為能力的規定關係到涉外合同能否順利履行。銀團及其境外律師希望中國律師查明有關中國當事人的問題與中國法律的相關規定，包括當時的內部（紅頭）檔所載的政策，在意見書出具後，貸款協議才能正式簽署。

案一，Y公司是明智的，及時請教中國法律專家為之提供有力的法律武器。若是X公司在懷疑所涉「兩通知」的溯及力以及

「兩通知」對其在中國C公司的權益構成徵收之時，在依據保險合同提請仲裁之前，同樣請求陳教授為其出具法律意見書，那麼效果是上佳的。畢竟若將爭議提交仲裁，由於X公司的現金投資是一千二百萬美元，保險額勢必不少於該數額（可能另加10%）其仲裁請求斷不少於此數額。而聘請律師要付費，向仲裁機構提請仲裁要交管理費（按請求金額的比例計算）、指定仲裁員的費用與仲裁庭的費用，與中國專家出具法律意見書的費用相比，後者是最合算的。

案二，根據筆者在前文提及曾經參與出具法律意見書的經歷，在準據法是紐約州法律的情況下，對中國當事人的屬人法，境外的律師從不敢掉以輕心，因為它關係到銀團與借款人之間的貸款合同是否存在落空的危險；更不會如Bunge聘請的中國律師般漠視。

本案是國際貨物銷售合同的爭議，雙方均來自《聯合國國際貨物銷售合同公約》（CISG）的簽字國，CISG成為新加坡與中國法律的構成部分。若不明確排除或減損其效力，那麼保留部分除外，CISG是否適用於本案？以英國法為準據法的合同爭議是否排除CISG的適用？依據陳教授援引的《羅馬公約》第3.3條：

當事人選擇外國法這一事實，無論其是否同時選擇外國法庭，如在選擇時一切與當事情況有關因素僅同一個國家有關，不應影響該國法律規定的適用，即該國法律規定（以下稱「強制性規定」）之適用不得以合同廢除之。

據此，上述法條表明，適用英國法不能構成對適用CISG的排除，那麼CISG第7（2）條規定：

本公約未明確解決的屬於本公約範圍的問題，應當按照本公約所依據的一般原則來解決，在沒有一般原則的情況下，則應按照國際私法規定適用的法律來解決。

依照CISG的上述原則，係爭合同Zhonghe的屬人法，對其以及對中國的銀行（包括它們的海外分行）的行為能力有約束力。在明知進口的食品（或食物的原料）被檢驗總局禁止的情況下，不得違反。對此，陳教授已經援引法條充分論證。

此外，是否還可以提及中國《合同法》第127條：

工商行政管理部門和其他有關行政主管部門在各自的職權範圍內，依照法律、行政法規的規定，對利用合同危害國家利益、社會公共利益的違法行為，負責監督處理；構成犯罪的，依法追究刑事責任。

上述法條從另一角度再次表明中國法律體系中強制性規定的約束力與違反的嚴重後果。

或許還可以告訴案二的當事人，如果仲裁庭漠視中國法律體系中的強制性規範，裁決可以向中國出口含有高毒性致癌農藥的巴西大豆，或者裁決Bunge勝訴，中國法院可以不承認與執行被申請人的勝訴裁決。因為危害消費者健康的食品是不可接受的。

裁決書中嚴重的錯誤構成對公共政策的違反。[221] 允許有重大缺陷的裁決書存在，不予更正，必將損害公眾對仲裁整體的信賴。[222] 這是國際上日漸流行的準則。這一準則現在已經鮮明地體現在聯合國國際貿易法委員會《國際商事仲裁示範法》第34條與第36條之中。這裡不妨援引一宗案例Telkom SA Ltd. v. Anthony Boswood QC，涉及仲裁員的處理不當（misconduct）導致裁決書的撤銷或擱置（setingaside）：

> 南非高級法院查明仲裁員出現（適用）法律的錯誤（commit errors of law），構成仲裁的重大違法（或不當）行為（to amount to gross irregularities），而撤銷（或擱置）裁決書。[223]

從陳教授的法律意見書中，仲裁員還可以學到些什麼？在裁決書的仲裁庭意見部分，仲裁員論述爭議焦點，交代與揭示其所查明或確認的事實，要全面、詳盡、條理清楚；要論述當事人的請求與反請求成立與否的理由。如果仲裁員具備這樣的能力，裁決才有說服力。

陳教授的法律意見書出具時間是二〇〇六年，當時中國與改革開放和市場經濟建設相配套的法律法規已經基本齊全。意見書中提及的所有法規均在陽光下，「紅頭文件」的效力逐漸消退。問題在於一個法律專家是否真的是行家裡手？若沒有深厚的理論功底與對所涉問題的深刻理解，又對所涉法規不能了然於胸、融會貫通，便不能多角度多層面地分析與論述，鞭辟入裡，結論清楚，釋疑解惑。

時代給他提供了機會，他無愧於時代賦予的使命。作為傑出的法學家，他的聲音在攀登的路上迴響。

料想，陳教授必定熟知馬克思所言：「外國語是人生鬥爭的武器。」他的英文著作代表中國國際經濟法學界與中國國際商事仲裁界在國際上發聲。非經多年的苦讀與苦練，不能以地道的英文撰寫專業文章並在國際仲裁的權威刊物上發表，進而得以結集出版。

《中國的吶喊》中披露，陳教授從一九五三年起作為年輕的法學教員轉入馬列主義的教學領域。一九八〇年，他年過半百後，才得以重回法學領域，研究國際經濟法。盛年之時，在「應衝刺的年齡才起跑」，也可以視為幸運。在中國改革開放與法制建設的春天，他「急起直追，以勤補拙」。據其弟子告知，陳教授往往工作到深夜或淩晨。三十多年中陳教授獲得了廣闊的舞臺，在流逝的歲月中留下了深深的足印，為光輝的時代留下了華章。

二〇〇五年他已七十六歲，猶以自勖詩句[224]表達其永不止步的決心：

蹉跎半生，韶華虛擲。青山滿目，夕霞天際。
老牛破車，一拉到底。餘熱未盡，不息奮蹄！

誦讀此詩，令人不禁想起美國詩人Robert Frott的詩《獻身》（*Devotion*，漢蓉譯）：

心靈視獻身，不比海岸高。

守候岸曲線，永數潮漲消！

（編輯：龔　宇）

Precise and Thorough Analyses—Illustrating a Guru's Profound Knowledge

—A Brief Commentary on *The Voice from China:*
An CHEN on International Economic Law

Huang Yanming*

Opening this great monograph titled *The Voice from China: An CHEN on International Economic Law (The Voice from China)*, I am very delighted with and impressed by Prof. Chen's scholastic achievements on the subject and his skills in mastering English.

Prof. Chen is an eminent jurist and the forerunner of China's international economic law discipline. He was the Chairman of the Chinese Society of International Economic Law in which I was once a member of the Society and a mere subordinate under his supervision. I wish to touch and simultaneously share my views on some aspects of the cases and the Legal Opinions in The Voice from China (Chapters 20, 21, 22 and 23 [225]) from the perspective of a craftsman—an arbitrator. In order to save space, abbreviated case names and subjects related would be applied.

Case 1, A UK Co. X v. a UK Insurance Co. Y. In December 1996, an entity from Cayman Islands and Chinese Co. B entered into a contractual joint venture agreement (**"the Agreement"**) and a contractual joint venture (**"the CJV"**) was established in China. Later Co. X replaced the Cayman entity. Under the insurance policy issued by Co. Y with Co. X as the assured, the risks undertaken cover losses arising out of acts of expropriation occurring during the policy period of February 20, 2001 to February 19, 2004. Due to the issuance of **Circular No.31〔1998〕** by the PRC's State Council and **Circular No.43〔2002〕** by the General Office of the State Council (**"the Two Circulars"**), Co. X claims that the Two Circulars constitute an **Act of Expropriation**, and therefore requesting compensation for losses from Co. Y by reference to the insurance policy that stipulated about (possible) compulsory take over by the Chinese government. Co. Y denies and Co. X refers the case to arbitration in British.

The key issues before Prof. Chen are whether the Two Circulars are of the nature or give such effects of an Act of Expropriation of the assets of the CJV; if the answer is affirmative, Co. X could base on the alleged Act of Expropriation to claim the coverage under the insurance policy, thereafter Co. Y would gain the subrogation (of insurer) from Co. X. In another word, the said issues could be expressed in a manner to cover situations where an agreement is in line with the provisions of the Act of PRC on Chinese-Foreign Contractual Joint Venture (**"CJV Act"**) and has received approval by some competent governmental authorities of China. Under such circumstances, have those internationally accepted basic legal principles, such as **"autonomy of the parties' will"** and **"no-retroactivity of law"**, been fully accepted by or already taken root in China as a country ruled by law?

Case 2, Xiamen Zhonghe Industry Co., Ltd. (Zhonghe) v. Bunge Singapore Pte. Ltd. (Bunge). Zhonghe as buyer and Bunge as seller on February 25, 2004 entered into the Contract S04-071**("the Contract")** with Brazilian soybeans of 55,000 metric tons as the subject matter. It is provided in the Contract that Zhonghe shall through a first-class Chinese bank acceptable by Bunge open a letter of credit in favor of the seller.

The kernel problems that Prof. Chen are faced with are whether **the prohibitions** (or **administrative ordinances, administrative prohibitive orders** or **mandatory regulations or rules**) by AQSIQ have comprehensive and powerful legal binding force over Chinese importers, Chinese banks and their respective branches overseas; whether China is the place of performance of the obligation to open the letter of credit under the Contract; **when English laws are applicable**, whether the mandatory rules or orders in Chinese legal system are of mandatory effects over Chinese legal entities and therefore the Contract was frustrated due to the said prohibitions and their binding force.

In his Legal Opinions, when dealing with issues pertaining to Case 1, Prof. Chen has not overlooked or missed out any provisions concerned from the Constitution to all the laws, acts, regulations, rules, and administrative orders and even the promises by China when entering into WTO. For instance, he lists some facts that as a member of WTO,

China has not only promised to "ensure the full conformity of its laws, regulations, and rules with the provision of the WTO Agreement" [226] but also taken measures in this regard. [227] When treating the problems relating to Case 2, he respectively identifies the Contract and the clause that "English laws shall be applied", and that the Contract was signed by Bunge's subsidiary Bunge International Trading (Shanghai) Co., Ltd. (**"Bunge Shanghai"**) residing in Shanghai with Zhonghe. [228]

Revealing his deep knowledge of the Convention on the Law Applicable to Contractual Obligations (**"Rome Convention"**), the effective Contacts (Applicable Law) Act 1990 (of British), the precedents established by English courts in their long established judicial practice and conflict of laws rules which have been refined and summarized by authoritative English scholars and widely accepted by the international community, analyzing their mutual relations and different forces, step by step, Prof. Chen discusses the issues and expounds his viewpoints by accurately referring to the relevant provisions of various acts or laws and legal theories.

Prof. Chen reaches his conclusion that in Case 1 the Two Circulars and their provisions are of no **Expropriation** effects, and confirms that the two major principles of law, ie., "**autonomy of the parties' will**" and "**non-retroactivity**" have actually taken root in China and are applicable to the case. And in Case 2, he firmly believes that the **administrative prohibitive orders** or **mandatory orders** contained in the Publication Announcements, such as the Announcements 71 by

AQSIQ are of binding effects over Chinese legal entities concerned, that China is the place of performance of the obligation to have the letter of credit opened and the Contract was frustrated due to the mandatory orders.

Perusing the Chapters, the author cannot help recall the days when China was at the initial period of reform and began to rejoin the international community. It was also the initial period of the rule by law in China. In 1985-1986, I once assisted a senior superior in his rendering of legal opinions. One of the legal opinions was for a banking group of Hong Kong, relating to the banking group as lenders and a Chinese company as borrower and two Chinese corporations as guarantors to the loan agreement with the laws of New York State of the America as the governing laws. The lawyers engaged by the banking group had to engage some lawyer in the mainland China to carry out inquiries to identify and confirm the status, the business scope, the financial standing and other conditions of the borrowers and the guarantors; that the matters relating to the loan and guaranty were normal and in conformity with the laws, acts, regulations or policies of China; that the borrower and his guarantors had got consents from competent departments of China; and the decisions relating to the loan made by the boards of directors of the borrower and the guarantors and representatives who would sign the loan agreement and other documents concerned. The main business of one of the two guarantors had been in Hong Kong for over 100 years, nevertheless its registration place of the business was in Beijing. Though it was of good credit in Hong Kong, it was required according to the regulations by the State Administrative Bureau of Exchange Control to apply for approval for the guaranty and to obtain the approval certificate. At that time, there were few statutes enacted or promulgated by National People's Congress or its standing committee, instead there were quite a lot internal documents or official documents of red colored titles ("hong tou wen jian" in Chinese). But it was obviously, while the applicable laws of the loan agreement were the laws of the New York State, the banking group and their lawyers relied expressly upon the provisions of the laws, acts, regulations or even the then popular internal documents of China containing some policies in this regard. All the legal issues or matters identified and confirmed in the legal opinions issued by the lawyer from mainland China were the pre-conditions for the finally conclusion of the loan agreement. The signing of the loan agreement was done upon the receipt of the legal opinions by the banking group and its lawyers.

In Case 1, Co. Y acts in reasonable manner, timely asking a Chinese legal expert for advice which forms as his basis for defence. If Co. X, when in doubt of the retroactivity of the Two Circulars and whether it is of the nature of expropriation, should have acted as Co. Y in asking a Chinese legal expert for advice, Prof. Chen's legal opinions would have been issued for him and such legal opinions would have even better effect. After all, Co. X had referred the case to arbitration, as his sum of investment was USD 12,000,000.00, the coverage of the policy would not have been less than that sum or probably plus 10 per cent and the sum claimed would have not been less than the sum either. In this case, Co. X had paid fees for his lawyers, for the arbitration administrative charges closely relating to the time spent by the registrar and his deputies and the fees for the arbitrator(s). If Co. X had asked for advice before referring the case to arbitration, the sum paid for a Chinese legal expert and his legal opinions would be a very small proportion comparing with the fees and changes that he would have paid for arbitral process.

Concerning Case 2, I have mentioned above that I was once an assistant to a senior superior in rendering legal opinions to a banking group from other jurisdiction. When the governing laws were those of the New York State, the banking group's lawyers had never overlooked the lex personalis of the borrower and guarantors of other jurisdiction. In contrast, in Case 2, the Chinese lawyer engaged by Bunge has given me an impression that he did not take proper notice or even probably turned a blind eye to the laws or mandatory orders of China.

The lex personalis of Zhonghe should not have been neglected, such as those pertaining to the capacity for private rights or duties, any Chinese legal entities should abided by them or the Chinese legal entities must be subject to those laws, acts, regulations or administrative orders. If there are any prohibitions on the importing or exporting to China food or material for food processing with **pesticide**, knowledge about these prohibitions or the absence of such knowledge would have different serious consequences. Prof. Chen has proved that he is well professed of all aspects of the matters concerned.

I would like to stress that the Contract is of an important feature in international trade. For example, parties are from the contracting states to the CISG, then the provisions of the CISG will be regarded as being integrated into their respective national law of P. R. China and Singapore. If the parties do not expressly exclude the application of the CISG or derogate from or vary the effect of its provisions, [229] save the reservations, doesn't the CISG apply to the case? When the governing law is of English law, does it mean that the CISG could be absolutely excluded?

I am fully accept that Prof. Chen is correct in quoting Art 3(3) of the Rome Convention "[T]he fact that the parties have chosen a foreign law, whether or not accompanied by the choice of a foreign tribunal, shall **not**, where all the other elements relevant to the situation at the time of the choice are connected with one country only, **prejudice the application of rules of the law of that country which cannot be derogated from by contract, hereinafter called 'mandatory rules'.**" [230]

It seems to me that the application of the CISG to the case could not be excluded. If the parties don't exclude the application of the CISG in the Contract, it will be necessary to look at Art.7(2) of the CISG:

> Questions concerning matters governed by this Convention which are not expressly settled in it are to be settled in conformity with the general principles on which it is based or, in the absence of such principles, **in conformity with the law applicable by virtue of the rules of private international law.**

If in the instant case the CISG could not be excluded, should we rely on the lex personalis of Zhonghe as Prof. Chen does and we may further refer to Art. 127 of the Contact Act of PRC:

The Administration of Industry and Commerce and other relevant administrative authorities shall, within the scope of their respective the functions, supervise and deal with any unlawful conduct by way of contract prejudicial and detrimental to national or public interest. **If such conduct amounts to a crime, criminal responsibility shall be pursued according to laws.** [231]

The provision contained in Art.127 above, once more from another angel reminds anyone of the binding effects of Chinese mandatory orders or rules and serious consequence of being against them.

In addition, I guess it might be better to tell Bunge and his Chinese lawyer, if they insists on the view that the mandatory rules or orders in the Chinese legal system could be ignored and the award should be made in favor of Bunge that under the Contract Brazilian soybeans containing highly toxic carcinogenic pesticide could be exported to China, the award should be set aside or its enforcement be refused. Some lines on a case revealing that misconduct of arbitrator "[W]hich justified setting aside an award Telkon SA Ltd. v. Anthony Boswood QC" are as follows:

The South African High Court found that the arbitrator had committed errors of law (emphasis added) which amounted to gross irregularities in the conduct of the arbitration and set the award aside.

We should be aware that nowadays any awards tainted with extremely serious or egregious errors amount to a breach of public policy. [233] To allow such fundamentally flawed awards to stand uncorrected would undermine confidence in the integrity of the arbitral process. [234] That concept or principle is expressly reflected in the Arts.34 and 36 of the UNCITRAL Model Law on International Commercial Arbitration.

From the Legal Opinions by Prof. Chen, we arbitrators could get some enlightenment. In our awards under the subtitle "the Opinions of the Tribunal", the tribunal should ensure that no issue and claim is missed out, all matters, key issues, facts and the merits of the case should be thoroughly explored. If arbitrators are short of that ability, failing to explain why a claim or counter-claim is sustained or refused, their awards rendered would be far from convincing in giving reasons.

It is in the 21 century that Prof. Chen issued his Legal Opinions. Sets of laws, acts, regulations or rules that are orientated towards the needs of a market economy have been basically enacted or promulgated. All the provisions he quotes are transparent in the sun. The effects of those "internal documents" are fading. Nevertheless, the problem lies in whether one is an old hand. Not familiar with all the aspects of the matters concerned, without profound knowledge and deep understanding of all the issues concerned, without skills in mastering in one's mother-tongue and English plus its legal terminology, one could hardly deal with those hard-nuts properly.

The era of reform and opening to the international community has provided Prof. Chen with a golden opportunity and in return for the era and on behalf of the discipline of the international economic law of China he advocates with admirable clarity and strength, his voice are echoing along the long road to the heights.

I guess Prof. Chen must be familiar with the saying of Karl Marx: "A foreign language is a weapon in the struggle of life." No pains no gains. Without decades of hard working, reading, writing and studying, no one is able to write in idiomatic English.

His professional papers are carried in authoritative journals and then collected in this monograph. Acting as a distinguish representative of discipline of the China's international economic law and the circle of China international arbitration, he has made his marks on the international stage and added academic literature thereon.

It is revealed in *The Voice form China*, that Prof. Chen as a junior teacher in 1953 shifted from law to Marxism and Leninism. When over 50 years old, in his prime years, he at last got the chance to return to the law field as he says that "Just stated to race at the age of spurt". On the other hand, it could be regarded as a matter of luck. In the spring of reform and opening to the outside, he has lost no chance to "rouse to catch up, overcome shortage by diligence". His doctorial candidates remember that he usually would not turn off his desk-lamp until midnight or early morning. In the past decades, he has never idled away. His brilliant works are reflecting the long road he has travelled.

In his poem of self-encouragement in 2005 even when he was aged

76, he revealed his determination that he would never stop in his academic researching and creating course:[235]

Regretfully it is so late in a daytime,
Half of a lifetime had been spent in vain,
Thanks to the setting sun so brightly shines,
The old ox insists in carrying a broken cart to the end,
Never stop in speeding up its hoof-pace in time,
As long as its surplus energy still remains.

That reminds me of the similar poem by an American poet Robert Frost:

Devotion
The heart can think of no devotion,
Greater than being shore to the ocean,
Holding the curve of one position,
Counting an endless repetition.

（翻譯：黃雁明）

十、獨具中國風格氣派　發出華夏學術強音

——評《中國的吶喊：陳安論國際經濟法》

石靜霞　孫英哲*

　　二〇一三年，中國國際經濟法學界的前輩陳安先生的英文版新書《中國的吶喊：陳安論國際經濟法》隆重面世。該書匯輯了

陳安教授自一九八〇年以來不同時期撰寫的二十四篇精品專論，受「國家社會科學基金中華學術外譯項目」支援，由國際著名出版社斯普林格（Springer）出版。

陳安先生學貫中西，素養精深，他就中國國際經濟法學的基本問題提出了許多真知灼見，並多次代表中國國際經濟法學界赴國外交流講學，被譽為「中國國際經濟法學的奠基人之一」。陳安先生並未拘泥於國際經濟法學的理論探討，而是積極投身實踐，代表中國參與多項國際法律實務。特別是，陳先生曾經先後於一九九三年、二〇〇四年，二〇一〇年三度受中國政府指派，就任「解決投資爭端國際中心」（ICSID）國際仲裁員，處理具體的國際投資爭端。

陳安先生《中國的吶喊：陳安論國際經濟法》一書共分六部分，系統梳理和分析了改革開放以來國際經濟法學術前沿的重大熱點和難點問題，在該書中，陳安先生將理論與實踐緊密結合，始終堅持實事求是，並以公平正義作為自身觀點的內在脈絡。其中，以第十一章「對近期謝業深訴秘魯政府案ICSID管轄權裁定的若干質疑：中國秘魯BIT是否應當適用於『一國兩制』下的香港特別行政區」（Queries to he Recent ICSID Decision on Jurisdiction Uponthe Case of Tza Yap Shumv. Republic of Peru: Should China-Peru BIT 1994 Be Applied to Hong Kong SAR Under he "One Country, Two Systems" Policy?）[236] 尤為突出。

近年來，國際投資仲裁發展迅速，中國企業的參與度正在逐步增長。中國企業近年來提起了三起國際投資仲裁案，[237] 其中包括兩件ICSID仲裁案。因此，ICSID仲裁實踐對於中國投資，

尤其是中國對外簽訂的雙邊投資保護協定（BIT）的具體落實具有重要意義。這篇文章以中國政府簽署條約首次在ICSID涉案的謝業深訴秘魯政府案（Tza Yap Shum v. Republic of Peru）的管轄權裁定為中心，探討了ICSID仲裁庭裁決的不當之處。案件的核心問題之一是，香港人是否可以援引中國政府在香港回歸之前與秘魯政府簽訂的BIT來尋求投資保護。陳安先生對此持否定態度。陳安先生在著重分析《中英聯合聲明》《香港特區基本法》以及《維也納條約法公約》（VCLT）等相關規定的基礎上，主要從兩方面論證了其觀點：首先，考慮到中國政府「一國兩制」的大政方針和《香港特區基本法》中的具體規定[238]，中國秘魯BIT不應自動適用於香港。其次，中國秘魯BIT於一九九四年簽訂時，香港尚未回歸，因此不能適用於涉及中國的爭議。

　　Lao Holdings N. V. v. Lao People's Democratic Republic案[239]也涉及類似問題，即澳門投資者是否可以援引中國老撾BIT對老撾提起仲裁。Lao Holdings N. V案仲裁庭在肯定了《關於國家在條約方面的繼承的維也納公約》（VCST）第15條「移動條約適用範圍原則」（moving treaty frontiers rule）與VCLT第29條均為國際習慣法，並對二者區別以及在此案中的聯繫進行分析的基礎上，認為中國老撾BIT應當適用於澳門特別行政區。[240]該案裁決雖然與謝業深案的裁決思路存在差異，[241]但在基本立場上繼承了仲裁庭在謝業深案中的立場，值得注意。首先，仲裁庭運用VCST第15條[242]對於國家繼承問題所發展出的分析框架進行了論證。第15條分為一般條款和例外條款，仲裁庭認為，如果適用一般條款，中國—老撾BIT可以對澳門適用；且是，如果第15條

的例外條款的規定得以滿足，則中國—老撾BIT不得對澳門適用。仲裁庭採用反推的方法，證明第15條B項中的3項例外條款中的規定均未在該案當中得到滿足。其中，在論證「中國—老撾BIT是否在另外被證明不能適用於中國領土全境」時，仲裁庭繼承了謝業深案的觀點。在謝業深案中，仲裁庭認為在中國與第三國已經簽訂BIT的情況下，香港自行與第三國締結BIT的權力並不必然多餘（necessarily redundant）。[243] 該案中的仲裁庭認為，中國—老撾BIT與澳門—老撾BIT的立法目標都是保護外國投資者和東道國的經濟發展。兩個BITs如果同時對澳門適用，不僅不會造成阻礙，反而會對實現這兩個BIT的立法目標產生促進作用。[244] 除此以外，在對BIT s重點概念的理解上，該案仲裁庭也基本認同謝業深案仲裁庭適用VCLT進行的論證分析。[245] 謝業深案仲裁庭認為，根據VCLT相關規定，[246] 在對中國秘魯BIT第8條第3款[247] 中規定的「涉及」（involving）一詞的「通常意義」（ordinary meaning）進行解釋時，應當將「涉及」理解為「包含」（inclusive）而非「僅包含」（exclusive)。因此，不能僅僅從表面上將第8條第3款中規定的「涉及」簡單理解為對於仲裁庭管轄權的限制。[248]

由此看來，陳安先生的主張雖然理由翔實，但並未受到國際仲裁實踐的完全認可。陳安先生的論證重點在於《中英聯合聲明》與《香港特區基本法》，但仲裁庭顯然對《中英聯合聲明》與《香港特區基本法》的分析著墨不多，而是著重於對BITs的分析。這啟示我們，作為中國學者，應當對中外聯合聲明的國際法律地位以及特區基本法的內涵進行深入研究，從而能夠引起國際

關注。

陳安先生文章的最大特色在於論證充分，尤其是完整論證了VCLT第31條、第32條在具體適用中的問題。總體上看，陳安先生的論證不僅對後案有所影響，[249] 同時還留下了一些值得深思的問題。首先，中國—秘魯BIT不能對香港特別行政區生效，是否可以直接等同於香港公民（Chinese nationals who hold a HKSAR passport）不能援引中國—秘魯BIT？中國—秘魯BIT中規定的「投資者」的範圍是所有「依照中華人民共和國法律擁有其國籍的自然人」[250]。而根據中國《國籍法》相關規定，[251] 香港公民具有中國國籍，則香港特別行政區的「高度自治權」是否可以阻礙香港公民憑藉中國國籍，獲取中國—秘魯BIT項下的投資保護呢？其次，作為一種法律論證技術（lawyering skill），如果謝業深不能獲得中國—秘魯BIT項下的投資保護，他是否可以根據英國於一九九三年與秘魯簽訂的英國—秘魯BIT(1994年生效）來尋求投資保護呢？如果謝業深因為「舊法（1995年生效的中國—秘魯BIT）不適用『新情況』[252]」而不能獲得中國—秘魯BIT的保護，則其是否可以依據「舊法（1994年生效的英國—秘魯BIT）應當根據『過去的情況』[253] 繼續適用」的邏輯尋求英國—秘魯BIT的保護呢？這些都是我們在陳安先生著作的啟發下，可以進一步考察的重要問題。

此外，陳安先生在該文中還從中外投資爭端的視角，詳細論證了有關《中英聯合聲明》《中國憲法》《香港特區基本法》以及中外條約彼此之間的關係等問題[254]，明確指出，《中英聯合聲明》明文規定，中國政府決定於一九九七年七月一日對香港恢

復行使主權，同日，英國政府將香港交還中國。從此時起，根據《中國憲法》第31條制定的「《香港基本法》構成管理香港特別行政區的憲政性文件」[255] 香港的一切事務均應按《香港基本法》行事。依據《中英聯合聲明》附件一第XI章以及《香港特區基本法》第153條規定，在「一國兩制」的特定條件下，「中國與外國簽訂的各種國際協定在一九九七年後並不能自動適用於香港。相反，這些協定只在中國中央政府徵詢香港特別行政區政府的意見，並決定適用於香港特別行政區後，才能適用於香港特別行政區」[256]。這些論證，對於當前中國所面臨的現實問題，包括任何人都無權藉口《中英聯合聲明》干涉中國內政、應以法治方式解決香港「占中」危機等，均具有重大的現實參考意義。[257] 具體說來，情況如下：

據香港《文匯報》二〇一四年十一月十八日報導，英國下議院外交事務委員會十七日舉行有關《中英聯合聲明》的聽證會。香港《南華早報》前總編輯范力行（Jonathan Fenby）在出席「作證」時稱，中國中央政府希望緊緊控制香港政治和經濟，香港特區政府比較重視與內地的關係，忽略港人的民主訴求。在港參與「占領」行動的香港大學學生Hui Sin Tung及香港中文大學學生Tang Chi Tak則稱，中國中央政府多次違反《中英聯合聲明》，包括「剝奪」內文訂明港人能繼續享有的新聞自由、集會自由及普及選舉權利，英國應該迫使中國「履行」《中英聯合聲明》並作出譴責，甚至重啟《南京條約》及《天津條約》。此外，香港民主黨主席劉慧卿十八日也通過視像向英國國會「作證」，稱英國有責任保障香港的自由和生活方式。另外，英美等外國勢力一

再插手香港內部事務，趁「占中」之機，他們插手頻率更是有增無減。二〇一四年九月底，英國時任首相卡梅倫稱，「英國與中國達成的協議中提到了在『一國兩制』框架下，香港擁有民主對未來的重要性」，十月中旬他又宣稱「英國應為香港人的自由權利站出來」。十一月，當「占中」行動在香港已陷入窮途末路之際，繼美中經濟與安全審議委員會年度報告用了二十頁篇幅對香港政改胡謅一通外，美國國會中國問題委員會又召開聽證會，邀請「末代港督」彭定康在倫敦透過視像衛星越洋「作證」，稱西方國家應公開對香港問題發聲。英國外交事務委員會的議員則計畫到港調查，結果被北京拒絕入境。對於英國的諸多讕言和花招，香港特區政制及內地事務局局長譚志源反駁說，英方對回歸後的香港無主權、無治權、無監督權，不存在所謂「道義責任」。香港工聯會議員王國興說，香港部分反對派人員「應邀作證」，是**公然配合外國勢力干預香港內部事務，是喪失國格的行為，對中國人民、香港市民構成極大傷害**。香港金融界立法會議員吳亮星也說，香港事務是中國內政，其他國家無權指指點點，有香港反對派議員「配合」出席聽證會，明顯是招引外國勢力干涉中國國家內部事務。[258]

中國政府對英國下議院外交事務委員會舉行有關《中英聯合聲明》的聽證會的荒唐行徑，也連續予以嚴詞譴責。早在二〇一四年七月二十五日，中國外交部發言人洪磊就指出，香港事務屬於中國內政，英方的做法是干涉中國內政，中國對此表示強烈不滿和堅決反對。中國政府反對任何外部勢力以任何藉口進行干涉。[259]二〇一四年十二月三日，外交部發言人華春瑩更加明確

指出，香港已於一九九七年回歸中國，是中國的特別行政區。一九八四年的《中英聯合聲明》就中方恢復對香港行使主權和過渡期的有關安排，對中英雙方的權利義務作了清晰劃分。英方對回歸後的香港無主權、無治權、無監督權，不存在所謂「道義責任」。英方有些人企圖用所謂「道義責任」混淆視聽，干涉中國內政，是不可接受的，也不可能得逞。〔260〕

　　顯而易見，中國政府二〇一四年的上述表態以及香港愛國人士二〇一四年的上述主張，與陳安先生早先在二〇〇八年作出的前述詳細論證，可以說是完全契合和互相呼應的。

　　陳安先生博學強識，書中很多對於國際經濟法學重要問題的觀點均來自於其畢生孜孜不倦的研習以及他與國際學術界的對話。陳安先生先後與Louis Henkin、Andreas F. Lowefeld以及John H. Jackson等著名國際經濟法學學家進行過深入的研討交流，不斷更新自己的知識，並將中國國際經濟法學界的新發展和新動向介紹給國外同仁。更可貴的是，在研究與實踐的過程中，陳安先生深刻洞察到國外國際經濟法學著作中所暗含的殖民主義氣息和單邊主義進路，尤其是美式雙重標準（US-tyle double standards）等，因此他畢生以呼籲改造舊式國際經濟秩序、建立新型國際經濟秩序為己任，堅持實事求是的態度，不懈探索真理，三十年如一日，積累彙聚而成《中國的吶喊》一書。「全書結構自成一體，觀點新穎，具有中國風格和中國氣派，闡釋了不同於西方發達國家學者的創新學術理念和創新學術追求，致力於初步創立起以馬克思主義為指導的具有中國特色的國際經濟法理論體系，為國際社會弱勢群體爭取公平權益鍛造了法學理論武器。」〔261〕

黨的十八屆三中全會決議將「構建開放型經濟新體制」上升到戰略高度，加強中國國際經濟法學研究、完善中國國際經濟法治建設，已成為因應「一帶一路」「走出去」、創設金磚銀行和亞洲基礎設施投資銀行的核心要求和必要保障。汪洋副總理撰文指出，應當加強涉外法律工作，積極參與國際規則的制定。[262] 本書正是陳安先生植根於中華民族利益、中國特色社會主義制度以及中國作為發展中國家經貿大國的發展現狀，對國際經濟法基本理論和熱點難點問題的重要回應。當前，多邊貿易體系前行緩慢，雙邊、諸邊貿易投資協定尤其是以跨太平洋夥伴關係協議（Trans- Pacific Partnership, TPP）、跨大西洋貿易與投資夥伴協議（Transatlantic Trade and Investment Partnership, TTIP）、區域全面經濟夥伴關係（Regional Comprehensive Economic Partnership, RCEP）等為代表的巨型自貿協定（Mega-FTAs）以及數百個包含投資規則的FTAs，正成為國際經貿法重構的重要體現。陳安先生在書中指出，「中外雙邊投資條約中的四大『安全閥』不宜貿然全面拆除」[263]，這對於在中美、中歐BIT談判中如何保護國家、民族利益等具有借鑑意義。此外，陳安先生在其著作中引經據典，從中國古詩詞到外國學界大師名著，可以很好地幫助讀者更深入地了解中國國際經濟法學者的獨特學術視野。

　　我們相信，陳安先生的巨著《中國的吶喊》一書，將乘著全球化浪潮和中國經濟高速發展的東風走向世界，代表中國國際經濟法學人，在國際法舞臺上發出華夏學術的強音。

（編輯：陳　欣）

Academic Voice with Chinese Characteristics
—A Commentary on *The Voice from China: An CHEN on International Economic Law*

Shi Jingxia   Sun Yingzhe*

In 2013, the English version of the book *The Voice from China: An CHEN on International Economic Law*, sponsored by Chinese Academic Translation Program, was published by Springer, a distinguished publisher across the globe. The book is a collection of the 24 papers written by An Chen, an emeritus professor of Xiamen University, the former chairman of the Chinese Society of International Economic Law, and one of the co-founders of the Society, in different times since 1980s.

An Chen, with profound attainments and a thorough knowledge of both western and Chinese law in the field of international economic law, has been honored as one of the founders of the discipline of international economic law in China. He has put forward a lot of insights on the basic issues in China concerning international economic law and, for many a time, he went abroad for international academic exchange and overseas lecturing. Not just limited to the theoretic exploration, he also devoted himself to the practice in the field of international economic law. In particular, he was designated by the Chinese government in 1993, 2004 and 2010 respectively as an international arbitrator in the International Center for the Settlement of Investment Disputes (ICSID) and engaged in the specific settlement of investment disputes.

The book, composed of six parts, systematically presented and analyzed the major heat issues and perplexities concerning international economic law faced with China since its Reform and Opening-up Program. In this book, Mr. Chen has combined theory with practice, insisted the principle of seeking truth from facts unswervingly, and regarded fairness and justice as the backbone of his arguments. In Chapter 11, the paper entitled "Queries to the Recent ICSID Decision on Jurisdiction Upon the Case of Tza Yap Shum v. Republic of Peru: Should China-Peru BIT 1994 Be Applied to Hong Kong SAR Under the 'One Country, Two Systems' Policy?" is a particular case in point.

In recent years, with the rapid expansion of international investment arbitrations, China has seen an increasing engagement in the settlement of investment arbitration. Enterprises in the Chinese mainland have in recent years initiated 3 international investment disputes, two out of which involve ICSID arbitration. Therefore, the ICSID arbitration practice is of huge significance to China's overseas investment and, particularly, to the implementation of China's BITs negotiated with foreign countries or jurisdictions. This paper, revolving the decision on the jurisdiction issue in the case Tza Yap Shum v. Republic of Peru in which a BIT negotiated by China was involved in ICSID arbitration for the first time, has explored the inappropriateness of the ICSID arbitral tribunal's decision. One of the focuses in the case was whether Hong Kongese could seek investment protection under the BIT negotiated by the government of the Chinese mainland and that of Peru prior to

Hong Kong's return to China. Mr. Chen adopted a negative attitude. After an analysis of the Joint Declaration of the Government of the United Kingdom of Great Britain and Northern Ireland and the Government of the People's Republic of China on the Question of Hong Kong (hereinafter referred to as "Sino-British Joint Declaration"), The Basic Law of the Hong Kong Special Administrative Region of the People's Republic of China (hereinafter referred to as "The Basic Law of the Hong Kong SAR") and the Vienna Convention on the Law of the Treaties (hereinafter referred to as "VCLT"), he based his argument on the two following aspects. The first was that Hong Kong had not returned back to China when the China-Peru BIT was signed in 1994, thus the China-Peru BIT could not be applied to Hong Kong; and the second was that in accordance with China's "One Country, Two Systems" policy and the relevant provisions in The Basic Law of the Hong Kong SAR, the China-Peru BIT could not be applied automatically to Hong Kong.

In the case Lao Holdings N.V. v. Lao People's Democratic Republic, a similar issue also arose whether investors in Macau may institute an arbitration against Lao under China-Lao BIT. The tribunal in the Lao Holdings N.V. case acknowledged both the Article 15 (moving treaty frontiers rule) of the Vienna Convention on Succession of States in Respect of Treaties (hereinafter referred to as "VCST") and the Article 29 of the VCLT as customary international law and held the view that the China-Lao BIT should apply to Macau SAR after distinguishing the above-mentioned two articles and analyzing the association therebetween in the present case. Although there existed differences in the jurisprudence between the two cases, it was noteworthy that the Lao Holdings N.V. case generally followed the positions adopted by the Tza Yap Shum tribunal. The Lao Holdings N.V. tribunal first used the Article 15 of the VCST to carry out the argumentation on the analytic framework developed by the state succession issues. Article 15 of the VCST includes general provisions and exceptional provisions. The tribunal observed that the China-Lao BIT may apply to Macau SAR if the general provisions were applied; but otherwise if the exceptional provisions were satisfied. The tribunal backwardly demonstrated that none of the three circumstances listed in Sub-paragraph B of Article 15 had been satisfied in the present case. To demonstrate that "the China-Lao BIT could not apply to all the jurisdictions of China", the tribunal had followed the Tza Yap Shum case. In the Lao Holdings N.V. case, the tribunal believed that under the circumstances where China has concluded BIT with a third country, Hong Kong's power to conclude of itself BIT with this third country was not necessarily redundant. In the tribunal's opinion, the legislative purpose of both the China-Lao BIT and the Macau-Lao BIT was to protect foreign investors and the economic development of the host state. If both of the above BITs could be applied to Macau, the legislative purpose, instead of being obstructed, may be otherwise facilitated. Besides, in terms of the understanding of some of the key conceptions in BITs, the Lao Holdings N.V. tribunal also basically followed the Tza

Yap Shum case which used the VCLT argument. The tribunal of the Tza Yap Shum case believed that according to the relevant provisions of the VCLT, when interpreting the ordinary meaning of the word "involving" in Paragraph 3 of Article 8 in the China-Peru BIT, the word "involving" should be construed as "inclusive", but not "exclusive". Therefore, it would be inadvisable to simply take the word "involving" literally as a restriction to the tribunal's jurisdiction.

It thus appears that despite that Mr. Chen had provided a detailed and accurate argument, his argument had not been fully acknowledged by international arbitration practice. Mr. Chen concentrated on the Sino-British Joint Declaration and The Basic Law of the Hong Kong SAR, while the arbitral tribunal mainly drew on the BITs. It thus reveals that we as Chinese scholars need to delve into the international legal status of the Sino-British Joint Declaration and the intension of The Basic Law of the Hong Kong SAR, so as to attract the attention of the international community.

Mr. Chen's argument was sufficiently presented in his paper, and the issues around the specific application of Article 31 and 32 of VCLT were fully discussed in particular. Generally speaking, not only has his argument created important influence on subsequent cases, but his paper has also brought up quite some food for thought. To name a few. Is the fact that the China-Peru BIT cannot apply to Hong Kong SAR equivalent to that Chinese nationals who hold a HKSAR passport cannot invoke the same BIT either? The "investors" in the China-Peru

BIT cover "all the natural persons who hold its nationality in accordance with the law of the People's Republic of China". Pursuant to the Nationality Law of the People's Republic of China, Hong Kongese possess Chinese nationality. Then, can Hong Kong's "high degree of autonomy" serve as an obstacle to Hong Kongese seeking investment protection under China-Peru BIT? In addition, as a lawyering skill, assuming that Tza Yap Shum cannot obtain the investment protection under the China-Peru BIT, whether there exists a possibility that it can get investment protection under the British-Peru BIT negotiated in 1993 (in force as of 1994)? If Tza Yap Shum cannot get protected under the China-Peru BIT because of the logic that "old law (the China-Peru BIT in force in 1995) cannot apply to 'new circumstances' ", can it seek protection under the British-Peru BIT by the reasoning that "old law (the British-Peru BIT in force as of 1994) should continue to apply to 'past circumstances' "? These are all inspiring questions posed by Mr. Chen's paper that need to be further considered.

Moreover, Mr. Chen also, from the perspective of investment disputes between China and foreign countries, expounded the relationships between the Sino-British Joint Declaration, the Constitution of the People's Republic of China, The Basic Law of the Hong Kong SAR as well as a series of treaties negotiated by China with foreign countries. He clearly pointed out that according to the Sino-British Joint Declaration, the Chinese government would resume the exercise of sovereignty over Hong Kong on July 1, 1997, and the British government would return

Hong Kong back to China on the same day. Since then, "The Basic Law of the Hong Kong SAR formulated according to the Article 31 of the Constitution of the PRC would be the constitutive instrument governing the Hong Kong SAR", and all the affairs in Hong Kong shall be subject to The Basic Law of the Hong Kong SAR. According to Chapter XI of the Appendix to the Sino-British Joint Declaration and Article 153 of The Basic Law of the Hong Kong SAR, under the policy of "One Country, Two Systems", "international treaties entered into by China with third countries would not automatically apply to Hong Kong after July 1997. To the contrary, they would only apply to Hong Kong under the prerequisite that the Central Government of China decided to extend their application to Hong Kong after consultation with the Government of HKSAR." These crucial arguments are of huge practical relevance to tackling the current problems faced with China, including the attempt of interference with China's internal affairs by using the Sino-British Joint Declaration as a pretext and the crisis of "Occupy Central", etc. The specific circumstances are as follows:

As reported by Shanghai Mercury, Hong Kong on November 18, 2014, the Foreign Affairs Commission of the House of Commons on November 17 conducted a hearing on the Sino-British Joint Declaration. Jonathan Fenby, the former chief editor of South China Morning Post, expressed when "testifying" that the central government of China wished to keep a firm hand on Hong Kong's politics and economy and the government of Hong Kong SAR prioritized its relationship with the mainland over the appeal of the Hong Kongese for democracy. Hui Sin Tung from Hong Kong University and Tang Chi Tak from Chinese University of Hong Kong, students who participated in the "Occupy Central" movement stated that the central government of China had repeatedly violated the Sino-British Joint Declaration by depriving the Hong Kongese of the freedom of press and assembly as well as the universal voting rights as stipulated therein, and Britain should compel China to "honor" the Sino-British Joint Declaration, make condemnations, and even resume the Treaty of Nanking and the Treaty of Tientsin. In addition, Liu Huiqing, the chairman of the Democratic Party of Hong Kong also "testified" to the British Parliament by video on November 18 that Britain should be responsible for the maintenance of the freedom and lifestyle of Hong Kong.

External influences from Britain and America keep interfering with the internal affairs of Hong Kong and this has become more frequent since the "Occupy Central". In late September, the British Prime Minister Cameroon said, "the agreement between the UK and China mentioned the importance of Hong Kong's democracy under the framework of 'One Country, Two Systems'." In mid-October, he once again proclaimed that "Britain should stand up for the freedom of the Hong Kongese." In September, when the "Occupy Central" movement met the dead end, the United States used 20 pages in the annual report of the U.S.-China Economic and Security Council to fabricate wild tales on the political reform of Hong Kong. After that, the Congressional-

Executive Commission on China conducted a "hearing", during which Peng Dingkang, the "Last Governor of Hong Kong" made an overseas "testification" in London through video satellite, claiming that western countries should speak out on Hong Kong issues. When the British MPs planned to conduct investigations in Hong Kong, Beijing denied their entry. Tan Zhiyuan, director of the Constitutional and Mainland Affairs Bureau refuted the British slanders and tricks, arguing that Britain has no sovereignty, nor administration and supervision powers over Hong Kong, and the so-called "moral responsibility" is nothing but nonsense. Wang Guoxing, a representative of Hong Kong Federation of Trade Unions, stated that the testification of the oppositionists in Hong Kong, overtly assisting foreign forces to interfere with the internal affairs of Hong Kong, was an act of losing national dignity and caused huge harms to Hong Kongese and the Chinese people at large. Wu Liangxing, a member of the legislative council on banking industry in Hong Kong, said affairs in Hong Kong belong to China's internal affairs with which other countries have no power to interfere, and the oppositionist senators who "cooperated" in the hearings conducted by foreign countries were obviously incurring foreign forces to do so.

The Chinese government also consecutively condemned the ridiculous hearings on the Sino-British Joint Declaration by the British House of Commons. As early as July 25, 2014, Hong Lei, the spokesman of China's Foreign Ministry, pointed out that affairs in Hong Kong belong to China's internal affairs with which the British hearings were interfering, and China would like to express strong dissatisfaction and resolute opposition to its actions. The Chinese government would oppose to any foreign forces interfering by any pretexts in China's internal affairs. On December 3, 2014, Hua Chunying, the spokeswoman of China's Foreign Ministry claimed in a more definite manner that Hong Kong had already returned back to China since 1997. Hong Kong is a special administrative region of China. It had been made clear on China's resumption of the exercise of sovereignty over Hong Kong and the relevant arrangements during the transition period in the Sino-British Joint Declaration of 1984. The respective rights and obligations of both China and Britain were also clearly defined. Britain had no sovereignty, nor administration and supervision powers over Hong Kong, and the so-called "moral responsibility" did not exist at all. It was unacceptable and untenable for Some British people attempted to use "moral responsibility" to confuse the public and interfere in China's internal affairs. This was unacceptable and untenable.

It is obvious that the statements made by the Chinese government and the patriots in Hong Kong in 2014 coincide perfectly with the detailed arguments brought up by Mr. Chen as early as 2008.

Mr. Chen is fast-learned and wealthy in knowledge, and many of his views in the book on international economic law come from his sedulous research and persistent dialogues with the international academia. He once had in-depth discussions about academic issues with distinguished scholars in international economic law, such as Louis

Henkin, Andreas F. Lowenfeld and John H. Jackson. He keeps renewing his knowledge and trying to introduce the new developments of the international economic law in China to international peers. What's more commendable is that Mr. Chen has detected the colonialism and unilateralism, especially the U.S.-style double standards, in the books written by foreign scholars in international economic law. Therefore, he devoted all his life to the reform of the old international economic order and the establishment of a new international economic order. He insists the approach of seeking truth from facts and finished the book *The Voice from China: An CHEN on International Economic Law* after 30 years of hard work. "With an even structure and novel views, this book features Chinese styles and characteristics by expounding innovative academic ideas distinct from those of the developed countries in the west. Dedicated to the initial establishment of the theoretic system of international economic law with Chinese characteristics under the guidance of Marxism, this book has forged a theoretical arm for the international underprivileged to struggle for equitable interests."

In the third plenary session of the 18th National Congress of the CPC, "to construct a new open-style economic system" has been promoted to a strategic level. To strengthen the research on, and to improve the rule of, international economic law has become the core requirements and necessary guarantees for the strategies of "One Belt, One Road" and "Going global", and the establishment of the BRICS Development Bank and the Asian Infrastructure Investment Bank.

Wang Yang, the vice premier of the state council of China, pointed out in an article that we need to intensify the foreign-related legal work and proactively engage in the formulation of international rules. Deeply rooted in the national interests of the Chinese people, against the backdrop of the socialist system with Chinese characteristics, and based on the status quo of China as a developing economic and trade power, this book has served as an important response to the heated and difficult issues on the basic international economic law theories. At present, it has been dragging on over the multilateral trading system and, the mega-FTAs such as Trans-Pacific Partnership Agreement, Transatlantic Trade and Investment Partnership and Regional Comprehensive Economic Partnership and hundreds of FTAs with investment rules have reflected the reconstruction process of international economic and trade rules. Mr. Chen pointed out in his book that "the four 'safety valves' in China's BITs with foreign countries should not be rashly dismantled", which is of critical relevance to protecting China's national interests in the negotiation of BITs with the United States and the Europe. Viewing the classics and ancient works cited in the book, no matter the ancient Chinese poetry or the masterpieces from the west, the readers can have a better appreciation of the peculiar perspective of a Chinese scholar in the field of international economic law.

Thus, we firmly believe that the book *The Voice from China: An CHEN on International Economic Law*, the monumental work of Mr. Chen, will surely be able to go global under the background of globalization and China's soaring economic growth, and the voice from China can certainly get heard in the international arena.

（翻譯：張川方）

十一、把准南方國家共同脈搏的學術力作
—— 評《中國的吶喊：陳安論國際經濟法》

孔慶江*

陳安先生的皇皇巨著 *The Voice from China: An CHEN on Internationil Economic Law*（《中國的吶喊：陳安論國際經濟法》，以下簡稱《中國的吶喊》）已由世界著名學術出版社Springer出版，此乃學界幸事。陳先生是中國國際經法學界的前輩，長期以來一直擔任中國國際經濟法學會會長（1993-2011）和榮譽會長（2012-），領導中國國際經濟法學界同仁，引領中國國際經濟法學研究的風氣。陳先生大作刊行於世，我等晚輩同儕無不奔相走告，以先睹為快。

《中國的吶喊》由多篇專論構成，既獨立成章，又相互支撐配合，形成一個相互關聯的體系。縱覽全書，主旨鮮明突出，即批評當今尚存重大合理性問題的現有國際經濟秩序，並在此基礎上，為構建著者心目中更公平合理的國際經濟法律新秩序提供建言。

二〇〇七至二〇〇八年全球金融危機後，舊的全球經濟秩序的弊端凸顯，如何重構全球經濟秩序已經成為刻不容緩的問題。

對此，大國之間也立即開展了新的國際經濟規則主導權的競爭。中國作為最大的發展中國家和崛起中的大國，自當發出自己的聲音，而《中國的吶喊》在此時代背景下應運而生，無論批評還是建言，都體現了著者對國際經濟秩序推陳出新和破舊立新的人文關懷。在一眾中外學者滿足於貌似完美的以「自由主義」為基石的現存國際經濟秩序的背景下，著者毫不隱晦其中國學者的身份，強調中國在國際經濟秩序重構過程中應該有的大國責任和大國風範，即應積極參與到全球國際經濟新規則的制定過程中。其視野其觀點，都不脫著者心目中不可或缺的中國視角和中國利益。這一切，反映出著者作為國際經濟法學家拳拳的愛國之心。著者的赤子之心，在字裡行間呼之欲出。

　　值得一提的是，著者絕非狹隘的民族主義者，其觀點無不浸潤著對發展中國家弱勢群體數十億大眾的利益關切和廣闊視角。從全球範圍內看，著者的這一巨著，不啻是在國際經濟秩序推陳出新和破舊立新方面，體現南方國家共同立場的學術力作。無論是對於現存國際經濟秩序的理論剖析還是對於各方觀點的細緻評判，都見解獨到而又發人深省。而在批判現存國際經濟秩序的基礎上提出的構建國際經濟新秩序的視角，則體現了一個心懷天下的國際經濟法大師的胸懷，為全球南方國家在這個破而後立的時代，點明了參與國際經濟規則制定的方向。

　　《中國的吶喊》的學術價值，還在於勾勒了塑造中國國際經濟法學發展面貌的諸多因素，豐滿了中國國際經濟法學發展維度的諸多細節，特別是指出了中國國際經濟法學發展的方向。這不但對於國際學者正確全面理解中國特色的國際經濟法學，而且對

於中國國際經濟法學者反思自己的研究路徑，都具有指導性的意義。

我相信，一方面，《中國的吶喊》將與任何嚴肅著述一樣，經得起歷史風雨的考驗；另一方面，該書的出版將使著者成為南方國家中有代表性的、有重大影響的國際經濟法學家。

（編輯：龔　宇）

A Highly Recommendable Monograph that Senses the Pulse of the South

Kong Qingjiang*

The Voice from China: An CHEN on International Economic Law (herein referred to as *The Voice from China*), which was recently published by Springer, one of the world's leading academic publishers, is a dear gift for the academic society. Professor Chen, who served as the President (1993-2011) and is acting as the Honorary President (2012-) of the Chinese Society of International Economic Law (CSIEL), is a pioneering explorer of international economic law in China. He helps inspire the researchers in this new discipline and guide their academic pursuits. It is no exaggerating to say that the academia, particularly the young generation was jubilant to learn of the publication of this brilliant monograph.

The Voice from China is composed of several chapters. These chapters—either concerned with investment regime or trade issues—are independent yet mutually supportive and therefore form an integrated academic work. Throughout the book, outstanding is the theme, which mainly purports criticizing the existing international economic order for its lack of rationality, and, proposing the establishment of a fairer and more reasonable international economic order.

In the aftermath of the global financial crisis of 2007 / 08, the old global economic infrastructure turned out to be defective, making the reform of the infrastructure a pressing issue. Hereto, the world powers are found to engage in a new round of competition to grab the leadership of international economic rule-making. As the biggest developing country and a rising power, China has to make her voice be heard. Under this circumstance, *The Voice from China* came out timely to reflect the author's humanistic concerns over innovative international economic order regardless of critics and disagreements. Where an array of scholars, home and abroad, are comfortable with and boasting the existing international economic order that is based on the seemingly perfect "liberalism", the author is not shy to disclose his identity as a China-born-and-bred scholar, advocate China's responsibility to contribute to the emerging new international economic order, and call for a China active in participating the international rule-making process. The author's perspectives and opinions, which originate from China' indispensable national interest, reflect nothing but the author's true patriotism as an international economic law scholar.

It is worth noting that the author is not a narrow-minded nationalist at all. His publication is a best example of how international economic law can be full of humane concerns on the interests of developing countries and the breath of billions of vulnerable people therein. From the global perspectives, *The Voice from China* insightfully presents and addresses the common concerns of the South in fighting for a fairer international economic order, thus making itself a great contribution. The meticulous theoretical analysis of international economic order and blatant critics of various parties' arguments are both highly relevant and thought-provoking. From the criticism of existing international economic order, to the proposal to have in place a brand new international economic order, what is evident is the image of a compassionate master in the realm of international economic law, who has great care about the whole world. At a time of setting up new rules after breaking down the olds, *The Voice from China* helps guide the South as a whole how to get involved in the rule-making for international economy.

Another academic value of *The Voice from China* lies in that it either sketches or details the development of Chinese international economic law, especially in that it points to the direction of how to advance the Chinese international economic law. It is of instructive significance to help international law scholars fully and properly understand the international economic law with Chinese characteristics, as well as to sharpen their research skills for the studies of Chinese international economic law.

I firmly believe that *The Voice from China* will, like any solemn monograph, undergo harsh testing of history and moreover, make the author a representative authority with significant contribution to the studies of international economic law.

（翻譯：于天琪）

十二、國際經濟法研究的「中國立場」
——讀《中國的吶喊》有感
李萬強*

　　廈門大學法學院陳安教授以「餘熱未盡，不息奮蹄」的精神與鬥志，在八十五歲高齡推出英文學術專著《中國的吶喊：陳安論國際經濟法》（以下簡稱《中國的吶喊》），令人可歎可佩！該書是繼二〇〇八年復旦大學出版社出版的中文五卷本《陳安論國際經濟法學》之後，面向國際學術界對陳安教授學術成就以及學術生活的一次全景式、立體化展現。

　　陳安教授是中國最早從事國際經濟法研究的學者之一。過去三十多年，陳安教授一直在這一領域辛勤耕耘，為中國國際經濟法學學科地位的鞏固與夯實做出了重大貢獻。他以一家跨國公司的投資專案為例，從六大方面釋明了國際經濟活動所需依賴和遵守的國際法律規範與國內法律規範、公法性規範與私法性規範、程式性規範與實體性規範，以及貿易法規範、投資法規範與金融法規範等，指明國際經濟法是應客觀現實之急需，不拘泥於傳統

法學分科，在學科交叉滲透的基礎上形成的獨立的、有機的邊緣性綜合體。[264]不僅如此，面對其他一些學者對初創的國際經濟法學的四種誤解與非議，即「不科學」或「不規範」論、「大胃」論或「貪食」論、「浮躁」論或「炒熱」論以及「翻版」論或「舶來」論，他撰文一一澄清或駁斥，進一步論證了這一學科定位的「科學性、合規律性和旺盛活力」。[265]

國際經濟法作為一種法律現象，可以有不同的研究視角和方法。陳安教授則「一貫堅持」南北矛盾的研究方法，「獨樹一幟」，形成並引領了頗具中國風骨與特色的國際經濟法學流派。這一立場，由於兩個方面的原因而對中國具有獨特的意義：一方面，崛起的中國已經觸碰到了某些發達國家「脆弱的神經」，它們對中國極力遏制；另一方面，中國由於實行不同的政治制度，被某些西方國家另眼相加，列入另冊，它們對中國嚴加防範。因此，建立國際經濟新秩序（NIEO），並在其中發揮積極的、建設性的作用，是陳安教授立足於中國實際所確立的國際經濟法研究的指導思想。為貫徹這一指導思想，《中國的吶喊》在學術層面進行了充分的論證與法理構建：

（1）身份：關於中國的國家「身份」問題，陳安教授的認識是一貫的。長期以來，他對國際經濟法中的經濟主權原則、南北矛盾與南南合作等問題傾注極大的心力進行研究，就是基於中國「作為全球最大的發展中國家以及全球弱勢群體的一員」這一認識。[266]

（2）定位：陳安教授提出，中國應當立足於自身的歷史，把握現有國際經濟秩序的大局，科學地、合理地從長遠角度確立

自己在建立國際經濟新秩序過程中的戰略定位。具體說來，中國理應成為建立國際經濟新秩序的積極推手，在國際經濟舊秩序尚未完全退出歷史舞臺的背景下，為了實現南北公平，中國作為發展中的大國之一，理應以公正、公平、合理的國際經濟新秩序作為長遠奮鬥目標，積極宣導和參與建設和諧世界；中國理應致力於成為南南聯合自強的中流砥柱之一，作為當代奉行和平發展方針的大國，應當具有大國的意識和風範，勇於承擔，與其他發展中國家一起聯合行動。〔267〕

（3）目標：陳安教授認為，中國與全球弱勢群體共同參與建立國際經濟新秩序的戰略目標，理應堅定不移，始終不渝。面對當今現存的各種國際經濟立法，包括WTO法制下的種種「遊戲規則」國際弱勢群體固然不能予以全盤否定，但是顯然也不能全盤接受，心甘情願地忍受其中蘊含的各種不公與不平。對待當今現存的各種國際經濟立法，正確態度理應是：以公正、公平為圭臬，從爭取與維護國際弱勢群體的平權利益的視角，予以全面的檢查和審查，實行「守法」與「變法」的結合。凡是基本上達到公正公平標準，符合改造國際經濟舊秩序、建立國際經濟新秩序需要的，就加以沿用、重申，就強調「守法」；凡是違反這種需要的，就要強調「變法」，並通過各種方式和途徑，據理力爭，努力加以改訂、廢棄或破除。〔268〕

在國際弱勢群體爭取建立國際經濟新秩序的過程中，國際學界也出現了一些頗為流行的理論，比如「新自由主義經濟秩序」論、「WTO憲政秩序」論、「經濟民族主義擾亂全球化秩序」論等。陳安教授研究指出，這些理論各有其合理內核，但其副作用

亦不可小覷。「新自由主義經濟秩序」論、「WTO憲政秩序」論可能是一種精神鴉片，會麻痺、瓦解國際弱勢群體的鬥志與信心；「經濟民族主義擾亂全球化秩序」論可能是一種精神枷鎖，會壓制國際弱勢群體的鬥志與信心。要警惕這些「時髦」理論取代「建立國際經濟新秩序」論！[269]

（4）途徑：面對當代國際社會「南弱北強」實力懸殊的戰略態勢，面對國際強權國家集團（七國集團之類）在國際經濟領域中已經形成的「長達三十餘年的霸業」格局，國際弱勢群體要求「變法」圖強，不應該單槍匹馬，各自為政。實踐反覆證明：唯一可行和有效之途徑就是南南聯合，動員和凝聚集團實力，不渝不懈，堅持建立國際經濟新秩序、「變法圖強」的理念和目標，一步一個腳印地邁步前進。也正是由於中國等發展中大國的綜合國力和國際影響的逐步提高，在WTO多哈會議、坎昆會議、香港會議、華盛頓會議、首爾會議的全過程中，中國與印度、巴西、南非和墨西哥等BRICSM成員曾多次通力協作，折衝樽俎，使得國際霸權與強權不能隨心所欲，操縱全域，從而為國際弱勢群體爭得較大的發言權、參與權和決策權。[270]

對於南南聯合自強及其成功經驗，陳安教授進行了歷史的考察。從歷史上看，通過南南聯合自強，逐步建立國際經濟新秩序的戰略主張，最初開始形成於一九五五年的萬隆會議，此後，建立國際經濟新秩序的進程迂迴曲折，步履維艱，儘管經歷了多次潮起潮落，但其總趨向是始終沿著螺旋式上升的「6C軌跡」或遵循「6C律」即Contradiction（矛盾）→ Conflict（衝突或交鋒）→ Consultation（磋商）→ Compromise（妥協）→ Cooperation（合

作）→ Coordination（協調）→ Contradiction New（新的矛盾）……每一次循環往復，都並非簡單的重複，而都是螺旋式的上升，都把國際經濟秩序以及和它相適應的國際經濟法規範，推進到一個新的水準或一個新的發展階段，國際社會弱勢群體的經濟地位和經濟權益也獲得相應的改善和保障。當然，盲目的樂觀也是有害的。陳安教授提醒，建立國際經濟新秩序的前途依然漫漫而崎嶇，要使它進一步發展成為康莊坦途，堅持南南聯合自強和南北合作仍是不二法門。必須假以時日，必須堅持韌性，二者不可缺一。[271]

《中國的吶喊》不單是不畏國際強權、力爭國際公義的吶喊，更是陳安教授赤誠的現實關懷與報國情懷的完美結合。陳安教授「蹉跎半生而重返法學殿堂」（先生語），卻思想活躍，能緊跟形勢，與時俱進。面對中國的實際問題，陳安教授殫精竭慮，奉獻了超凡的智慧。無論是在改革開放之初還是在「1989年政治風波」之後，陳安教授都及時撰文，宣講中國的開放政策，澄清事實，消除誤解。[272] 在中國對外開放的複雜形勢面前，一些學者和官員在國際投資法重大問題的立場方面出現了疑慮與彷徨。陳安教授多次撰文條分縷析，周密論證，闡述中國應當採取的立場與做法，提出四大「安全閥」不宜貿然拆除等真知灼見。[273] 在中國《仲裁法》頒布之初，陳安教授即對中國的涉外仲裁監督機制進行了批判分析。[274] 在WTO運行一段時間後，陳安教授以其學術敏感，撰文綜合評析十年來美國單邊主義與WTO多邊主義交鋒的三大回合，揭示美國學者主權觀的兩面性以及當代條件下經濟主權原則之不可動搖，為國內學界再次敲響警鐘。

〔275〕……總之，作為中國國際經濟法學界的泰斗級人物，在關涉中國國際經濟法研究與實踐的重大問題與重大事件時，幾乎都有陳安教授振聾發聵的「吶喊」！

（編輯：龔　宇）

A Chinese School of Jurisprudence on International Economic Law

Li Wanqiang*

It is admirable that Professor An Chen finished his monograph in English at the age of 85. This monograph, titled as *The Voice from China: An CHEN on International Economic Law,* is a quintessence of his five-volume book series published by Fudan University Press five years ago and some of his articles thereafter. Nevertheless, it reflects a three-dimensional panorama of Professor Chen's academic achievement and activities to the international academia.

Professor Chen is one of the rare pioneers in the research field of international economic law (IEL). Since the inception of China's policy of reform and openness (CPRO), he has been concentrating his energies on the IEL and the CPRO. As a founding member and former Chairman of Chinese Society of International Economic Law, he has played a leading role in the establishment and enhancement of the discipline of the IEL in China. He takes an international investment project as an example to show how an international economic transaction may be governed by international law and domestic law, public law and private law, substantive law and procedural law, as well as trade law, investment law, tax law and financial law etc. Based on this practical analysis, he points out that IEL is a novel branch of legal discipline in response to the objective reality. This legal discipline adopts an interdepartmental and interdisciplinary approach of investigation and is an organic marginal independent synthesis. [276] Facing some misunderstandings and suspicions to the IEL, such as so-called "nonscientific or nonnormative", "polyphagian or avaricious", "fickle fashion or stirring heat", and "duplicating version or importing goods", he wrote an article to rebut or correct these opinions one by one, which prove the scientific and normative nature and the strong vitality of the IEL from different perspectives. [277]

As a legal phenomenon, the IEL can be reviewed and treated from different approaches. What Prof. Chen has been taking consistently is the "South-North Contradiction" approach. Thanks to his achievements and influence, a Chinese School of Jurisprudence on the IEL featured by this approach has come into being in China. Based on two factors, this school of jurisprudence on the IEL is of special significance to China. One is that some developed countries adopt "containment strategy" in response to China's rise. The other is that some western countries treat China in an alien way because of China's political system. According to Prof. Chen, establishing New International Economic Order (NIEO) is a way for developing countries like China to be treated justifiably and China shall play an active and constructive role in this process. In checking and reshaping the IEL, the following points shall be adhered to:

Firstly, the identity of China as a developing country must be recognized. Prof. Chen holds it is a fact that China is one member within the disadvantaged groups as well as one of the biggest developing countries in the world. [278] Based on this standpoint, he has attached great importance to the study of the basic issues in IEL such as economic sovereignty, South-North conflicts and South-South cooperation.

Secondly, the goal China shall firmly pursue is the establishment of a just, fair and reasonable NIEO. Facing the existed IEL, including varieties of "rules of game" for international economic and trade affairs, neither "accepting all" nor "denying all" is a right attitude. Prof. Chen holds a full review and investigation shall be carried out from the perspective of campaigning for and maintaining the equal rights and interests of the international weak groups, and law-abiding and law-reforming shall be combined together. For each and every rule which is in violation of justice and fairness, the weak groups shall seek to reform, abolish, or eradicate it through all possible ways and approaches. [279]

Accompanying the advocacy for the NIEO, some other theories have prevailed to some extent, such as "Neoliberalistic Economic Order", "Constitutional Order of the WTO", and "Economic Nationalism's Disorder of Globalization". Although the core of these theories is reasonable in some sense and could be utilized critically, Prof. Chen reminds that the former two can be a kind of mental opium and disintegrate the unions of the weak states, while the latter one can be a kind of mental shackles and prevent the weak states from establishing the NIEO. [280]

Thirdly, the role China is playing in the course of establishing the NIEO shall be one of the driving forces. China shall act ideologically and in style as a large nation, be brave in assuming responsibilities, and join force with all other weak states in advocating and participating in the establishment of a harmonious world.

Lastly, the pathway to achieve the goal of establishing the NIEO is South-South Cooperation. Since the South is far weaker than the North in contemporary international society and the group of international powers (such as G7) has maintained the dominant position for as long as over 30 years in international economic fields, the international weak groups' demand for law-reforming to strengthen themselves up shall not be expected to be accomplished once and for all, nor shall they take actions dividedly and single-handedly. Prof. Chen points out the only feasible and effective way is through South-South Coalition to keep mobilizing and agglomerating the collective power unswervingly with the aim to establish the NIEO. [282]

The significance of the South-South Coalition has been embodied in the South-North Contradiction. For over 60 years, the struggles between the South and the North usually temporarily paused when the two sides reaching a compromise, after which new conflicts would arise from new contradictions. As for the historic course and practice of South-North struggle, Prof. Chen proposes a generalization of the "6C Track" or "6C Rule": Contradiction→Conflict→Consultation→Comp romise→Cooperation→Coordination→Contradiction New... But each new circle is on a spiral upper level rather than on an exactly repetitive old one, thus pushing International Economic Order and the relating IEL towards a fairer level at a higher development stage. Consequently, the economic status and rights of the international weak groups are able to acquire corresponding improvements and safeguards. [283]

The Voice from China is not only an advocacy of struggling against international hegemony and striving for international justice, but also a convergence of Prof. Chen's patriotism and realism. Although starting his legal research as late as the inception of China's Openness Policy, Prof. Chen has endeavored to keep pace with the times. He has dedicated vast energy and wisdom to the research of Chinese reality. He wrote papers to eradicate the misunderstandings and suspicions to China's Openness Policy both at the earlier stage of 1980s and 1990s. [284] Facing the complicated issues in international investment law, he presented constructive suggestions to the decision makers through his painstaking research work. For example, his viewpoint that the "Four Safeguards" in Sino-foreign BITs can not be hastily and completely dismantled is of great importance to the protection of China's economic sovereignty. Soon after the enactment of China's Arbitration Law, he did a critical research on the law and proposed suggestions on how to reshape it.[286] He made an analysis on how America interacted with the WTO in the first decade of this organization and revealed America's "double standards" to the sovereignty. It is a reminder that the sovereignty shall be stuck to for developing countries at any time[287] ... To sum up, as an authority in Chinese academia of IEL, Prof. Chen's voice can always be heard at each critical moment or about each critical incident concerning the IEL, which has always been an advocacy for the rights and interests of the international weak groups.

（翻譯：李萬強）

十三、不為浮雲遮眼　兼具深邃堅定
——評《中國的吶喊：陳安論國際經濟法》
韓立餘*

　　收到陳安教授惠寄的Springer出版的 *The Voice from China: An CHEN on International Economic Law*（中國的吶喊：《陳安論國際經濟法》，不禁心潮澎湃。為其觀點，為其成果，為其精神！

　　初次面見陳安教授是在一九九八年於深圳大學召開的中國國際經濟法年會上。其時，陳安教授力倡「以文會友、以學報國」，那鏗鏘有力的聲音和抓鐵留痕的信念深深地印記在我的腦海裡。此後，幾乎在每次年會上，或聽取陳安教授的大會報告，或參與陳安教授主持的討論，或是私下裡的交流，我都沐浴在陳安教授的思想光輝中。作為後學，自己取得的些許研究成果，一

定程度上與陳安教授的影響、關懷和鼓勵是分不開的。雖由於生活經歷、成長年代、求學背景、研究興趣等的不同，也有與陳安教授不同的具體想法，但那份尊重和敬佩深植心中、依然如故。

如陳安教授自己所言，其英文巨著是在其五卷本中文版《陳安論國際經濟法學》的基礎上進一步修訂、更新、補充而完成的。今將其思想、觀點、成果以 *The Voice from China* 為題出版英文版，陳安教授在國際層面進一步踐行了「以文會友、以學報國」的信念和追求。陳安教授的思想獨樹一幟，且一以貫之，不為浮雲遮眼，兼具深邃堅定。這一特點在國內如此，在國際上亦如此。其思想觀點並非一時心得，而是建立在扎實的歷史事實和教訓之上。正因為如此，其聲已超出個人之音，而具有歷史和現實之義，理應向國際傳播。

由於多方面的原因，特別是由於歷史和語言的原因，中國學者對中國社會的描述，對國際社會的看法，不能盡達於國際社會。即便有些著述，或因篇幅所限，或因管道所困，或因話語語境，不能充分而全面地闡述中國學者的立場觀點。國際上一些漢學學者，由於經歷、環境不同及興趣所限，亦不能很好地反映中國的情況和觀點。陳安教授立足中國，放眼國際，不滿足於國內取得的學術成就和影響，志在基於中國現實和視角向國際社會表達中國學人的立場和觀點，努力地有計劃地在國際刊物、國際場合發文出聲。在年屆耄耋之際，陳安教授深耕細作，集其觀點大成，推出八百多頁巨著 *The Voice from China*，向世人展示其中國觀和世界觀，學術生涯達到新的高度。令人敬佩的是，陳安教授在堅持自己觀點的同時，積極宣導、推動學術爭鳴，提攜後進進

行獨立研究。雖德高望重，但平等待人、平等交流；堅持一家之言，鼓勵百家之說。筆者個人認為，其英文著作名稱取「The Voice from China」而沒有選取「The Voice of China」，亦體現了其虛懷若谷的風範。

作為中國國際經濟法學的奠基人之一，陳安教授對國際經濟法的諸多領域均有很深的造詣，並且以學者、律師和仲裁員三棲身份，言行一致地踐行其觀點。*The Voice from China*收錄的文章，既有對建立中國國際經濟法學科的詳細論證，也有對國家經濟主權理論和國際經濟新秩序的深刻剖析，還包括親身參與國際仲裁和訴訟的睿智實錄。透過各種重大議題，如國家主權、南北關係、國際秩序、國際投資、「一國兩制」等，再現了中國改革開放以來的激蕩歷史和中國人民參與國際事務的偉大實踐。有的文章成文雖早，但仍不失其現實意義，這進一步體現了陳安教授所見所期之遠之大，亦為後學所敬仰追隨。

The Voice from China，洋洋巨著，灑灑數百萬言。任何介紹或評論性的文字都無法充分展示其豐富的內容和精髓。筆者在此也不作該等無謂努力，相信讀者會從中見仁見智、相遇金屋玉顏。

最後，想對「國家社會科學基金中華學術外譯專案」致以敬意，感謝其立項資助陳安教授將中文著作推廣到英語世界，讓英語世界的讀者認識、分享其思想觀點，並引發對中國問題更深入、全面的認識。沒有這一資助，陳安教授的「以文會友、以學報國」的理念或許無法實現到今天這樣的程度。

（編輯：龔　宇）

Never Covered by Cloud, Insisting Profound Insight

—Comments on *The Voice from China*

Han Liyu*

On receiving the monograph *The Voice from China: An CHEN on International Economic Law* of about 800 pages written by Prof. An Chen, published in 2013 by famous publisher Springer, I could not help being moved by the book, the opinions, and the spirit of Prof. An Chen.

It was in 1999 when the annual meeting of Chinese Society of International Economic Law(CSIEL)was held in Shenzhen University that I first met Prof. Chen. This was also the first time I attended the activities of CSIEL, almost every attendants of the meeting being stranger to me, but I was deeply impressed by Prof. Chen, then the President of CSIEL, when he gave a speech in his characteristically robust style, calling for "meeting friends with writings and rewarding home country with knowledge". Since then, either during the annual meetings of CSIEL or in other occasions, it was normal to listen to speeches of Prof. Chen, seek advices from him, and discuss with him. To some extent, what I have achieved in my legal research should be attributed to the influence, care and encouragement of Prof. Chen, though he was not my academic adviser in strict sense. This does not mean that I fully agree with all opinions of Prof. Chen owing to diffident ages, education backgrounds, life experiences and research interests etc. between us, but my respect for Prof. An Chen lasts forever.

Just as Prof. Chen said himself in his book, *The Voice from China* was a updated English version of his five-volume An CHEN on International Economic Law in Chinese published by Fudan University Press in 2008. The English version not only reflects Prof. An Chen's deeper thoughts on International Economic law, but also his effort to voice Chinese message on international plane, which in broader extent puts into practice his belief "meeting friends with writings and rewarding home country with knowledge". Prof. Chen is determined and thoughtful, and his thoughts on International Economic Law are consistent, neither blocked by intricate developments nor for occasions. He has supported his conclusions with good reasons and facts. Readers, either domestic or international, will find perfect combination of historical lessons and modern thinking in *The Voice from China*.

For some time Chinese scholars' views on domestic issues and international affairs have been not easy to be heard and understood by international community because of various reasons, including factors of language, history, media, and cultural context. On the other hand, Sinologists, owing to lack of rich experience in China and having their own special research interests, cannot accurately and fully reflect the real views of Chinese scholars and the complex reality in China. Born in Old China, experiencing the invasion of Japan, witnessing the change and development of China, and trained in Harvard Law School, Prof. Chen is in a good position to tell China's story to international community. Not satisfied with the reputation of one of most famous scholars in

China, Prof. Chen has broken through and made his academic career to a new height at the age of more than 80, with *The Voice from China*, which is based on China's perspective and world outlook. As a matter of fact, this is not the first time for Prof. Chen to voice his views in international forums. For many years Prof. Chen has been doing his efforts to hold or attend international conference, to publish articles in international journals, so as to make voice from China to be heard by international community.

As one of noble character and high prestige and one with own special perspective on International Economic Law, Prof. Chen has been paying due respect for different opinions of different people in different ages. "Respect for different opinions" is his long-held belief. Prof. Chen always encourages younger scholars to express their own views, and the more difference with his views the more encouragement from him. As far as I know, many Chinese young scholars pay high respect for Prof. Chen, though they don't agree with Prof. Chen in some points. Prof. Chen is always modest, and in my judgment his book titled "The Voice from China", not "The Voice of China", also show his modesty.

Being one of the founders of CSIEL, Prof. Chen has an extremely good knowledge of International Economic Law. Besides a professor of Law, Prof. Chen is also an arbitrator and a lawyer active in the field of international transactions. The essays collected in *The Voice from China* include different focuses, not only arguments for separate status of International Economic Law discipline in China's law education system, theoretical analysis of state sovereign and the new international economic order, but also arguments with wisdom for international cases he handled. With discussion of important topics such as state sovereign, South-South or South-North relationship, international order, international investment, and "One Country Two System" etc., Prof. Chen has revealed the surging history of opening-up and reform in China and active practice of China's participation in international affairs since 1979, and made his own contribution in his own way as a Chinese scholar to the new international economic order. Some essays, though finished long time ago, still have inspirational implications for current international affairs, with deep insights into future. This also implies that the academic style of Prof. Chen sets an example for younger scholars.

It says that there are a thousand Hamlets in a thousand people's eyes. So I won't attempt to make detailed comments on the contents of *The Voice from China* of about 800 pages, and I know my any effort of this kind would be an effort in vain. I encourage readers themselves to read *The Voice form China*. I'm sure readers all over the world would find his own Hamlets from *The Voice from China*.

Last but not least, I want to express my own appreciation for the work of the National Social Science Fund of China. Without its project, i.e. the Chinese Academic Foreign Translation Project (CAFTP), The Voice from China would not, I guess, been published in English by international famous publisher; readers in English world would not have this privilege to have a better understanding of modern China through the lens of Prof. An Chen; and the dream cherished by Prof. Chen of "meeting friends with writings and rewarding home country with knowledge" would not come true so soon.

（翻譯：韓立余）

十四、任你風向東南西北　我自巋然從容不迫
—— 國際經濟新秩序的重思：

以陳安教授的國際經濟法研究為視角

何志鵬*

國際經濟法研究的兩大流派

作為法學的一部分，國際經濟法的研究顯然不可能完全脫離法學研究的主流路徑而完全獨樹一幟。法學的主流研究模式分為實證法學派和自然法學派，[288]因而國際經濟法的各種研究手段也可以大略總結為描述性研究和規範性研究兩大流派。描述性研究主要是對既有的國際經濟法律規範和組織、運行進行說明，通過語義分析闡釋規範的含義，通過資料統計分析揭示實際運行的狀況，或者通過案例研究研討規範在實踐運行中取得的成就和存在的問題。[289]這種研究是作為一般法學方法的實證主義研究在國際經濟法中的體現。規範分析一般前設一套正當性原則，通過批判性、反思性地考察相關的規範或者實踐，或者比較不同的規範、不同的實踐或者進程，來判斷相關的規則和實踐是否正當，

或者說明相關的國際經濟法進步的領域和方向何在。[290] 這種研究方法是作為法學方法的自然法學派在國際經濟法領域的具體體現，是一種顯在的價值分析的研究方式。

這兩種方法雖然表面上並不相同，實質上卻有很多聯繫。一個令人信服的價值分析必須建立在扎實的實證研究基礎之上，很多實證研究在背後也都隱藏著一些基本的價值判斷。[291] 進而言之，偏好實證分析的學者和偏好價值分析的學者有必要保持相互尊重和欣賞，而不必偏執地認為，只有自己才是正確的，另一種方法則是錯誤的。所以，好的法學研究雖然會在研究手段上有所側重，但二者不可偏廢。

陳安教授作為中國頂級的國際經濟法學者，不僅在國際投資法的實證研究上作出了很多重要的努力，而且在國際經濟法的發展方向的批判研究上也進行了卓有成效的嘗試，提出了很多發人深省的觀點。其中，關於國際經濟新秩序及中國的立場的研究就是非常具有代表性的部分。

國際經濟新秩序的興衰

陳安教授從歷史實證的角度考察了建立國際經濟新秩序的背景與進程，同時也探討了現代社會中宣導國際經濟新秩序的重要性。起源於二十世紀六〇年代的國際經濟新秩序運動，可以理解為殖民時期基本結束後自決權的延續和拓展。新獨立的發展中國家不僅在歷史上受到侵略和盤剝，在現實中也被國際經濟體系所傷害。[292] 原來的宗主國，繼而成為國際經濟體系的主導者、國際經濟法的主要制定者的發達工業國家確立起一套國際經濟規則

體系，繼續將利益輸送到發達國家，卻使得多數發展中國家積貧積弱，這種法律體制很難說是公正的。[293]正如陳安教授所揭示的，國際經濟法立法過程最常見的三大弊端是：少數發達國家密室磋商，黑箱作業，缺乏國際民主；國際經濟組織體制規章中存在不公平、不合理的表決制度；全球唯一的超級大國在世界性經貿大政的決策進程中，歷來奉行的「國策」是「美國本國利益至上」和「對人對己雙重標準」。[294]

國際經濟新秩序的主張就是一種試圖除舊布新、繼往開來的努力。但是，這種努力顯然會影響到發達國家的短期、局部利益，所以它們對於國際經濟新秩序的主張反應並不積極。[295]來自發達國家的學者也更傾向於論證載有國際經濟新秩序主張的國際檔不屬於國際法、沒有約束力，不能確立國際義務。在很大程度上是由於二十世紀七〇年代初能源危機的壓力以及冷戰政治平衡的需要，[296]發達工業國家才允諾了包括普惠制在內的一些推進國際經濟新秩序的條件。

在冷戰結束以後，發展中國家追求國際經濟新秩序的聲音馬上被新自由主義和全球化這兩個相互聯繫的浪潮所淹沒。去除管制、私有化、自由市場成為壓倒性的聲音。以世界貿易組織、世界銀行和國際貨幣基金組織為代表的國際經濟體制也主要以這些自由主義的理念為尺度去確立新的國際經濟法，國際經濟法的發展似乎走向了自由主義一枝獨秀的「歷史的終結」。建立國際經濟新秩序的努力進入了消沉的階段。

實踐是檢驗真理的唯一標準。歷史顯然沒有終結，自由主義的普世宣講不僅在很多時候沒有造福於發展中國家，而且「金融

創新」的泡沫使發達國家自己也陷入了麻煩之中。

國際經濟法的未來，究竟何去何從？

國際經濟法的中國立場

國際法的變化，既可以從實體規範的層面進行，也可以從程式規範的層面進行；既可以是全域層面的變化，也可以是局部領域的變化。但所有的變化，歸根結底來自於行為體層面的推動。這種行為體，雖然包含國際組織、非政府組織、企業和個人，但最有力量、最有影響、行動方式最為方便的，顯然是國家。如果一個國家不能夠明確地形成自己的立場，並以學術、政治和法律的方式表述自身的觀念，則國際體制的變革就會失去該國家的話語，不僅有可能有害於該國的利益，而且有可能影響整個國際法的發展進程。

正是站在不同的利益取向上，帶有不同的國際機制設計觀念的國家在一起通過協商、談判而形成的國際法律機制才能在多樣化的基礎上做到相對均衡。當然，絕對的平衡是不存在的，只有相對的平衡。這是因為，即使在所有國家都表述自己觀點的前提下，作為一種國際博弈，強國與弱國之間的力量差異會轉化成談判過程中的討價還價能力的對比，並最終在國際法律體制中表現為絕對的不平衡。

在中國的發展與國際經濟法的發展兩者互動的進程中，中國面臨著多重任務。在很多學者看來，融入現有體系、了解現有體系、參與現有體系就已經很不容易了，甚至是值得稱道的成就，但是在陳安教授看來，中國還有一項更為艱巨、複雜，同時也非

常偉大的任務，那就是變革現有體系。這項任務在有些學者看來似乎是不必要的，如果將WTO這樣的國際經濟法體制視為「模範國際法」，或者國際法治的典範，那麼變革現有體系的正當性就不明顯。同樣，如果認為中國的國家利益在當今的國際體制中並沒有受到重大影響，那麼中國自身要求變革的動力就不大。如果我們認為中國還不是一個具有話語能力和話語影響的國家，那麼中國要求進行變革的影響也不大。

陳安教授顯然不是這麼認為的。他強調：「作為全球最大的發展中國家和正在和平發展中的大國，在建立國際經濟新秩序的歷史進程中，中國理應發揮重要作用。」[297] 具體說來：「首先，中國應成為建立國際經濟新秩序的積極推手。……其次，中國理應致力於成為南南聯合自強的中流砥柱之一。……第三，中國與全球弱勢群體共同參與建立國際經濟新秩序的戰略目標，理應堅定不移，始終不渝。……第四，中國在建立國際經濟新秩序進程中自我定位，理應旗幟鮮明，和而不同。」[298]

WTO這樣的國際經濟法體制較之以往的體制，誠然取得了長足進步，但是至少就發展中國家的利益而言，其公平性仍然不足。[299] 烏拉圭回合之後對於發展中國家確立的一系列特別待遇，多為「軟措施」，或者予以「過渡期限」，難以達到提升發展中國家發展能力的目標；[300] 中國的「入世」議定書中存在著對於中國非常不利的條文，以往的一些案例已經展現了這些條文對中國的損害。而中國已經躍升為全球性的經濟和政治大國，此時，如果仍然不能展現出一個大國的風範，擔負起一個大國的責任，不能代表如中國一樣科技、產業不夠發達，人均GDP較低

的眾多國家，去爭取更好的國際體制，則不僅中國自身的發展會受到負面影響，國際社會的公正、穩定、健康、持續發展也無以維繫。

所以，中國必須有所作為。以陳安教授為傑出代表的學者們所提出的宏觀立場和具體建議，恰恰是中國在國際經濟法和國際經濟秩序破舊立新進程中理應有所作為的學術表現和實踐基礎。

陳安教授的學術貢獻

陳安教授勤於研究、認真思考，心懷理想、碩果纍纍。陳安教授在國際經濟法基本理論、國際經濟法的中國立場、國際投資法、仲裁法等領域都出版了大量的著作，其中既包括高水準的論文，也包括很多教材和專著。

從這些研究可以看出，陳安教授在對國際經濟法進行價值分析方面提出了很多具有啟發性的觀點。對於那些認同和高度評價現有國際經濟法體制的專家和學者而言，這些觀點未必能獲得他們的贊同，但應當是可以激起進一步思考和討論的重要闡釋。其中體現的對國家利益的關切、對國際經濟法發展方向的關切、對國際社會未來的關切，既有著一個學者追求學術真理的理想成分，也有著對於國際社會格局堅實認知的現實基礎。

陳安先生的研究成果是國際法律文化的重要組成部分，這些著作是他貢獻給中國學界和國際學界的寶貴財產。作品中不僅相關的內容和論斷值得我們一再學習，而且其顯示的獨立學術品格，深切民族關懷，以及批判的研究方法也值得我們認真對待和深入借鑑。換言之，陳安先生放眼全球，立足中國，任你風向東

南西北，我自巋然從容不迫，堅毅探求國際經濟秩序之公正合理發展，由此鼓呼中國之立場方向，此一大端，中外學人已受益或將受益者必多。

（編輯：龔　宇）

Disregarding Whither the Wind Blows, Keeping Firm Confidence of His Owns
——A Revisit to Prof. Chen's Research on NIEO
He Zhipeng*

1. Two Mainstream Approaches of International Economic Law Research

As a part of the science of law, the studies on international economic law cannot really deviate from mainstream approaches of legal studies and create something totally new. Since the mainstream approaches of legal studies may be categorized into positivism and natural law theory, [301] the means of studying international economic law may also classified into two streams, namely, descriptive studies and normative studies. Descriptive studies mainly try to illustrate existing rules, organizations, and operation, to explain the meaning of rules through semantic analysis, to discover the status of operation by analyzing statistics, or demonstrate achievements and problems arising from the enforcement of rules in practice based on case studies. [302] Normative studies need a set of principles of justice as prerequisite, and then, their main task is to make judgments on whether relative rules and practices may be regarded as legitimate through a critical, reflexive examination of such rules and practices, or to specify the area and direction of international economic law for improvement. [303] This approach is the specific embodiment of natural law approach from the field of legal theories into the field of international economic law, and should be regarded as an express value analysis.

Although at the superficial level these two approaches are different, they are closely related in many ways. A convincing value analysis must be based on solid positive studies, and many positive studies may implicitly include some basic value judgments behind it. [304] Thus, those who prefers positive studies and those who prefers values analysis should respect and appreciate each other instead of regarding implacably their own studies as the right approach and the other approach as wrong. Therefore, a good legal study may emphasis in a certain approach, but not choose one and abandon the other.

Professor An Chen, as one of the top scholars in international economic law in China, has not only achieved a lot in positive studies in international investment law, but also tried much in critical studies in the orientations of international economic law, and put forward many inspiring points of view. The research on new international economic order (NIEO) along with the position of China in the process of it is a typical and representative part.

2. The Rise and Fall of NIEO

Professor An Chen examined the background and history of setting up NIEO, and probed into the importance of NIEO in international society even in the 21st century. The NIEO movement, originated in the 1960s, may be understood as the continuation and upgrading of self-determination after the end of colonial times. The new independent states were not treated fairly since they had been invaded and exploited in the history and were still harmed by the international economic system at the time being. [305] The former suzerains, now acting as the promoter of international economic system and the creator of international law, took welfare and interest to their own territory by the rules they established, and made the developing states poor and weak. Such system cannot be legitimized. [306] According to Professor An Chen, there are three most commonly observed defects of international economic law-making process: 1) It is up to the heads or representatives from several most developed countries to consult and manipulate secretly before a basic framework is determined. 2) Unfair and unreasonable voting mechanisms are enacted into the regime of global economic organizations in advance. 3) US, as the only superpower of the world, has been constantly pursuing the policy of "the superiority of US national interests" and "double standards towards itself and others" in her participation in the decision-making process of global economic issues. [307]

The proposition of NIEO should be regarded as efforts to get away with the old and set up the new, as well as a critical examiner of past traditions and a trail blazer for future generation. However, these efforts would definitely influence short-term and local interest of the developed countries. Hence, the developed countries' reaction towards NIEO was far from enthusiastic. [308] Some scholars from developed countries are inclined to argue that the documents proscribing the advocates of NIEO are not legally binding and cannot establish international legal obligations. The developed industrialized states reluctantly accepted some conditions such as the Generalized System of Preferences (GSP) to carry forward NIEO, to a large extent due to the pressure of Energy Crisis during the 1960s-1970s, plus the need for political balance during the Cold War. [309]

As soon as the Cold War ended, the voice of developing countries seeking for NIEO was submerged by two interlinked waves, namely neo-liberalism and globalization. De-regulation, privatization, and free market became overwhelming voice in the world. Main international economic institutions in the world, such as the WTO, the World Bank, and IMF, engaged in the establishment of "new" international economic laws based on the liberalist notions. It seemed that the development of international economic law was in the track of unilateral hegemony of liberalism and went directly to the "end of history", meanwhile, the striving for NIEO was in a depressed stage.

Practice is the sole criterion for testing truth. The history has not meeting its end. The universal dissemination of liberalism, in many occasions, has not made benefit for developing countries, and even made developed countries themselves in trouble by the bubbles named "financial innovation".

What should the future of international economic law be?

3. China's Position in International Economic Law

The change of international law may occur in substantive matters, or in procedural matters. The change may be in a general and overall dimension, or may be in a specific and regional level. However, all changes must be initiated by the will and activities of actors. Such actors, although including intergovernmental organizations (IGOs), non-governmental organizations (NGOs), multi-national companies (MNCs), and individuals, mainly appear as states. Because states are the most powerful, most influential, and most convenient to appear in international stage. If a State cannot form its own status clearly, and demonstrate it by academic, political, and legal means, the change of international regime may lose discourse of that state. This circumstance may not only affect the interest of a state, but the whole developing process of international law.

A comparatively balanced international legal system may only be possible based on the negotiation of states with various preference of interest and various idea of international mechanism, and such a negotiation may create deliberate democracy in international society. It is necessary to mention that an absolute balanced mechanism in international law never existed. Even in the case that all states have the opportunity to express their views, as a type of international game, the asymmetric powers of states may change into the contrast of bargaining power in international negotiation, and then result in a status that could be unfavorable for the weak parties.

During the course that China interacts with the current system of international economic law, China is faced with many tasks. For many scholars, it is a demanding mission, or even a considerable accomplishment for China to be involved in the current system, to understand the current system, and to participate in the current system. But for Professor An Chen, this is not adequate. China still faces a more arduous, complicated, and significant task, that is to change the current system. This task seems to be unnecessary to some scholars because they regard international economic law regimes like the WTO as "model of international law", or a perfect example of international rule of law. If it is really so, the change of the current system is not so desirable. Moreover, if the national interest of China is not substantially influenced by today's international regimes, China would not have the initiative to demand changing the present system. Further, if China is not a country with negotiation power and discourse influence, the impact of China's efforts on changing the present system would not be significant.

Surely, Professor An Chen doesn't think so. He stresses: "As the largest developing country peacefully rising in the world, China should play an important role in the historical course of establishing the NIEO." [310]

"Firstly, China should be the driving force of the establishment of the NIEO... Secondly, China should dedicate herself to becoming one of the mainstays of 'South-South Self-reliance through Cooperation'... Thirdly, China should adhere firmly to her strategic objectives and principles accompanied by cooperating with all the weak states in the course of the establishment of the NIEO... Fourthly, China should take a clear-cut stand and be in harmony with other countries while reserving differences in the course of establishing the NIEO." [311]

It is true that international economic regimes like WTO has made substantial progresses compared with what we had before. However, judging from the interest of developing countries, they still lack fairness. [312] The special treatment for developing countries in the WTO after the Uruguay Round cannot really achieve the goal of capacity building for developing countries since most of them are just "soft measures" or merely setting up period of transition. [313] There are provisions in the Protocol on the Accession of the People's Republic of China which are obviously unfavorable for China, and cases have already shown that such provisions may take disadvantages to China. Now, China has already gained the position of a political and economic great power in the global scale, if she cannot show the image as a great power, assume the responsibility of a responsible states, cannot endeavor to establish a better international regime on behalf of a great number of states who, like China, are not advanced in science and technology, and not developed in industries, has a low GDP per capita, the development of herself would be negatively affected, and a just, stable, healthy, and sustainable development of international society would be difficult.

Therefore, China must take some positive actions. The position and specific suggestions that submitted by scholars of whom Professor An Chen is a distinguished representative, may lay a solid foundation in academic and practice level for China's discourse in the evolution and innovation of international economic law & international economic order worldwide.

4. Professor An Chen's Academic Contribution

Professor An Chen is very diligent in making research, he thinks about legal issues critically with a set of ideal based on third world interests, and has contributed a lot in fundamental theories of international economic law, the position of China in international economic law, international investment law, arbitration law and many other fields, by many works including high level articles as well as textbooks and monographs.

From these research works, it is not hard to find out that Professor An Chen has provided many inspiring views in critical analysis on international law. These works embodied the author's concerns on national interest, concerns on the orientation of international economic law, concerns on the future of international society. They expressed the ideals of a scholar's seeking for academic truth, as well as a solid realistic basis for the constellation of international society. For those who agree with international economic law mechanism status quo and highly endorse it, these views may not be acceptable; however, they definitely present important discourse arousing further thinking and discussion.

Professor An Chen's research achievements form an important part in international legal culture, and should be deemed as a treasure he contributed to the academia in China and the whole world. In his works, not only the substantive contents and conclusions are worth leaning repeatedly, but the independent academic spirit, deep concern on national interest, and critical research methodology are all worth taking seriously and drawing useful experiences. In other words, disregarding to whither the prevailing wind blows, Professor An Chen has kept a firm confidence of his owns. His contributions are saliently featured by holding a firm Chinese stand while taking a global broad view, and by insistently pursuing the fair and reasonable development of international economic order, and thus advocating for China's self-position and orientation during this process, regardless of all kinds of voices otherwise preaching. With no doubt, scholars of international economic law, domestic or abroad, have greatly benefited from Professor An Chen's works both in the sense of substantial viewpoints and methodological approach, and will keep benefiting therefrom in the future.

（翻譯：何志鵬）

社科文庫・國際財金研究叢刊 AA101017

中國特色話語：陳安論國際經濟法學 第四卷 上冊

作　　　者	陳　安
版權策畫	李煥芹
責任編輯	林以邠

發　行　人	陳滿銘
總　經　理	梁錦興
總　編　輯	陳滿銘
副總編輯	張晏瑞
編　輯　所	萬卷樓圖書股份有限公司
排　　　版	菩薩蠻數位文化有限公司
印　　　刷	百通科技股份有限公司
封面設計	菩薩蠻數位文化有限公司

出　　　版　昌明文化有限公司

桃園市龜山區中原街 32 號

電話 (02)23216565

發　　　行　萬卷樓圖書股份有限公司

臺北市羅斯福路二段 41 號 6 樓之 3

電話 (02)23216565

傳真 (02)23218698

電郵 SERVICE@WANJUAN.COM.TW

大陸經銷

廈門外圖臺灣書店有限公司

電郵 JKB188@188.COM

ISBN 978-986-496-535-9

2019 年 9 月初版

定價：新臺幣 560 元

如何購買本書：

1. 轉帳購書，請透過以下帳戶

合作金庫銀行 古亭分行

戶名：萬卷樓圖書股份有限公司

帳號：0877717092596

2. 網路購書，請透過萬卷樓網站

網址 WWW.WANJUAN.COM.TW

大量購書，請直接聯繫我們，將有專人為您

服務。客服：(02)23216565 分機 610

如有缺頁、破損或裝訂錯誤，請寄回更換

版權所有・翻印必究

Copyright©2019 by WanJuanLou Books CO., Ltd.

All Right Reserved　　　　Printed in Taiwan

國家圖書館出版品預行編目資料

中國特色話語：陳安論國際經濟法學. 第四
卷 / 陳安著.-- 初版.-- 桃園市：昌明文化
出版；臺北市：萬卷樓發行, 2019. 09
　　冊；　　公分
ISBN 978-986-496-535-9 (上冊：平裝)

1.經濟法學

553.4　　　　　　　　　　108015601